The Splendour of a Tear was an absorbing read from start to finish. Written with passion and conviction, Bridget takes you on a personal adventure of risk, faith, sacrifice, and beauty. The driving narrative tells of a God who uses ordinary people to accomplish his transformative work. Through the ministry of Hope House God's love is changing lives. He might just change yours as you read this wonderful account that gives witness to a compelling mission and gospel message that values and prioritises the infinite worth of every life.

- Rev. Joel Small,
Senior Pastor
Erina Community Baptist Church

As I read Bridget's story that weaves in and out of different stages of her life, bringing her to her destiny; I could not put it down. I read into the night, I read more early each morning and was not satisfied until I had finished.

- Pamela Ann Sun
Author

I am so privileged and blessed to read a book about

lives given totally to serve others – not by one, but two people who have taken God's word and put it into practice; forsaking 'all' for the cause of Christ Jesus.

My husband and I were privileged to be Bridget and Greg's pastors during their journey with Hope House.

This book is so full of "raw honesty" – The journey of Bridget, Greg, and the beautiful girls of Hope House, encourages and also challenges us as to what 'we' are doing with all that God has blessed us with.

- Ps. Sandra Piefke
Pastor – House of Praise

This is Bridget's story! A story of childhood poverty, a mis-spent youth, a spiritual awakening, the dramatic submission to the personal call of God, the eventual success, but heart-breaking and drama-filled journey to commence Hope House refuge.

- Jeffrey Blair

THE SPLENDOUR OF A TEAR

Hope House Peru

BRIDGET BONNER

The Splendour of a Tear: Hope House Peru

by Bridget Bonner

Print ISBN: 978-0-6452676-0-0

Ebook ISBN: 978-0-6452676-1-7

Subjects: Peru – Street kids – Mission – Ordinary people – Ecuador –
Nurses – Faith – Culture – Missionaries – Adventure – Risk –
Sacrifice

A portion of the proceeds from the sale of this book will be donated
to Hope House Peru.

Poems 'Never Alone' & 'Love or Lust' by Bridget Bonner

The Poem 'Tears' by Fini Kuipers is used with permission.

Bible quotations are taken from THE HOLY BIBLE, NEW
INTERNATIONAL VERSION

Cover Design: Believers Book Services

Cover Photo by Mark van Tongeren

Interior Layout: Ben Wolf (www.benwolf.com/editing-services)

Dedicated Above All:
To the one who first loved me.
I am forever His!

For Greg:
None of this would have ever happened without you.
Words are not enough to express my love and gratitude
for all you are to me. Thank you for loving me.

Oh! And thanks for the encouragement, support,
tea/coffee and snacks that you fed me while I was
writing.

To Anna & Carmen:
Whom I love more than life itself.

To Luke, Patrick, Nick, Sophie, Anna & Carmen:
I want to acknowledge the sacrifice you made in our
being absent for so long and thank you for graciously
making it possible for Greg and me to go to Peru.

To all our Grandchildren:
When and if you read this story, may it help you in
some way to better understand your respective
grandparents and may our God
one day become your God too.

To Adriana Kuipers:
Fini, my late mentor and friend.
You were always such an encouragement to me.
Look forward to when we meet again,
on the other side of eternity!

CONTENTS

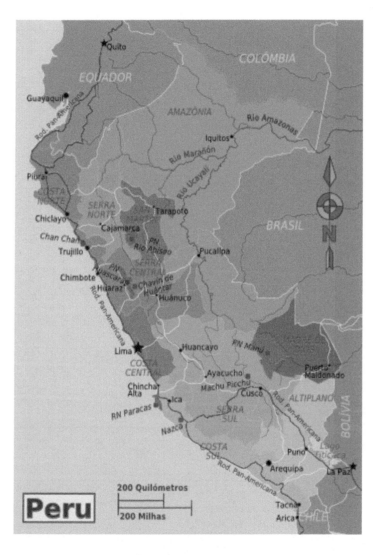

**MAP SHOWING PERU &
NEIGHBOURING ECUADOR**

INTRODUCTION

Everyone has family. This real-life story is about young girls running away to escape the sad, hostile environment of their family life. The girls, shaped by the cruelty they refused to accept, run to the streets hoping to eke out a living as best they can, but find only disappointment. Ever optimistic, they keep on searching for the love they desperately need.

Some chapters include actual journal entries, but the entire narrative is a true account of what happened as seen through my eyes.

The narrative begins with a child's desperate escape, which connects with my own subtler story of escape. For all of us, life's journey involves a kaleidoscope of feelings and emotions almost impossible to pen. I have endeavoured to paint a picture, using words to carve their way through the landscape of my life and theirs.

Surpassing peace, found while meandering through Ecuador, finds a resting place, Peru. Here a gentle flow intricately weaves my life with the lives of the girls on the streets of Lima. Their stories unfold, and I begin to understand what underprivileged really means. I must do something to help!

Construction of a place called home begins but is fraught with disappointment and tainted by the shocking betrayal of a trusted carer. Eventually, a new beginning dawns – the home is renamed "Hope House," and optimism returns.

For I am the least . . . and do not deserve . . . but by the grace of God I am what I am, and I am not about to let His grace go to waste.

— 1 Corinthians 15:9-10 (NIV/Message)

Chapter One

IRMINA

Disturbing voices wake Irmina in the early hours of the morning; she tries hard to stay asleep because she knows something bad always happens when her father is angry. The familiar babble gets louder and louder, so she sits up in bed and rubs her eyes. The dim light shining through the crack in the curtain hanging over the doorway helps her to focus. Irmina hears her mother's voice crying out and then a thud to the ground. Her heart begins to pound as she runs to see.

Peering through the curtain, she sees her mother lying on the floor, crying. She watches her mother's petite body being hauled up by her father's fist grabbing the front of her light-coloured slip; her mother screams and struggles, trying to lash out while hurling abuse at him. He slaps her hard across the face. Irmina is terrified and doesn't know what to do. She wishes her big brother was there, but there's no one. Her mouth is dry, and she is paralysed with fear, but her misty eyes can't stop watching.

Her mother is struck again and again; her screams become more desperate, and her slip is tarnished with crimson as she tries to resist. Like a rag doll, she is smashed to the floor and the screaming stops. Deadly silence follows, but just for a moment, then the sound of her father's drunken ranting starts again.

Irmina runs towards her mother's lifeless body, looking to the ground in horror. She bolts out the door and runs as fast as her little legs can carry her. Scared for her life, she runs and runs until her lungs are about to burst; gasping for breath, she stops and lets her hands rest on her knees, breathing deeply. Beads of sweat roll down her face as she becomes aware of the dark alley in which she finds herself. Exhausted, Irmina wipes her fringe sticking to her forehead and weeps bitterly.

Amidst the beauty of Peru and the loveliness of its people, the sub-culture of domestic violence, child abuse, and poverty is impossible to hide. Irmina is just one of the many tragedies that entered my life during my time in South America. My journey, however, began in Ecuador some months before our paths crossed.

Chapter Two

AN AMAZON AWAKENING

Journal Entry:
Hospital Vozandes Del Oriente Shell, Ecuador
10th September 2003

Everything is new. The culture, the food, the climate, and my new home located on the edge of the Amazon rainforest. With just a small population of 5,000, Shell is a remote little town about two hours by bus from the nearest city with a shopping centre. That means fast food is now sold on the street stalls instead of MacDonald's, and the tiny pieces of deep-fried pigskin look incredibly different from the French fries.

I'm discovering that my Spanish is not as good as I thought it was. Rolling one word into the next, the fast-talking people pause only to draw breath. Sometimes I don't catch a word.

Already three shifts have passed at the Hospital and I'm still so unfamiliar with the routine. Names of people are like tongue twisters and when I am given a patient's address to organise their discharge, I don't know whether it's North, South, East, or West.

Back in Australia, my field of speciality is in Midwifery; now I find myself in all manner of situations ranging from receptionist to admissions clerk and even cashier. I have learned to be versatile very quickly.

Hospital Vozandes Del Oriente was established in 1958, a small, twenty-eight-bed mission hospital with a grand total of sixty staff. The team consisted of nurses and physicians from North America, Australia and Germany, as well as Ecuadorian nationals. Though a little run-down and lacking in resources, the hospital provided general surgery, obstetric and some orthopaedic services, as well as outpatient facilities. Diagnosis of tropical diseases such as leishmaniosis (parasites), tuberculosis, pyomyositis (bacterial pus-filled abscesses), malaria, and dengue (a mosquito-borne virus) were frequently treated.

I was happy to sacrifice my time and especially my salary because the hospital treated people of all faiths, and in many cases, people without money.

Poor supplies of pre-washed bandages and unsterilized gauze filled the antiquated dressing trollies. Plastic Coca-Cola bottles had been recycled into "sharps bins", and grey, wrinkled sheets were commonplace. Even though fresh from the hospital laundry, the dirty-looking sheets were very different from the pristine white sheets I was accustomed to in Australia. Also, they were riddled with patches neatly hand-sewn into the worn parts. All of this was so different yet, in some way, acceptable given the scarcity of resources. More difficult to come to terms with was the fact that there was no pain relief for women in labour and that wounds were aggravated by lack of sterile dressings.

It was my first day when an overdue pregnant woman arrived by plane from a remote part of the jungle. After an ultrasound showing an abnormally large foetus, she was admitted. This petite Quechua woman went into spontaneous labour soon after arrival. Her labour was complicated with shoulder dystocia, a condition where the baby's shoulders are broader than the birth canal. The normal procedure in Australia is to deliver by caesarean section. However, the baby's bones are flexible and normal delivery is possible, but it is always a long, difficult labour requiring pain relief, and the risk is that the baby can become stuck. In this case, in Ecuador, the procedure is a technique where the midwife can reach in and break the baby's collarbones.

To avoid this, I had the poor woman try every position imaginable. She was so willing and compliant as she tolerated twelve and a half hours of excruciating pain without any analgesia. Her efforts paid off, and final relief came at the birth of a baby boy, clavicles intact. He came out quite traumatized, not breathing and with floppy muscle tone. But he responded to resuscitation with impressive cries, beautiful to my ears. On examination, he was perfect. As I placed him in his mother's arms, the woman kissed and caressed my hand, softly uttering words in her tribal language. Without a hint of complaining, she accepted the ordeal and endured with absolutely no pain relief. I didn't understand what she was saying, but I was stunned at her expression of gratitude and felt very humbled.

The native people from villages deep within the Amazon jungle had little or no exposure to the Spanish language. There were four distinct dialects spoken: Shuar, Achuar, Quechua, and Huaorani. I concentrated all my efforts on learning only one, Quechua, because it was the most common dialect and the Quechuan people were friendly.

I learned from experience that not all the indigenous people were as likeable as the Quechuans. On one occasion, I approached a middle-aged woman who was sitting by her bed in a corner. As normal, I greeted her in Spanish. She just glared at me in silence. Not knowing which tribe she was from, I tried again, this time in Quechua. 'Ali Pumsha' (Good morning), is all I said.

To my astonishment, she abruptly stood up and eyeballed me from head to toe; then, she picked up her chair and turned to face the corner with it. She promptly sat down and completely ignored me. I never really understood why she was offended, but I felt so intimidated that I had to walk away.

Later experiences showed me that the Huaorani

tribe often displayed this type of antisocial behaviour. I considered that since it was in my own lifetime that the Huaorani people had still been cannibals, they had actually come a long way. The friendlier Quechua patients talked kindly to each other and even nick-named the little Cessna aircraft Alas de Socorro (Wings of Mercy) because it had rescued them from certain death.

During my stint as cashier, one of the dilemmas I commonly faced was when a patient could only pay his bill with the currency of coconuts, live chickens, or some other animal. The first time I dealt with this was when a patient presented me with a live pig. His bill only cost a portion of what the pig was worth, and he wanted the change!

This was in the "too hard" basket for me; bemused, I scratched my head and pondered on what to do for a moment. I had no idea, so I left the man waiting with his pig at the front desk while I went to find some help. I consulted one of the other nurses. 'Oh! Happens all the time', said nurse Paredes. 'You simply weigh the pig.'

The solution was more than obvious to her, but not to me. I must have looked dumbfounded as she began to spell it out for me. 'Currently, pork is worth U.S. $4.00 per kilo. Just do the math', she exclaimed. With that piece of information, I realised that all I had to do was weigh the pig, as she said – easy!

I walked back to the front desk and ushered the man to follow me. Hauling his pig along by a tattered twine around its neck, we found the room where the scales lived. The tiny square on the scales was obviously not designed for a four-legged beast, least of all a pig. What was I to do? Puzzled, the owner and I looked at each other. Then I stooped down, picked up the grimy pig, and stepped onto the scales. The dirty pig looked quite a spectacle against my pristine-white uniform. I felt my face glowing hot with embarrassment as the man looking on grinned from ear to ear. Ignoring my humiliation, I noted the weight down and quickly did the sum.

'The pig weighs 18kg, and your bill is U.S. $50.00', I said sharply. The blank look on his face told me that he didn't understand, so I reiterated using a great deal of sign language and pointing. This time I got a few nods in the affirmative, followed by a long silence. He still didn't get it. Trying not to raise my voice, I said, 'You will need to give me 12.5kg, that's approximately ¾ of the pig, to cover your bill.' The man nodded repetitively again and, at least in my mind, problem solved. Then in his extremely expressive sign language and his broken Spanish, the man asked, 'Do you want the head or the tail?'

I responded, breaking into laughter, 'Is this a trick question?'

'No, no, no!' he exclaimed. The look on his face caused me to know that he was serious. 'You can choose', I responded. Immediately his countenance lit up. He went off smiling to the kitchen, dragging the not so happy pig behind him. There the pig was slaughtered, and the pork was used for the patients' meals. His choice was the *tail*!

BRIDGET WITH THE LOCAL NURSES ALL STANDING FOR THE PHOTO AT HOSPITAL VOZANDES DEL ORIENTE ECUADOR

After a long but interesting day, I was exhausted and glad it was over. I usually have no trouble sleeping, but that night a deafening bang followed by what seemed like explosions blasting off outside my bedroom window caused a rude awakening. In the early hours, I ran to the window where the shutters violently banged open. All I could see were flashes of lightning in the sky, and I heard the pounding rain hammer loudly on the tin awning. A storm like no other raged and shook the whole house. I remember how the room lit up brightly and how almost immediately thick darkness followed; then, an enormous thunderbolt caused the glass to vibrate in the window frames. Another flash of lightning lasted just long enough to read the words on my wall, "Be still." Instantly, they vanished into blackness before I finished reading. Even so, I knew them well. They had been etched into my heart a long time ago. Within seconds, another flash of lightning pierced the darkness, and spontaneously the words reappeared… "and know that I am God".

'Really?' my doubting mind scoffed. Then a furious clap of thunder blasted back, like an angry God responding in defiance. Fearful yet fascinated by the power and the energy generated, I was reminded how as a child, I was petrified during a storm. My mother's wrath was always terrifying, but never in a storm. Her words were strangely soft and comforting, 'It's just the angels moving their furniture', she would say.

Those words brought instant relief, just as they did when I was a kid. I reflected on the simplicity of a child; how complex life had become. Through the glass, the tempest continued. I watched the rain, irresistibly transfixed, as it invaded every crevice. Slowly it seeped into the tiniest of gaps, soaking everything in its path. Nothing was left untouched. Unconsciously, I likened the rain to the Spirit of God, my life to a desert plain – and with a sense of knowing, I was being enticed heavenward. I could not escape.

Another incredibly humid day followed that stormy night. At twenty-nine degrees in the shade, it was far too hot to sleep in. Instead, I spent the morning trying to stay cool in a cold shower knowing that the afternoon shift, with no air conditioning, was unbearable. Within minutes of stepping outside into the scorching sun, I was drenched in sweat again. The heat was relentless.

I had only just arrived on the ward when Doctor Jeff Moulding approached me. He summoned me to follow him. I knew when I struggled to keep up with his urgent pace that something was seriously wrong. He led me to the emergency room, where a teenage girl lay on a stretcher, seemingly lifeless and obviously in the third trimester of pregnancy. Wings of Mercy had just brought her in. With a grim expression on his face, Jeff said, 'She's been in labour for four days; she's not responding.'

'Is there a foetal heart rate?' I asked. He immediately passed me the fetoscope, a tubular fibreoptic instrument. As I lifted the covers, my nostrils filled with the stench of death. I knew it was too late for the baby. Still, I placed the fetoscope on the girl's abdomen, 'Nothing', I reported shakily. Focusing on the girl, I palpated her jugular vein. 'Her pulse is faint but definitely present', I stated. But while I was speaking, the pulse waned gradually to nothing. 'It just stopped!' I said.

'She's in cardiac arrest', Jeff responded in a very controlled but raised voice. He quickly inserted an ET tube and bagged oxygen into her lungs while I commenced cardiac compression. With more urgency in his voice, Jeff yelled out for an auxiliary nurse to draw up Adrenalin plus Atropine. Soon another doctor arrived and injected the drugs intravenously as we continued with our rhythmic attempts of bagging and cardiac massage. The seconds passed slowly, and still, there was no response. We continued in the over-whelming heat for another five minutes. The other doctor noticed the sweat streaming down my face and offered to relieve me. 'On the next count', I said.

As he took over, I breathed a massive sigh of relief, although the battle wasn't yet over. Jeff requested a repeat of the same two medications. I prepared the syringe but hesitated to give the injection as normal protocol in Australia is for doctors only to inject these drugs. Jeff asked me to hurry, and given there was no one else available, I injected the drugs into her vein. Still, there was no response. We continued to work desperately on her for several minutes longer; even so, she continued to be unresponsive. We had to give up. She was gone. She and her baby, both gone.

A deadly silence now engulfed us. I managed to fight back the tears, but the lump in my throat was choking me. The two doctors, the auxiliary nurse, and I stood motionless in absolute silence, just staring at this lovely young woman.

Jeff's voice quivered as he spoke, 'I think we should pray.' We bowed our heads, and Jeff, choking back the tears, somehow composed himself and spoke in a stronger voice. His first words were, 'Gracias Dios' (Thank you, God). He continued in Spanish; trans-lated, his words said, 'Thank you God for your love. In spite of death, we know that you love us. We pray for the girl's father waiting outside and for the community, that you would comfort them.'

More words were said in his prayer but what really touched my heart was that even in this awful tragedy, despite not getting what we hoped for, Jeff was able to say thank you. His prayer had a profound effect on me. Those powerful words lifted my spirit out of the despair I was feeling, and I knew deep down that despite our inadequacies and failures, God still loves us.

Jeff opened the door to face the father with the bad news. The others left the room, but I remained. After a moment, the father came into the room and walked slowly towards the stretcher where I was standing. He looked at his daughter, shaking his head, and the tears began to flow. He sobbed quietly. Silent tears are the worst, I know. At these times, no words are sufficient. I stood beside him and tried to be present with him without uttering a word. I literally felt his pain, but still fragile, it was too much. We sobbed together in complete silence.

Journal Entry:
Morete Cocha, Shell, Ecuador
25th November 2003

> *Life or death hangs in the brink depending on the*
> *torrential rain; it has a lot to answer for. This type of*
> *rain is predictable every evening without fail for at*

least an hour. When it continues all through the night, the aircraft are often grounded for days. Imagine the frustration of a pilot knowing that a woman is in trouble with obstructed labour or perhaps a man with a venomous snake-bite, yet he's not able to help because his craft is grounded.

Today we are a team of seven and now the frustration is ours. In spite of the fine weather in Shell, the two-way radio informs us that there is a storm at the other end. Our destination is Morete Cocha, a remote village less than an hour's flight away, much longer by canoe down the river or several days on foot. The storm is expected to clear in about two hours.

I was so excited to be included on this trip. Doctor Vinicio encouraged Doctor Ulrich and me to join him on the chartered flight paid for by his employer, AGIP Oil Ecuador. This large oil company offers free medical supplies and services to the indigenous people in return for the inconvenience of their oil rigs in the rainforest.

Over the three-day period in Morete Cocha, I was to administer the Hep-B vaccinations to school-aged children and the normal childhood vaccinations of Diphtheria, Polio, Tetanus, and Rubella to the babies. The two doctors were to treat "anyone" who presented at the Clinic. The rest of the team was comprised of two fumigators who brought spray guns and large back-packs full of chemicals to disinfect against malaria. Malaria is now uncommon in these parts of the

Amazon due to regular treatment. The final team members were a dentist and a bodyguard.

THE TEAM WAITING TO BOARD ONE OF 'ALAS DE SOCORO' AIRCRAFT

Waiting for two hours in the hangar allowed us the luxury of introducing ourselves and getting to know each other. We watched the pilot meticulously weigh everything going on board the small craft. He explained it was especially important on this trip since the dentist had a heavy generator to power his drill, and there was always the possibility that an urgent case may need to be picked up on our return.

During our conversations, I learned that some communities didn't approve of the oil companies and had demonstrated this by trying to sabotage the efforts of medical teams sent out. This news, combined with the presence of a bodyguard, made me a little nervous. I approached the bodyguard, scanning him for weapons, but saw no guns or knives; all I could see was muscles, huge muscles. He was short and solid, built like brick. After talking with him for a while, I discovered that his only weapon was a machete. This, he assured me, was only to protect us against dangers such as deadly snakes and other wild animals. I felt more at ease and believed what he told me.

Finally, our plane lurched into the air. As far as the eye could see lay a thick blanket of vegetation, interrupted only by the winding Amazon River carving its way through the vast expanse of lush green. The verdant land below drifted by for miles and miles, and I imagined that infinity must be like this.

The Amazon Rainforest in Ecuador alone covers over 5.5 million square kilometres. With too much noise for verbal communication, the pilot indicated our descent with a "thumbs down".

Soon the wheels screeched along the bumpy landing strip, rattling and shaking the craft more than I was comfortable with. The others reassured me that this was all "perfectly normal".

Children were running along each side of the plane as we taxied down the narrow airstrip. At the end of the strip, the children joined a large gathering of people at the point where the plane came to a sudden halt.

Immediately on exiting, the indigenous group swarmed around us. They babbled in words incomprehensible to me. The gibberish seemed to go on and on forever until my attention drifted towards a little boy, and then it faded into the background.

The boy was intriguing; he played, unaware of his nakedness. Oblivious, he played with his makeshift slingshot, and I felt, for the first time, a deep sense of the selva (jungle). These really were tribal people.

Most of the adults were half-dressed, none wore shoes, and generally, their clothes were dirty. With no running water and with daily torrential rain, they struggled to keep clean from mud. One bare-chested woman wearing a faded polka-dot skirt resembled a mixture of two cultures; it seemed that they had adopted part of the Western culture too.

There were children everywhere. Some wore nothing but a string around their abdomen, while others wore a dirty T-shirt; all had messy hair, with their feet and bottoms bare. I was sad to see the white man's influence in this way.

We walked in extreme heat, carrying our personal belongings. Initially, the path was well marked around the huts, but a thick undergrowth of vegetation veiled it between one group of huts and the next.

The bodyguard led the way as he hacked through the flora with his machete. He commented that the undergrowth only took a few days to re-grow because of the climate.

The Amazon had a greater variety of plants and animals than any other place on the planet, he informed us. Then he casually warned us to look out for the snakes and the tarantulas.

TYPICAL THATCHED HUT IN MORETE COCHA

We passed several groups of huts approximately an hour apart. Passing another cluster of thatched huts, I observed a long tree trunk lying on the ground, protruding out of one of the doorways. Curiosity compelled me to peer into the doorway. Inside, an old woman beckoned me, 'Ven, ven' (Come in, come in), she said, waving her arms. Stepping inside, I saw two shorter logs placed at angles on the floor, merging into each other. The smouldering ends of the logs sat on glowing embers in the centre of the hut with a cooking pot balanced on top. Lifting the lid, the woman eagerly ushered me over. I saw green bananas still in their skins bubbling and boiling away.

I was told that the logs, some too long to fit inside the hut, were gradually pushed towards the centre of the fire until they burnt down to nothing. The hut seemed quite bare, apart from some small straw mats scattered on the dirt floor, which were used for sitting. The beds were wooden slats slightly elevated off the ground, and there was nothing else. Realising that I was lagging behind, I thanked the woman and hurried off to catch up with the others.

After passing the final cluster of sparsely spread-out huts, at last, we arrived at the clinic. Located at the farthest point from the clinic was a block of toilets with six porcelain toilet bowls. There was just one catch; the toilets didn't flush. Although fitted out with plumbing and pipes, there was no means of pumping the water from the river. The disgusting odour was unbearable.

A spokesperson introduced us to a couple of indigenous health promoters who spoke both Quechua and Spanish; they proved to be invaluable throughout our stay. Already many indigenous people had gathered outside the clinic. Some had walked barefoot for two or three days from the surrounding villages and had been waiting all day in the hope of seeing a doctor.

Despite our long, arduous walk in the heat, we went to work straight away unpacking supplies of medicines, dressings, syringes, and sterile solutions. Doctor Ulrich suggested that I set up a triage area outside to treat the minor ailments until the crowd became more manageable. I was to send those I couldn't manage to him in the clinic.

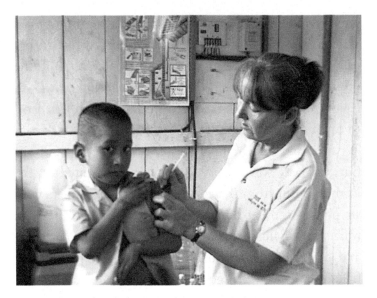

*BRIDGET ADMINISTERING VACCINES IN MORETE
COCHA*

Bacterial and fungal infections were rife, as the hot, humid climate made for a perfect breeding ground. I treated many open cuts, mainly on the feet and lower limbs, which really just needed to be cleaned and dressed. For wounds that looked even slightly infected, I gave antibiotic ointment. With verbal consent from Doctor Ulrich, I also gave numerous oral medications, including antibiotics and treatment for parasites and pain relief. The health promoters translated any follow-up instructions, but I noticed that nothing was ever written down. When I suggested making reminder notes, I was told that the indigenous people were mostly illiterate.

Some children had eye infections resulting from the

flies, while others had boils and tropical ulcers. Many children had chronic diarrhoea, vomiting, stomach-aches, and fevers. Some even had developmental problems. The lack of fresh, clean water only frustrated my attempt to promote good hydration. That's when I learned that the stream close by was contaminated. I also discovered the awful truth that most of these health problems were a direct result of the pollution from oil spills.

A twelve-year-old boy I examined was so full of energy that he was hardly able to stand still. His complaint was puzzling; there were several unusual lumps on his scalp and behind his ears. As I palpated the lumps, I found that they were soft and squishy, not firm enough to contain fluid. Although these lumps were almost the size of golf balls, the boy had no pain to the touch, and no inflammation was apparent. 'Definitely one for Doctor Ulrich', I thought aloud as I brought the boy into the clinic.

'Ah yes', he said in his confident German accent, 'zis is quite common here'. Pausing from his work, he grabbed a stool and sat the boy down. 'You vill find zis very interesting', he said nonchalantly. 'Come and vatch'.

I stood close and observed him clean the soft mass with yellow-brown betadine solution; he then shaved a tiny patch of hair. Without explaining what he was about to do, he incised the bald patch, making a slit about half an inch long. As he dabbed the blood away with gauze, he motioned me to draw near so I could see clearly. He then inserted his forceps and, to my horror, pulled out a long, wriggling, writhing worm on the end of them. I let out a shriek as my stomach churned, and I jumped back almost a meter. Ulrich cracked up with laughter, which increased as the boy and then others in close proximity joined in.

Ulrich seemed somehow more human, his expression more relaxed. And his intense, serious demeanour was gone in an instant. Obviously, I produced the desired reaction, but I didn't think it was funny at all.

Still recovering from the shock, I asked how such an enormous worm could get into the boy's scalp. As Ulrich stitched the wound, he explained how blowflies lay eggs within small scratches on the surface of the scalp. The skin then heals over, and left untreated, the eggs hatch into parasitic larvae, which thrive in these perfect conditions and keep growing bigger and bigger. In this particular case, they had been growing for many months. Ulrich was right; I did find it very interesting. However, the thing that interested me most was the side of Ulrich that I had never seen before.

The Clinic, a large thatched hut divided into three rooms, was the only hut with a concrete floor. At the end of the day, we transformed the back room into our personal space. It was to be our haven where muddy boots remained outside, and we protected ourselves by setting up mosquito nets over our mats on the floor.

The ground outside was soft and muddy from the storm, so with each step I took, I seemed to sink deeper and deeper. I wondered if I stood still for long enough, would the mud overflow into my boots, and if so, could I get stuck there permanently? I never stood still long enough to find out.

The children played outside most of the time. They rarely attended school. In the dry parts of the day, they played a game with stones, throwing them into a circle scratched in the dirt. I didn't understand it fully, but it intrigued me. The way they interacted with each other was hilarious, especially when their stone landed outside the circle and they jumped up and down and yelled at each other.

In the late afternoon, every day, torrential rain hammered down, but the boys and girls didn't seem to mind at all. Completely oblivious, some kicked around a sodden soccer ball that was made of natural fibres, while others used large banana leaves as umbrellas.

QUETCHUA BOYS USING BANANA LEAVES IN TORRENTIAL RAIN

After a hard day's work, I was feeling hot and sweaty, but at last, we were finished. In need of a shower, the river became very inviting. I approached our helpful interpreter and convinced him to take me on a joy ride down the river in his canoe. When the rest of the team got wind of it, they too wanted to join in. The long and narrow dugout canoe rocked frantically, almost capsizing, as each of us boarded. Again, my screams of fear and excitement initiated laughter, but this time I could join in. When we were all seated, the precarious canoe seemed a little more stable. We paddled up the stream; the owner stood on the bow of his canoe with his long paddle working hard against the current, yet making it look easy to maintain the balance.

As we paddled up the Amazon, I took a good look around. Many shades of green against the deep blue sky and the sun about to set stimulated all my senses at once. I was overwhelmed by the beauty! 'Surely this is you, God, dazzling me with your handy-work', I pondered. Feeling truly privileged and extremely grateful for this amazing moment in time, I took a deep breath and inhaled.

As the canoe turned in the opposite direction, my thoughts were interrupted. Now gliding along effortlessly with the current, our host asked if anyone would like to have a go at steering the canoe. No one else volunteered. To my own amazement, I found myself raising my hand and offering to have a go. No sooner had I stood up, even before I reached the bow, the canoe rocked, and I lost my balance and splashed head first into the water. On the way, I inadvertently tipped the canoe, and everyone else followed.

The refreshing water put a smile on my face, but amongst the splashes, I heard Ulrich frantically yelling out, 'Is zere any piranhas in zis vater?'

I laughed as he panicked, but secretly I was thankful that the answer was, 'No.'

SOME TEAM MEMBERS IN A DUG-OUT CANOE AT MORETE COCHA

Journal Entry:
Quito, Ecuador
4th December 2003

My time here in Ecuador is fast approaching its final days. During the past three months, I have been humbled and stretched in every which way possible;

after some deep searching of the soul, I realise that my life will never be the same again.

In both the good experiences and in the difficult ones, I have tasted a much more personal level of relationship with God. I see my need of this all-powerful God and I feel irresistibly drawn to surrender everything I am to Him. I want to go deeper. I am persuaded that this is a healthy dependency on God and I feel safe enough to develop it.

The cares of this world had kept me from seriously seeking God. The little connection I had was strangled out by the hard knocks in life. Ecuador, however, was a turning point in my faith where I began to accept God with my heart rather than my head. All those years, I never really allowed God to be God, and I began to realise that my disappointments were a direct result of my unrealistic expectations.

I needed to make some changes in my life; I needed to allow time-out with God. As strange as this may seem, I deliberately sought quiet times alone every single day. I spent many hours just waiting on God. Being a thinker, keeping my mind still and waiting was the hardest task for me. But I did it; I waited and waited. Sometimes during the busiest part of the day, when even five minutes seemed like an eternity, I stopped everything and waited. Other times, it was in the stillness of the early hours that I lay awake listening and waiting. In the solitude of that time, I became aware of God's presence. It was a powerful sense of connection with God, not a feeling but a knowing. His presence left me with such a tremendous sense of peace that my heart was lighter; nothing else seemed to matter. After a time, I became aware of God speaking to me, not with voice or vision but often through His word in the Bible and, sometimes, through people. I finally came to really know God more deeply, and I was certain that He was calling me to long-term missions. What puzzled me was the uncertainty. I didn't know where, or when, or with which mission organisation. I only knew that I didn't want to go my own way any longer. I wanted God to plan my course; I wanted to go His way. I met with my Ecuadorian pastor, Horacio, to talk, and we prayed together. By the end of our meeting, I knew that all I had to do was trust and take one step at a time. I was excited.

Before I returned to Australia, I daydreamed of three things I wanted to realise, but I didn't know how to make them happen since I barely had the funds needed to do so. My first and most important wish was to visit Malinda, my sponsored child in Peru.

My second aspiration was to visit Cali, Columbia, a desire that came about after watching the documentary *Transformation*. I felt strongly motivated to see for myself if the community of Cali really had been transformed through the power of prayer. I wanted to be a part of the 60,000 people who piled into the soccer stadium every ninety days, to pray!

My third was a burning desire to get a glimpse of

Cuban life. I had no real purpose for this trip; it was merely a pipedream. I had always been fascinated by Cuba and wanted to experience the culture, the music, and to meet the people of Havana.

I had a few free days before my flight home to Australia and decided to spend them in Quito, the capitol of Ecuador. After walking around all the old churches and cathedrals and visiting the sites, I still had time to spare. I couldn't stop thinking about Peru, Columbia, and Cuba, so I spent the rest of my time making enquiries about the cost. I went to the Embassy of Cuba in Quito first, just to see how much a visa cost.

The person behind the enquiry desk answered all my questions regarding the visa, then he said, 'When are you planning to go?' I explained that I wasn't sure if I could afford it and was just making the initial enquiries. He then asked if I could do him a favour. 'A favour', I said suspiciously. 'Yes, can you bring a much-needed laptop computer to a pastor in Cuba?' he said. I had some reservations but continued to listen. As he talked, I felt that perhaps this was the 'purpose' I needed. I listened carefully. Our conversation covered so much ground. He explained that the pastor and his wife had a guest room in Havana where I could stay in return for bringing the laptop. Then he mentioned his sister, Luisa, in Peru. I began to feel more comfortable as he told me all about Luisa. Luisa was a single woman about my own age who apparently accommodated voluntary workers from all over the world. He offered to call her on my behalf, and from there on, I felt that

God was making a way for me. New plans just fell into place when I managed to extend my return flight home, and my dreams began to materialize with a new flight, destination…Peru!

Back at the hospital, a farewell dinner was held for all the medical and nursing missionaries who were leaving for one reason or another. I felt very privileged when both long-term and short-term missionaries were thanked and appreciated for their contribution and sent off with a blessing. I caught up with Klaus-Dieter John and his wife Martina, two doctors I had worked with over the past three months; they had been working at Hospital Vozandes for many years. Although both Klaus and Martina were from Germany, their accents were more American than German. After a long conversation with Martina, I learnt that they were finishing up at the hospital and were headed to Peru just a week before me. When we realized that we would both be in Lima at the same time, at least for a few days, we arranged to meet up in the Swiss Mission Guesthouse. Martina asked if I could pick up her mail and pass it on to her. We all said our goodbyes to one another; it was the end of a season for all of us, and even though I felt that I would return to Ecuador, I still felt a little sad. Especially with regard to leaving my prayer partner Christi Leyva, a beautiful young American woman who was willing to be honest and transparent with me—we had many amazing prayer times over those months.

The abject poverty I had experienced in Ecuador

made such an impact on my life. The sickness and disease that permeated the jungle huts, the common tragedy of death in childbirth, even the brutal storms and the pig experience had totally re-shaped my world-view. The more I saw, the more I realised how privileged a life I had lived. My own exposure to poverty and the many monsters I faced as a child deceived me into thinking I had a handle on what "poverty" really meant. Despite growing up with very little, I did have a good education, and I had free access to health care. Hot school dinners and brand-new uniforms and shoes were all provided free of charge. The hunger I experienced was only temporary, and I was able to escape my reality through the blissful world of literature and the creative illustrations found in books at the local library.

In Ecuador, although public libraries do exist in populated areas, their entire stock is all reference books, and none can be taken home. In truth, I had never suffered hardship such as these people suffered; I had not known the meaning of true poverty.

I reflected on the babies admitted to Hospital Vozandes on the brink of death, with sunken, glazed eyes and feeble, almost non-existent signs of life. I remembered how many died from simple dehydration before they reached the hospital and how numerous more cases died from prolonged vomiting and diarrhea caused by contaminated water. Others died from common childhood diseases such as measles. The injustice of oil companies becoming wealthy at the expense of these indigenous people infuriated me. Adults likewise perished from simple pneumonia or appendicitis, all because of lack of access to medical attention. Some died from tropical diseases and snakebites for the same reason.

For a moment, I felt a heavy kind of hopelessness as if I could never make a difference. But then I realised that my hope was no longer in myself; it wasn't all about me anymore, it was Christ in me. I felt empowered, and I knew that I wasn't alone.

Chapter Three

PERU'S ABANDONED

Journal Entry:
In flight to Lima, Peru
9th December 2003

From my window seat, looking out through the plastic I can see that it's a clear day: bright for 5.30 pm. How magnificent the land of Ecuador appears from a distance; then, my view wanes into a white carpet of cotton wool clouds before disappearing completely.

With plenty of mind-space for the next two-hour flight, my thoughts wander towards Malinda. I have known Malinda for the past four years, but only through correspondence and photos with my sponsor-child program; Malinda will soon be leaving the program because she is seventeen years old. The thought of meeting her makes me feel extremely happy. It's something I've always wanted to do, but never imagined I would be able to, and now it's really happening. I wonder if we will get on well together. I wonder if she will be allowed to spend some time with me.

In no time, the flight was over, the plane landing safely in Peru and surprisingly on time at 10.30 pm. My missing luggage, however, caused a long delay. An hour later, still no joy. Then, finally, I was handed a ticket and told to return the following day.

Now travelling light, I stepped through the airport exit only to be set upon by a bunch of taxi drivers. I recalled some advice given by Pastor Horacio back in Ecuador. At the time, his words of warning seemed to drone and fade into nothing, but now they echoed loud and clear and seemed to be significant. 'Taxis are not safe; only get into an official taxi and always agree on the fare before you get in.'

The babbling drivers were virtually in my face, each voice trying to override the other. My indecision only seemed to make things worse, and they became even louder. I just wanted to escape and forcefully brushed past the manic crowd walking aimlessly outside. A couple of persistent drivers followed me into the dark night, pestering me with offers of cheap fares. I felt intimidated and became a little nervous, so I stopped. I turned around to face them and asked, 'Are you official taxis?' One man scurried off into the shadows while the other immediately pulled out his photo license. We agreed on the fare, and I was ushered to a long line of taxis; his taxi stood in the middle.

I was glad to arrive unscathed at the hotel but soon learned from the receptionist that I had been ripped off. I had been charged in American dollars instead of nuevo soles (in Peruvian currency, one nuevo sol is worth about one-quarter of an American dollar). Though money was tight, I didn't care; I was safe.

I could see from the drive to Mira Flores that it was an up-market part of town by the flash hotels and the classy restaurants. Despite the late hour, Mira Flores was buzzing with life and activity, cars blasting their horns and loud music playing from the bars. I felt wide awake and energized, and I was hungry; I had to go out into the hustle and bustle to investigate the food scene and to get a feel for the place.

Again, vague warnings of danger from the pastor began to ricochet in my mind—cautions about the high crime rate and how tourists were always a target: 'Be alert for bag snatchers. Don't open your mouth, or they will know you're a Gringo!'

Expecting the worst, I took off my rings, my watch, and my earrings and hid them in the room with my handbag. I felt a little nervous and prayed for protection. Then I rammed a handful of Christian tracts into my pocket before leaving, a habit I had developed in Ecuador. The tracts gave a precise explanation of the message of salvation.

The moment I stepped out of the hotel into the

street, I felt a heightened sense of awareness; my heart was pounding as I walked along, and the street was noisy, with people mulling around everywhere. A chorus of laughter and chatter echoed from a crowd of young people inebriated with alcohol. The restaurants and shops were packed. I didn't feel safe.

Something caught my attention. Just a few metres away was a young child, possibly six or seven years old, peering curiously into a huge plate-glass window. It was a hotel window, and it was tinted. I couldn't see anything inside. The little girl was leaning forward as she cupped her hands around her eyes, pressing her face intently against the glass. I wanted to see what she could see. Captivated, I found myself walking towards her, somehow lured by an unseen force. I stood beside her, peering into the window myself in a similar fashion.

What I saw was beautiful. The round tables were tastefully decked-out in fine white linen tablecloths and silver cutlery, and it looked so very inviting. Some of the tables were occupied, and some were empty. Interrupted by the little girl tugging on my clothes, I gazed down to see her big dark eyes looking up at me; her hand held out. To my surprise, she said, 'Money, money', in English!

The girl, far too young to be out so late and too vulnerable to be alone, had soiled clothes and matted hair. I asked her, 'Donde está tu mama (Where's your mum)?' With a blank look on her face, she ignored the question but responded instead with, 'Money, money', again.

Ignoring her demand, I asked her what her name was, but her little mind, still grappling with the first question, blurted out, 'No tengo mama (I don't have a mum)!'

'Aaaah Jaaaah', I said with a nod, trying to slow down the pace of our conversation. After a short pause, I continued in Spanish, 'So, who's looking after you?' With an air of confidence beyond her years, the little girl straightened her shoulders as she proudly said, 'I look after myself.'

I responded, 'Where do you live?'

'I live with my friends.' After a quick pause, she continued, 'Mira Flores is my home.' I couldn't believe this was true, so I asked her to show me where she lived. She brought me to a nearby shop-doorway; there were newspapers spread out on the concrete slab, and the shop was closed. I looked closely at her in disbelief. She only had black socks on her feet, no shoes, and her clothes were ragged. Could she really be telling the truth?

My thoughts were broken, interrupted this time by the little girl's voice. She spoke softly, in a less demanding voice, 'Tengo hambre (I'm hungry)', she said. I was slow to respond, still trying to process, then her voice hardened as she insisted, 'Money, money', repeatedly. I gave her a coin, and before I knew it, she ran off into the night.

I continued walking but couldn't stop thinking

about her. How could such a defenceless little girl be living on the street? I wondered whether she was telling me some imaginary fairy tale. The only English word she knew was MONEY. Suddenly a boy approached me asking for money; he was about twelve years old. I looked at him intentionally. Although he wore shoes, they were way too big, and his ankles were black with caked-on dirt, no socks. This time I asked more questions and scrutinized him as he answered. His clothes were dirty, and he claimed to live on the streets too.

The boy said, 'There are lots of kids like me around here'.

While scanning for evidence to dismiss his claims as false, the boy offered to take me to a place where a crowd of street kids met together. I was unsure; reluctant to go with him, I declined. Instead, before giving him some money, I gave him a tract and asked him to promise me he would read it. The boy was silent but nodded his head in affirmation. I gave him a coin, and without hesitation, he ran off.

It seemed that I couldn't get more than a few metres down the street without this same thing happening again and again. There were children selling cigarettes to adults who seemed to be indifferent or oblivious to their plight. How could they not see? I spoke to so many young children that night; to each one, I gave one nuevo sol and a tract. How could I pass them by? My heart went out to them; I felt that I had to do something to help, but what? All I could do was to give them a miserly coin and a tract. That certainly didn't ease their situation, nor did it help the ache in my chest.

The advice from the Lonely Planet book *South America on a Shoestring*[1] didn't prepare me for the street children. Even the hotel I stayed in was a one-night special included in my airfare, and I knew I would have to find somewhere cheaper, much cheaper, after that first night. In spite of my desire to help, my shoestring was getting shorter by the minute, and I felt absolutely helpless.

Eventually, I located a supermarket called Vivanda and bought bread-rolls, fruit, cheese, and a large bottle of water, hoping that this might stretch out for several meals. I set off to the hotel. Although relieved to be back in the safe comfort zone of my room, I had no peace. Repeated flashbacks of young children out there alone in the dark shadows broke my heart.

The flashbacks continued. I couldn't rest; visions of hungry children had carved their way into my conscience, leaving a deep sense of sadness. It was more than I could bear; I was left feeling numb. My own childhood seemed almost charmed compared to the plight of these children.

Woefully, I made up some bread-rolls. I took a bite but could hardly swallow past the lump in my throat. My appetite was gone. How could I eat when they were hungry? Conflicting thoughts darted around my head: 'There must be something I can do. Go and find them and bring them back and feed them. Would they come with me? Would the porter of my hotel even let them in?'

I remembered that there was a kids' helpline in Australia and wondered if there was anything available here in Peru. In desperation, I grabbed the yellow pages and found "Street Kids' Project" listed. I rang the number, but there was no answer, only a recorded message. Then I realised it was one in the morning. What was I thinking? Below this listing was the Swiss Mission. I knew it was late, but I rang anyhow, hoping they could help. The woman who answered was very kind. She listened patiently as I told her about the little girl and the 12-year-old boy who were genuinely hungry. With great sensitivity, she explained that there were many children like them, and yes, it was a terrible situation because there was nothing in place to help them. I asked her about the Street Kids' Project, but she said she had never heard of them. When I asked her, 'What can we do about it?' she responded sympathetically, 'Sorry, I can't do anything, and I don't know what you can do!' Then she ended our conversation, reminding me it was very late.

I put the phone down, quite bewildered. 'She can't do anything! Well, I can't do nothing', I thought. Then in a feeble attempt to do something, I began to make up the remainder of the bread-rolls and put them back into the paper bag along with the fruit. I could at least give them some food.

My heart pounded fiercely, 'Is it safe to go out again at this late hour? What if someone pulls a knife on me?'

I felt angry at my own thoughts. 'But they're just kids', I rationalized. Before I left, I prayed earnestly, 'God, go with me, protect us, the children and me, and help me not to be so angry.'

While people were still milling around the less active streets, I saw a boy selling caramelos (lollies) who appeared to be alone. In fact, after talking to him, I discovered that his mother was begging further down the road. Then I saw the boy I'd met earlier sitting on the pavement. Excitedly I walked straight over to him. His smile indicated that he recognised me. He didn't ask for money, but I noticed him eyeing the brown paper bag in my hand, so I motioned to hand it to him. Without saying anything, he snatched the bag out of my hand and couldn't open it quickly enough. I asked him his name. Before thrusting the bread-roll into his mouth, he said, 'Miguelito.' I asked him if he had read the tract I had given him. He pulled it out of his back pocket and waved it about as he munched away with bulging cheeks.

'Yes, but did you read it?' I insisted. With his head downcast, looking less than proud, even ashamed, he quietly said, 'I can't read.' As he spoke, food dropped out of his mouth.

I felt bad, like a dagger had been thrust into my heart; how could I be so far removed from his situation? I had read that Peru had one of the strongest economies in the Americas with its booming tourist industry, so how could a child of twelve be living on the streets and not be able to read? This was Lima, with its first-world amenities and upscale nightclubs and casinos.

I talked with Miguelito at length; I wanted to know what it was like for him, and he seemed more than willing to tell me. As I listened to his story, my eyes filled, and I was cut to the quick. Living on the streets took on a whole new meaning, just as my under-standing of poverty did. For Miguelito it meant being very alone with no help from anyone. All he knew was rejection and isolation. The boy had poor self-esteem; he had never been to school and was unable to read; he had never had adult guidance. He didn't even know his own birth date, let alone celebrate it. He had never experienced what it was like to be loved. I just wanted to put my arms around him and make him feel that I cared. I didn't; I couldn't—it seemed inappropriate!

By the time I returned to my room, I was totally broken. Thinking about Miguelito brought back memories of my early years. I had felt isolated at school; I was so shy with very low self-esteem. But I always had a home to go to, a mother, a father – even if they weren't perfect, they were there. Though we couldn't afford to buy books, I learned to read and grew up with a love for it.

My contribution to fixing the problem was like applying a tiny band-aid onto a gaping wound. I realised how feeble an attempt I had made; it was a quick fix, and it was all wrong. I sat on the bed and sadly contemplated my failure to change the injustices of the world. I paused to reflect on the life journey that first drove me to volunteer to help the people of South America. It was a long journey – some 40-plus years in all – and I realised again that God is in control, that He wastes nothing but instead, He uses even our bad experiences in life for His purposes if we let Him.

Before giving in to sleep, I desperately cried out to God, 'What can I do?'

Chapter Four

AMAZING GRACE

Born into a Catholic family in Dublin in the 1950s, I was the second youngest of five children; my brother was the youngest and the only boy. Hard times began when my father had a stroke; it affected his speech, and he couldn't work. The domino effect meant that he lost his business and then slowly lost his mental health, his independence, and his parental role. We lost our father, our security, our possessions, and our home. In the late fifties in Ireland, social welfare was unheard of; if you didn't work, you didn't eat.

I was five years old when everything fell apart; the only thing I remember is the empty, hollow feeling inside. At night, my growling stomach made it hard for me to go to sleep. Sometimes it churned enough to wake me up too. Wide-eyed, I lay there listening to the monster inside me.

My spirited mother went from church to church asking for food. Initially, the priest would give her a box full of food, but when it became a habit, the door was slammed in her face. In desperation, she would beg, borrow, and even steal rather than see her offspring go hungry. At night, she resorted to breaking and entering grocery stores. Mum took Mary, my eldest sister, with her. She would smash a small window and let Mary in, and then Mary would open the door for mum. Once inside, they would fill the pram with food and wheel it home.

Eventually, mum realised that Ireland had nothing to offer a family of seven with no breadwinner at the helm. Mum stopped going to church, but she made sure that we all went. I often thought that maybe if she came to church, she wouldn't be so angry. When we stepped out of line, she lashed out in a terrible rage and beat us severely.

Mum left the Emerald Isle she loved and coura-geously took all of us across the sea to England to live in greener pastures (all except my father). He refused to go, so she left him. Six months later, she went back for him, and he reluctantly joined us.

The next monster I faced was the communal wash-house in Manchester; the tiny two-up and two-down terraced house we lived in had no bathroom. This was commonplace with government housing. Once a week, if we were lucky, we went to the washhouse, and we all shared the same bathwater. We couldn't afford the luxury of separate baths. I was somewhere at the end of the line, so by the time I got in, the water was cold and soupy. The towel was worse.

School was a nightmare for me. In the midst of five hundred students, I felt isolated. Clip-clopping around in my sister's hand-me-down shoes and wearing baggy clothes made the playground the hardest place to be. The situation improved when we received a grant to buy brand new school uniforms. That meant a new pair of shoes, and they actually fitted me. I was grateful that England was so good to us.

My mother tried to protect us from sexual predators, especially my uncle, but somehow, she didn't seem to think that playing on the streets was a problem. She never knew about stranger danger, nor that we often did exactly what she told us not to do. I never talked about the incident with the man in the back alley; it was my secret. I couldn't express the shame I felt, so I never said a word.

I left the Catholic Church and became a rebellious young woman drifting further and further away from God. I moved from one dead-end job to another and from one boy to another, shielding my heart along the way. From factory worker to sewing machinist, then check-out-chick to barmaid, never feeling settled anywhere.

Mum tried to rort the system wherever she could.

She surprised me in the supermarket one day, turning up at my till with a trolley full of food. Her bill was forty pounds, and she only gave me a fiver. I had to make the till balance by the end of the day. It was a busy place, and somehow without being caught, I managed it. When I got home that evening, mum sternly scolded me, saying, 'Next time, make sure you give me some change.'

I found it difficult living at home. I became dissatisfied and was so unhappy. Again, I changed jobs, always looking for more pay. My need for money was insatiable. I decided to train as a croupier. Approved by the Gaming Board for Great Britain, I soon found a full-time position at the Blenheim Casino. The money was excellent, and the hours from 9.00 pm to 4.00 am suited me. To get out of the house, I worked a second job as a waitress during the afternoons. I was happy, at least for a while. On top of my two pay packets, I was earning lots of money in tips at both jobs.

Dealing American roulette and Black Jack was a real buzz. The ambience hummed with excitement, and I loved wearing the elegant, full-length evening gown, which was the uniform. Sometimes, to add to the thrill, when a client had a big win on my table, I would receive a big tip. After only a short time, though, the men started to harass me.

Once, when I was dealing roulette, I felt the eyes of a short, overweight man watching me. He was a regular client. I caught his gaze and stared back at his worn face. Deep wrinkles bore into his skin, and his listless eyes just stared shamelessly. He was an older man with a fringe of grey hair around his balding, mottled scalp. I felt repulsed and looked away. I spun the ball. As the wheel slowed down, I called, 'No more bets, no more bets now.' The ball dropped. 'Six, red', I called as I placed the dolly on the winning number. The table was completely covered with chips piled high. It was a big win; it was his win. On receiving his winnings, the man arrogantly tossed a chip valued at one hundred pounds on the table in front of me. He never said a word. It was an unusually big tip, but I thanked him and took it gratefully. At the end of my shift, as I left the casino, this grotesque man approached me and wanted to take me home. I was disgusted; even so, I hesitated. Shocked by my momentary hesitation, I fumbled for my purse, handed him his money, and walked away. That night I realised how close I was to prostitution. I wondered if the man had been a young, attractive type, would I have fallen to the temptation. I knew the answer, and I never went back to that job again. Without giving notice, I left that very night.

I needed another job and began to look at nursing. My sister Carmel was enjoying her work as an Enrolled Nurse, and she was excited about her imminent plans to move into the Nurses' Home. I lacked that noble desire to help others. For me, nursing was simply a way out. The main thing was that I would receive a salary during the training. Even though the pay was a pittance, the Nurses' Home was affordable.

I commenced training as a Student Enrolled Nurse

and finally began to feel settled. I realised that I was doing something worthwhile. The upshot of this was profound; I actually began to feel good about myself. I made some great friends along the way. Deborah, in particular, and I had many fun times together. On completion of the two-year course, Deborah invited me to visit her father's holiday apartment in Majorca, Spain, to celebrate. We had worked hard, and we decided that it was time to play hard.

Let loose in Majorca, Deborah and I experienced a newfound freedom. Meeting so many young men who took a keen interest in us made us go wild. Mum's saying "rules were made to be broken" kicked in, and there was no stopping us. We broke all the rules.

Damian and his friend Antonio were both hand-some, hot-blooded young Spaniards who didn't speak a word of English. We laughed so much it didn't matter. They were best friends, and by some means, the four of us hit it off really well. Sangria has a lot to answer for! We continued seeing them for the rest of our stay in Majorca; we had a good time, and the two weeks passed quickly. Learning some Spanish words along the way was fun, but soon the fun was over, and we said our goodbyes.

After a short time back at the Nurses' Home, I received a letter from Spain. It was from Damian. I couldn't make any sense out of that first letter; the English was so poor. I purchased a Spanish dictionary and tried to figure it out. I wrote back by looking up words and just connecting them together. He didn't understand my letter either. We persevered with writing for ten months, and gradually my Spanish improved.

In a letter from Damian, I received an unexpected invite. He explained that he had found a job for me so that I could live in Spain for a while and learn the language. The job was for a qualified nurse to care for an elderly English gentleman in his home. I jumped at the opportunity and went without hesitation. I didn't have a work permit, so it was illegal, but I didn't care. I lived according to my own rules.

Damian and I lived together in a rented flat on the fifth floor overlooking the beautiful Palma Nova Beach. Life was bliss for a while, and the Spanish language came easily to me. Unfortunately, only a few months after my arrival, the English man died, and I was out of a job. To pay the rent, Damian had to find himself a second job, and we still couldn't make ends meet. I was bored at home and desperate to find work. Without a permit, it was difficult, and I ended up selling ice-cream on the beach for a while. It was great during the peak season, but when winter came, that job ended. Again, we struggled financially, but by this time, Damian and I were inseparable. It was a hard decision, but I knew the only thing to do was to go back home. Damian agreed and asked me to find him a job in England.

We continued writing to each other for a couple of months, and then a job came up in a Spanish restaurant, The George and Dragon, where all the waiters spoke Spanish. Damian had never worked as a waiter before, but he came to England to give it a go. He had many mishaps in the restaurant, but he had such an amiable personality that he got away with it. Damian didn't ever get the hang of serving food, but his English was so bad he couldn't do anything else, so he persevered.

I found employment with the Ambulance Service of Great Britain, and we both worked hard. Earning good money and living with Carmel, we were able to save up. Despite doing well money-wise, Damian was unhappy in England. He hated the rain, he hated the cold, he hated the food, and he didn't like the "Poms", though he was the one who never stopped whinging. The only thing he liked was his pay packet.

My sister Alice and her husband had migrated to Australia, and when Damian saw a photo of them on a 1000cc motorbike, he immediately wanted to go too. Since he couldn't settle in England and I couldn't settle in Spain, we decided to migrate to Australia. The first attempt failed; however, it was said that we would have a better chance if we applied as a couple. Up until then, we had never given marriage a second thought. Strangely enough, this seemed like a good idea to me. I was nonchalant about marriage as I felt that if it didn't work, I could always walk away. Damian was all for it, though he was keener to go to Australia than anything else.

Without any pomp or ceremony, we married in a registry office, and our second application to migrate was successful. Australia was an exciting adventure that brought us closer to each other. We worked hard and made a good life in Australia. We both had two jobs and saved up like crazy. I worked full time as an Ambulance Officer, and because Damian worked seven days a week as a sub-contract painter, I drove a taxi on my days off. We set ourselves some goals, and after six years, we reached our first goal of purchasing a house. They had been happy years, and I was ready to start a family. Damian, on the other hand, tried to delay having children for as long as he could. I tried to reason that we didn't need to work so hard and began some gentle persuasion. After some time, though not fully convinced, he gave in to having a family.

Anna's birth changed the dynamics of our relationship quite dramatically. Damian became acutely aware that he didn't have my undivided attention; he struggled with feeling "left out" from the day she was born. For me, it was entirely different; her birth was the catalyst to a wake-up call that started me asking some hard questions about life and about God. This didn't help Damian's feelings of rejection, but I was unaware at the time. I believed that we had a good, solid relationship and blundered through life naively, ignoring all the warning signs. We remained relatively happy for some years, but deep down, we knew something had changed.

Carmel in the UK contacted me by cassette tape; this was unusual as we normally wrote to each other. The tape told of her born-again experience. I knew her voice. It was definitely her, but she sounded like some crazy fanatic.

Reciting large chunks of scripture just wasn't the Carmel I knew. I thought she had lost her marbles. I knew that she had just split up from her husband and felt that she might be heading for a breakdown, so I gave her some slack and responded very carefully.

We continued to communicate, at a much deeper level, by audio tape. Carmel began to sound more and more like a "Jesus Freak" to me. Every second word out of her mouth was "Jesus". It seemed that she was involved in some sort of cult.

I found myself trying to convince her of this most of the time, and although I had left the church long ago, I found myself defending it. I just couldn't let go of my Catholic beginnings.

Then in one of the audio tapes, Carmel challenged me: 'If you can show me that the Catholic Church is the only true church, through the scriptures, I will come back.'

Feeling that Carmel needed help, I took on the challenge. I soon realised that I knew nothing about my own faith and needed to find out a few things before I could put her straight.

First, I started attending church. I then volunteered to give Catechist lessons, purchased a Bible, and began to read it. The Bible wasn't very helpful; it was like Double Dutch, making no sense at all.

To make things worse, teaching the Catechist to 7-

year-old children only added to the chaos in my mind. I was left very bewildered.

Almost everything that we did in the Catholic Church was nowhere to be found in the scriptures (the sign of the cross, eating fish on Friday), and some things were even contrary to scripture (confession to a priest,[1] calling the priest by the name of "Father"[2]).

So many questions troubled me. I needed answers, so I brought them to the priest. Though he tried his best, he really didn't have a clue. On numerous occasions, when he didn't have the answer, he simply said, 'Real faith is blind faith.'

I began to realise that I was blind, and I was following the blind. I was following the traditions of men, not scripture. Catholicism and scripture did not harmonize well at all.

Still, I just couldn't let go. Even though I knew things weren't right, I couldn't break away from a lifetime of indoctrination.

I think pride played a big part as well; after all, how could I be wrong? That meant my mother, my grandmother, and generations before me were all wrong!

I tried to talk to Damian about how I was feeling and the dilemma with Carmel, but it was pointless. He was indifferent about faith. He couldn't understand why I even bothered to respond to Carmel.

Annoyed that I was interested at all, he would say, 'Just drop it.' The road of least resistance was easier for me. I kept the peace and quiet for a time. Going into denial, I shelved the whole thing, but ultimately, in my heart, I just couldn't deny the truth. Whether I liked it or not, my worldview began to crumble.

In 1986 when Carmen was born, I was captivated a second time. I loved her deeply, but I experienced the very same surge of emotions that I had felt at Anna's birth. Those same doubts and feelings of inadequacy rose again.

During the following five weeks, my every moment was all-consumed with the girls and dealing with my own feelings of inadequacy. Damian seemed happy enough; more than anything, he was obsessed with work.

Damian worked long, hard hours; by the time he was home, the girls were asleep, and, within a short time, he too was snoring on the couch. Flashbacks of heated discussions prevented me from waking him up. I couldn't bear another row.

I knew that money had become his idol, and I felt powerless. No amount of encouragement would persuade him to take a day off.

Damian often dreamt of winning the lotto, and he spoke endlessly on how he would spend his fortune. His humble beginnings in Spain left him money-hungry, just as did my own wretched childhood, the only difference being that Damian had become a workaholic.

He was doing what he liked to do most – work,

work, work. I tried not to concern myself with his lack of involvement with me and the kids.

On the other hand, I needed to settle on the issue of faith once and for all. I decided to grab it off the shelf with both hands. I guess I was doing what I wanted to do, too. I began to reflect on my own personal faith or lack thereof.

For the first time in my life, I began to talk to God. No more "Hail Mary" or "Hail Holy Queen". I just talked to God as though he were my friend. I didn't go to church, but I persisted in reading my Bible.

Carmen's christening was difficult for me. Having read the scriptures about baptism, I felt that infant christening was just another fabricated tradition of men. I could see that Damian was determined, though, and I didn't want to rock the boat.

I gave in to him. Giving in was easier, at least for a time.

Carmen was about three months old when a letter arrived from Spain. It was from Damian's family. His father was sick, and his uncle was asking us to return to Spain to help. Damian was in the middle of a contract at work and insisted that he had to finish it.

After much discussion, he was adamant that he could not go. That night I hardly slept. Burdened by a compelling tug on my heartstrings to go, I found myself talking to God through the night. I knew that I could help Damian's father, and I knew I was free to go.

The next day was Sunday. Damian was working, so I got up extra early to catch him before he left. I suggested that I could go to Spain with the girls and he could follow when his contract finished. Speaking as he rushed out the door, he said, 'I'm not sure, but I'll think about it.'

Over the next few hours, I couldn't stop thinking about it. The more I thought, the more I began to fear that maybe I wouldn't be able to manage. So many anxious thoughts filled my mind. What if I couldn't understand them. My Spanish wasn't that great. What if the old man deteriorated and died! Would the girls be all right?

A glance at the clock showed me it was only 9.00 am. Maybe I could go to church. I still had time. I needed reassurance from somewhere, so I quickly dressed the girls and off we went. The Mass seemed almost foreign to me, but the sermon hit between the eyes. The priest talked all about honouring your parents.[3] I was convinced that God was speaking to me through this priest and felt reassured that He would take care of us.

Damian came home from work with his mind already made up; he agreed that I should go. This was the final confirmation I needed. The following weeks of preparation were exciting; I felt good about the whole thing and was confident that God would move in Damian's heart while we were gone.

With a 2-year-old and a 3-month-old in tow, it was a long, arduous journey. The worst part was the final leg of the trip, on the train from Madrid to Jaen. Anna had crashed with her head on my lap, and Carmen fell asleep at the breast. I struggled to keep my eyes open.

My thoughts drifted to Damian's father, Antonio, intrigued by the fact that his father's older brother, Enrique, and his younger sister, Chacha, still lived with him. They were in their seventies, and neither had ever married.

Suddenly, I woke up with a start thinking I had missed my stop. As I enquired in my rusty Spanish, a kind middle-aged woman assured me we hadn't passed Jaen. I must have seemed stressed as she continued, 'It's another three stops yet.' She gently asked, 'Where have you come from?' When I told her I had come from Australia, she was quite shocked; within minutes, the whole carriage was talking about the girl from Australia, and they all wanted to know more. I was relieved to get off that train.

At last, our taxi arrived outside the house, in the tiny village of Andujar. I knocked on the door gently at first, but no answer. I knew someone had to be home, so I knocked harder.

I waited for some time, then just when I was about to give up, I heard a series of bolts sliding on the other side; it was like Fort Knox. The door creaked open until barely ajar, and a man appeared wearing a black, felt beret. He was unshaven and grubby; I hardly recognised him.

When he mumbled something in his manly voice, I knew it was Enrique. I couldn't make out what he was saying, but after a moment, he recognised me and slowly opened the door a little wider. His bushy mono-brow crumpled over his eyes as if to protect them from the sunlight. Slowly, a smile crept over his well-worn face, and he started to laugh in disbelief. 'Brijeet… Brijeet de Australia', he said repeatedly.

Eventually, I was ushered in. A pungent smell filled my nostrils as soon as I entered the house. Antonio was in bed, but he appeared to be fully dressed in layers of dull, faded clothing. He looked very sick.

His once olive skin, now pale and lacklustre, sagged over his cheekbones. His emaciated body barely moved, and his voice was weak. Indifferent to the girls and me, he immediately asked for Damian. A grunt of disapproval was all he could manage when he heard that Damian wasn't with me.

'He's too sick to take any interest in us', I told myself. I tried to encourage him that Damian would be coming soon, but his only response was a contemptuous nod.

Chacha, too was sick in bed. She had always been thin and frail, but now she looked better than her brother did. Her sad eyes lit up, and she let out a piercing cry of excitement when she saw the children. Her outstretched arms ushered me over, and she gave me a kiss. As we embraced, the overpowering smell of urine almost bowled me over.

DAMIAN'S FAMILY; SPAIN

The house was filthy; a film of grease covered the dirty mosaic tiles that fully lined the kitchen walls. Above the stove, oil slowly dripped from the ceiling. An opened sac of rat poison stood slumped in the corner. Upstairs, a foul stench reeked from all the bedrooms. I discovered it was from the chamber pots under the beds. The only toilet was outside, and it was winter, so I understood. I took a deep breath and weighed it all up, and then I told myself, 'You can do this.'

The first thing I did was to get a doctor to come to the house. It was a battle with Antonio because he didn't trust doctors, but fortunately for me, he was too weak to win. It turned out that he had pneumonia. The doctor must have known that Antonio would be noncompliant with his medication, so, on the spot, he gave a single shot of antibiotics via injection. Chacha was diagnosed with anaemia, for which a weekly iron injection was prescribed. The doctor was happy to hear that I was a nurse. He gave me a couple days' supply of intramuscular injections and a script for more, and then he carefully instructed me how to administer them, as if I didn't know.

Secondly, I learned the run of the house. I discovered which meals they favoured, found the best places to shop, and knew when to expect the panero (bread man), quesero (cheese man), and lechero (milk man). Each one had a bugle or horn to blow with a distinctive sound to alert the people. But for Antonio's household, they made an exception because they knew it was worth knocking on the door. Even so, it was easy to miss these important deliveries if the response wasn't quick enough.

Over the ensuing months, I focused on cleaning the house. It was a mammoth task, so I just concentrated on one room at a time. The first room I tackled was the kitchen. The kitchen was wall-to-wall with Moroccan ceramic tiles. Heavily covered with grease, cleaning them was a tough job; I was exhausted after just a tiny section of wall. There was so much to do that I was overwhelmed. From that moment, I decided to clean only one single tile a day. In between breastfeeding Carmen and caring for Anna, a very active toddler, I cooked the meals, and I ran up and down those stairs all day long. I never did finish those tiles.

Antonio's health improved day by day. His appetite increased, and the colour returned to his face, but he was agitated and unhappy most of the time. I knew he was getting better when I swept his bedroom one day. He jumped to his feet and nearly bit my head off. He almost had a seizure; the veins on his neck protruded as he snapped at me ferociously. In my pile of dirt, I had swept up what I thought were filthy socks, but it turned out that they were filled with cash, carefully rolled up with elastic bands. He made it crystal clear that I was not to change his sheets either. I rarely saw poor Antonio smile; he was just a cranky, cynical old man.

Chacha was a serious woman who forced a smile only occasionally and who let out a strange shrill sound to express herself whenever she was excited or threatened. Most of all, Chacha loved to talk. The conversation was often one-way; she didn't need any responses. She just needed to talk. Giving her the injections was ghastly. The pong was so overpowering—I had to hold my breath. She was so thin that the needle went straight through her withered gluteus maximus, almost hitting the bone. I'm sure Chacha hated me for it. It was difficult to like her, too. Often, when I was busiest, she would call out my name relentlessly in her high-pitched voice, 'Brijeeet, Brijeeet', until I went up to her room. When I got there, all she wanted to do was talk. She never made eye contact as her head stooped, allowing her only to stare at the bed cover. Initially, I did stand there to listen, but I was impatient, and her habit of picking her nose as she talked repulsed me. After a time, I rarely listened to her, and eventually, I even tried to ignore her calls completely.

One winter's day, I was flouring the fish for dinner, and my fingers felt frozen. Like a wailing banshee, her call grated on my brain all morning. As I glanced down to the floor, where the opened bag of rat poison once stood, a sudden wicked thought entered my head, 'I could so easily add some of that to the flour', I thought secretly. I was shocked and dismissed it instantly. I really did not like my own thoughts and feelings towards Chacha. 'God, forgive me for even thinking such a thing', I said to myself.

To my relief, Chacha made a miraculous recovery. I'm sure her sudden revival had more to do with the dread of those needles than anything else. She barely picked up her feet as she slowly shuffled around the house, and her shoulders stooped badly. Like a gloomy shadow, Chacha followed me around, wringing her hands, not knowing what to do with herself. She didn't have the strength in her hands to do much. Washing up was out of the question, too, as she was convinced that she would catch pneumonia by simply touching the water. She always found some excuse to do as little as possible. Her oily black hair, plastered against her leathery olive skin, was tied back in a low bun. It desperately needed a good wash.

When I tried to get her to have a shower, she responded vehemently. 'A shower, that would kill me', she squealed in her usual high-pitched tones. Before I could respond, she scurried away and hid in her room. I had never seen her move so fast. I resigned myself to the fact that a shower was out of the question.

My perception was that everything was becoming more and more difficult. I was just coping, and I reassured myself that Damian would come to the rescue soon. Determined to manage, I did manage, at least until the day that Antonio left his bed. The stronger he became, the more difficult he was. He kept me on my toes, ordering me around, and his eye was always on the clock. If dinner were late, he would complain. If someone were at the door, even if I were up to my elbows in flour, he would yell for me to open it. Before I knew it, I seemed to be responsible for everything. The more I did, the more Antonio demanded of me. I began to feel anger and resentment towards him. Perhaps the loss of his wife to cancer all those years ago had left him bitter. Whatever the reason, he was just an ungrateful, mealy-mouthed man who sucked all the joy out of life. I preferred it when he was sick in bed.

The bitterness and ill-will I felt on the inside towards Damian's family really bothered me. This was not what I expected. With good intentions, I had planned to care for them, to show some kindness, even to love them. But I couldn't do it. As much as I tried, I just couldn't love them the way I wanted to.

One evening, it was later than usual before I could prepare dinner. Carmen was asleep, but Anna was unsettled, and I had to read several stories before she finally closed her eyes. When I went downstairs, Antonio paced up and down, watching me while I made the dinner and set the table. I could sense he was angry. At last, we sat down. The first thing he did was to point to the watch on his wrist and complain. I told him I was doing my best. He then picked up a lettuce leaf from his plate and said with an irritated voice, 'This isn't washed properly.' I looked closer at the dangling leaf to see a tiny fruit fly. I felt furious and lost my temper. Instantly, I stood up, 'You can wash your own lettuce if you're not happy with my efforts.' I snapped back. Just then, I could hear Anna crying again; not waiting for his response, I left the table in stony silence.

Upstairs, I found Anna not so much crying as whinging. She repeatedly groaned, 'Read me a story, read me a story;' her voice added to my frustration. In a silent rage, I screamed bitterly to God, 'This is not what I expected!' In anger, I reminded God, 'You are supposed to be taking care of us.' Anna's voice persisted relentlessly, so I grabbed my Bible, opened it to a random page, and began to read. I kept on reading, but I was so distressed that I didn't hear the words. Anna became still, and I was shocked to see the words on the page were somehow superimposed; I thought I was going insane. I looked at Anna—she was sound asleep. An eery silence followed. I gazed back to my Bible, my attention now riveted to the words as they seemed to jump off the page. In the stillness, I began to hear my own voice reading them. It was uncanny how personal and relevant they were to me. I felt that God was speaking directly to my heart and that He was letting me know that He fully understood exactly how I felt. I read:

"With words of hatred they surround me; they attack me without cause. In return for my friendship, they accuse me, but I am a man of prayer. They repay me evil for good and hatred for my friendship." (Psalm 109:3-5)

I continued reading those words over and over. I felt utter relief. My distress melted away. I was in awe that God would speak to me. I didn't go back downstairs that night; instead, I lay next to my two girls sleeping in the single bed we shared and instantly fell into a deep sleep.

The next morning, my eyes shot open with the sound of Chacha bellowing, 'Brijeeet, Brijeeet', from her bedroom. Negative thoughts filled my head; I perceived that nothing had changed. I dragged myself out of bed thinking, 'And so...it begins!' I made my way to her room, wondering if something was wrong, but instead, I found her looking comfortably propped up, ready for a good chinwag. I stopped a distance from her bedside, as I always did, due to the smell. I asked, 'Que pasa (What's the matter)?' Patting a space on her bed, she ushered me over to sit with her. 'Ven, ven (Come,

come)', she said quietly. I hesitated, too close for comfort; I had never wanted to get that close to her before, but I felt drawn like there was another force beyond my own. Slowly I moved closer and sat beside her. I found myself just listening and realised I had never really listened to her before.

As she spoke, I looked at her closely, and for the first time, I began to see her through different eyes. It was as if I could see beyond her dull and wrinkled exterior. Somehow, she was not the same; I no longer felt repulsed by her. In this new light, she began to shine. I had a warm feeling; a sense of compassion radiated from deep within. I saw that Chacha was just a needy old woman longing for some company. How could I have been so cold and indifferent to her? I felt ashamed of myself. Why hadn't I listened to her before? She continued talking, satisfied with just a reassuring nod of the head here and there. I sat for a while and for once was riveted to her every word. I began to hear her and felt stirred by her loneliness. I wanted to put my arms around her and make her feel loved. Just like the little boy on the street, I didn't, I couldn't. Then she came to an end of talking and strained to look up at me. In a magic moment of silence, we made eye contact, a most unusual occurrence. Then she took my hand and softly stroked it as she said, 'Thank you for listening, Brijeet.' A lump formed in my throat, and my eyes watered. I knew she really meant it. Touched to the core, I responded by enclosing her hands in mine and squeezing them.

At that moment, my stony heart began to melt. Later that same day, seeing through new eyes, even Damian's father appeared softer and more accepting of me. I became more understanding of him, and he seemed less angry. The amazing thing was that it just happened; I didn't try to force it. In fact, I stopped trying so hard to please. I felt that I was being empowered somehow; I was no longer moving in my own strength. Also, I stopped trying to pretend that I understood the language when I didn't.

The next evening, I picked up my Bible with excitement and again the words spoke into my heart. They said, 'If you love those who love you, what credit is that to you? Even sinners love those who love them.'

Not long after, I will never forget the feeling I had when I glanced over at Antonio. He caught my glance, and his eyes crinkled as he smiled for the first time, and a most unusual expression came through his eyes; he actually looked happy. I discovered that he did have a heart after all, and like my own, it was beginning to melt. That evening, warmth from the embers beneath the tablecloth seemed to penetrate deep into both of our hearts.

The challenges and responsibilities hadn't changed, but something extraordinary was happening. I was changing, and it wasn't due to my stubborn determination. Feelings of love and compassion towards my new family continued without any effort from me. I tried to share those feelings, but no one I talked to seemed to understand. I called Damian, but our phone call was awkward, almost painful. Then I called Carmel (she was the only one who understood what I was experiencing). From then on, our communications by tape messages over the ensuing months became a great comfort to me.

In my mind, there was only one church, the Catholic Church, so I started going there. But, I found it oppressive with its candles and its hypocrisy. I still didn't fully understand everything; I only knew that God was real, and that was enough for me. I knew now that God was not confined to the walls of the church and stopped going altogether. God continued to speak through His Word, and as the whole situation turned around, I began to understand.

Five months passed, and at last, the day came when Damian arrived. We put a "Welcome Home" sign with balloons up in the living room. We were all so excited to see him. I couldn't wait to talk to him privately, but I didn't have the chance until later that evening. As soon as we were alone, I told him everything; about how sick his father had really been, how difficult the situation became when he recovered, how resentful I had felt, and how God had spoken to me through the Bible. Damian listened to every word, but by his reaction, I knew that he just hadn't understood. I was so disappointed. He looked at me in a most uneasy way and said, 'You need a holiday!'

I thought Damian seemed sympathetic but soon

realised that wasn't the case. He was condescending, and he treated me as if I was out of my mind. He said that I was overworked and needed a good rest, and he arranged a holiday for the girls and me to visit Carmel in Manchester.

Our short stay with Carmel was delightful. After telling her all, she was overjoyed, and we both knew we had found something very precious. We felt closer than ever before. The first Sunday there, the girls and I happily went along to Victoria Park Fellowship with Carmel and her three children.

This was the first Pentecostal church I had ever been to. It was daunting at first; so strange how the people lifted their hands and sang with gusto. Sometimes a still quietness fell upon the whole congregation, even the children. Then a loud voice prayed earnestly. I didn't know what to think, but I listened intently to the voices praying around the auditorium, one after another. My attention stolen by the children and their needs during the sermon made it impossible to follow, but I was drawn in and had to go back by myself.

That evening, I returned to Victoria Park Fellowship alone and was able to pay full attention to the sermon. The preacher, Noel Procter, played a tape recording of a man's testimony. I heard the accent of an Irish man's voice speaking. It was so deep and strong that I imagined him to be a big, burly character full of wild tales to tell. Instead, I heard him breaking down, weeping bitterly. His voice, high-pitched and barely intelligible, gave a powerful witness of a life totally changed. Following the tape recording was a message, and then the penny dropped. Suddenly, as if a light switched on, I understood the meaning of the Gospel. It all made perfect sense. The tears rolled as Noel gave an invitation to accept Jesus. My heart pounded, and I almost ran down the aisle to the front. There I stood, sobbing uncontrollably. I desperately wanted Jesus in my life. Seeing the floodgates open, Noel offered his handkerchief and gave me a moment to compose myself. The tears still flooded; I couldn't hold back. I repeated the sinner's prayer, and I knew from that moment, without a shadow of turning, that I was different. So, so happy! For the first time, I stood before my God unashamed, justified, and whole. Such sweet relief; I will never forget it. A heavy weight lifted off my shoulders, leaving me feeling euphoric as if I was floating six inches off the ground. I knew forgiveness. I knew I was accepted, warts and all.

I caught the bus back and got off at the bottom of Carmel's Street. Reliving the moment over and over as I walked up the hill, feeling very content. Before I knew it, I came to the "T" junction at the top of the street. I had been so elated and so immersed in my own thoughts that I drifted past the house completely unaware. I just grinned and turned around. As I spun in the opposite direction, I had a vision that my life had just taken a "U" turn.

Chapter Five

A BROKEN VESSEL

After a year in Spain, we moved back to Australia. Changing from the Catholic Church to the Evangelical Church had more of an impact on Damian than I could ever have imagined. At first, he was uninterested in my conversion and remained apathetic for a while. Anything to do with God was foolishness to him. Damian really believed that my interest would fizzle out over time. He loved me as much as he was able; he just hated my God.

Damian became more and more of a slave to work, working seven days a week without ever taking a break. He was so tired all the time, but persuading him to take a day off was impossible. If I so much as mentioned the idea, he went into an angry rage. He rarely spent time with the girls and me, and he seemed to snap at the least thing. At times, his outbursts caused terrible upset for all of us. One of the rare times when Damian sat down to the table, he yelled out as we began to say grace over the meal. 'You should be grateful to me; I'm the one who puts the food on the table!' he blasted. I hardly got a word out before he raised his voice even higher, saying some extremely bitter things. The meal was ruined; I no longer had an appetite. It was like treading on eggshells. I remained silent until his anger simmered down; otherwise, we would end up in a terrible row.

Carmel migrated to Australia with her three children during the ensuing months. Initially, they lived with us, which somehow made my life easier as Damian tried to be polite and put his best foot forward.

Once Carmel moved out, the rows crept back in. A big quarrel erupted when I tried to finalize some plans to go camping together, but Damian changed his mind and didn't want to go anymore. He was unhappy and complaining; I couldn't bear to listen anymore. I reached a tipping point and exploded. I stood up so abruptly that the chair went crashing to the floor, and without a word, I silenced his rantings by grabbing the car keys and taking off. Screeching out of the driveway, I sped off with my foot to the floor, crying and overcome with emotion. I gave myself a scare when I glanced at the speedometer – and I started to slow down. Thoughts of leaving my two little girls in such a rage made me feel upset. I started to pray as I drove. It was one of those "Why is it so hard?" conversations with God. I really didn't want to return home. Then the fuel light began to flash. I didn't have my purse with me, and mobile phones were non-existent at that time, so I pulled up on the side of the Camden Highway, wondering what to do.

After a few hours of praying, I stopped feeling sorry for myself and knew I had to turn around and go back. Damian was my husband; he was a good provider, and he never raised a hand to me or the girls. I loved him, and that's all that mattered.

In spite of the flare-ups, God was teaching me how to forgive Damian and how to really love him. As I picked up his clothes off the floor, instead of complaining, I found myself praying for him. I ironed his shirts and rolled his socks with tender loving care. Damian liked the "new me" for a time, but he said it wouldn't last. I learned to become more submissive; he really noticed that. But Damian observed other changes as well, less favourable in his eyes. Church involvement increased, and gradually swear words began to disappear from my vocabulary. Getting drunk and other bad habits began to fade, and in his eyes, I became "boring". He also resented my attempts to stop cheating on our tax returns (which I always completed).

Damian was accustomed to picking up "freebies" from his workplace. He brought back a whole box of chocolate bars and couldn't understand why I wasn't happy about it. My intention was to discourage him from taking anything else, so I asked him not to give them to the kids. He was so angry and reminded me that I was the biggest thief under the sun. I tried to explain that was my past life, and God was helping me to change, but any talk of God made him furious. I didn't try to defend myself; instead, I silently prayed as he erupted. I knew he could never understand until he was born again.

Submission was not easy for me, but I did submit; I loved him, and I believed I could win him over. Damian only took advantage of that. He didn't want me to go out to work. He didn't want me to study. It seemed that he didn't want me to do anything. Despite having the finances to buy a second car, Damian refused. The more submissive I became, the more controlling he became. He moved from complacency to out-and-out antagonism. Like his father, he became very demanding. There were many concerns, but I made a conscious effort to let go of them all. When it came to the kids' schooling, I tried to reason with him and persuade him to send them to a Christian school. It was useless! He blankly refused. I felt a tremendous sense of helplessness that progressively grew worse. I tried to talk to him, but he was quick to anger, and we always ended up in conflict. The last straw was when Damian demanded that I stop going to church and get rid of my Bible. I felt very restricted, but I stopped going to church, and I only read my Bible in secret. Even so, nothing appeased Damian. And after a time, life became unbearable. I felt completely powerless. In the end, I just couldn't live with his controlling ways.

I chose the most appropriate time, sat Damian down, and asked him to listen without interrupting. I explained exactly how I was feeling, affirming that I did love him but that I was done! Finished! I couldn't live with him anymore. To my amazement, Damian didn't explode. He spoke quietly and seemed to relent. I saw a softening in his eyes as he expressed that he felt second best. He felt that God had come between us as if there was another man in my life. My heart melted at his utter confusion. He really didn't understand what was going on. We both ended up in tears. I couldn't leave him.

We muddled through the next few months, but after only a short time, again, he became terribly controlling. I prayed long and hard, but our situation only deteriorated. When I came to the realisation that nothing had changed, I did something drastic. I told him it wasn't working and that I would be leaving in a week's time. His response was cold and accepting; he simply became silent and nodded his head. I felt that he wanted me to go. This time I did leave him.

I moved to a rented house closer to Carmel's place and enrolled the girls into Bethel Christian Academy, the same school their cousins attended. The kids thought this was great, and moving to a new house with a swimming pool seemed like a big adventure. When Damian and I told them that daddy would be staying in the old house, Anna was distraught and cried bitterly. It was heart-wrenching for all of us. Carmen, only five years old, was too young to process what was going on and appeared less affected.

The school provided a good environment both emotionally and spiritually. Anna and Carmen, inundated with birthday-party invites, made many friends.

They seemed happy and carefree. Sometimes I wondered if they even noticed their father's absence, they were so used to it, and they rarely asked for him. I continued to pray with confidence for the restoration of our marriage, and I felt at peace.

Six long weeks passed before Damian came around. But when he did, he seemed very different. He seemed genuinely contrite. He took me by the hand and gently said he was sorry. I could see remorse in his eyes, and I knew he meant it. Finally, it was he who really wanted our marriage to work.

We agreed on many things that day, both trying hard to meet in the middle. We agreed to buy a second-hand car, to sell our original home so that the girls didn't have to move schools again. Damian agreed that I could study, and I agreed I would only do part-time study. When he conceded that I could attend church, I promised I would only go every second week. Then Damian even agreed to spend some time with us on alternate weekends by taking the Sunday off.

Reunited again, we both began to work on our marriage. Damian became more considerate to both the girls and me. For a time, it was bliss. My faith soared like never before. Damian moved into the rented house, we sold our family home, and together we searched to purchase a new home.

Over that period, I gained entry into the University of Western Sydney to pursue a B.A. in Nursing, and we purchased our second home. Damian and I spent more time together as a family. Anna and Carmen were clearly pleased to have their dad back, and they remained in Christian education. Damian kept his part of the bargain, and I kept mine. We were happy. I finished my nursing degree and went on to complete a Graduate Diploma in Midwifery.

Before long, our close friends Alfredo and Isabel, who were very Catholic, became born-again Christians and started going to a Spanish-speaking Pentecostal church. Alfredo was Argentinian, and Isabel was from Spain. Alfredo shared his faith on many occasions with Damian; they had a lot in common and trusted each other.

Eventually, Alfredo invited Damian to attend his church. Damian went along, but he insisted on going alone at first. After a few weeks, the girls and I started going with him. What a glorious time that was; we were all so incredibly happy. Life was good, and we grew closer as a family. Then Damian responded to an invitation to be baptised. It seemed too good to be true, but I was just so grateful I praised God for it.

In the back of my mind, something was a little odd. As far as I was aware, Damian had not yet responded to the Gospel, but I just wanted to believe the best, and I left it between him and God, encouraging him all the way.

Not long after his baptism, right out of nowhere, Damian had a yearning to visit his homeland. I knew what it was like to be homesick, and I encouraged him to take a few weeks' break. He went to Spain to stay with his father for a month.

The month passed slowly, and we were looking forward to his return. On the day of his return, as planned, Damian called to organise pick-up from the airport. I was happy to hear his voice. After a few words of greeting, I asked, 'What time do you land?' A long silence followed, and I knew something was wrong.

Then in a serious tone, he said, 'I'm not ringing to tell you when to pick me up.'

'OK, so when do you get back?' I responded curiously.

'I'm not coming back', he said in the same tone.

I thought he was teasing but soon realised from the deadly silence that he wasn't. His words still resonate in my head. His solemn voice confirmed, 'It's over.'

My eyes began to fill with tears; I couldn't bear to hear another word and calmly put the phone down. In denial, I told myself, 'It's not true, he'll be back', and wiped my eyes. Instantly the phone began to ring again, but I just couldn't pick it up. I froze. I couldn't think. I continued to ignore the ringing until it rang off the wall, then finally, silence. No more tears. All I could do was grapple with the thoughts crowding in on me. He never said goodbye to the girls; his clothes still hung in the wardrobe; does he have someone else? Why? The ringing started again. This happened several times, but each time I didn't pick up. As though trying to convince myself, the thought 'He'll be back' kept repeating itself over and over in my mind.

Some months passed, and I continued to wait. I told myself that Damian was going through a mid-life crisis, and I continued to firmly believe that God would restore our marriage because God hates divorce.

Damian did come back, but not to me. There wasn't another woman. He just wanted out. Soon it became apparent that Damian's only reason for returning to Australia was to claim his portion of the house and move on. We came to an amicable agreement without any need to involve the courts. Settlement was all so very civilized, but I refused to divorce him. Contact with Damian over the following three years was brief, through Anna and Carmen. Even so, with tenacity, I clung to my belief and persisted in prayer, waiting expectantly for restoration.

I never stopped loving Damian. Being apart was hard, but I never wavered. I never looked at another man, nor did I respond to any attempts of friendship for fear of jeopardizing the chance of getting back with Damian. I encouraged the girls to respect him, and I cooperated with any contact he wanted to have with them. Then, in 2002, the moment I had been waiting for arrived. Damian asked me if I would be willing to have another go at our marriage. I was more than willing.

We didn't live together, mainly because I didn't want to. I needed to know that there was no other woman. Also, there were some concerns in our relationship regarding communication, which we definitely needed to deal with. We spent the next year courting and ironing out these issues. Damian continued to live and work in Sydney, a two-hour drive from the Central

Coast where the girls and I lived. We saw each other on weekends, and sometimes they turned into long weekends.

Though it wasn't easy at times, it was a happy year for me. I was optimistic about the future. For Damian, who knows? I only know that he booked a weekend in Melbourne for our twenty-third anniversary, only to tell me on the second night, 'It's over!'

Those words cut deeper than the first time because this time, I knew it was final.

Unrequited Love
My Love burns as a blazing fire,
Lavished on one with no desire.
Depreciated, lost on hardened heart,
Yearnings remain never to depart.
Hopeless truth for endless time,
I am my lover's, but he is not mine!

At one time or another, we all struggle to find purpose in life. It's often an inward struggle, a well-kept secret that makes life appear "normal" on the outside. For me, that time began. I ached for my husband, just like the first time we split. I couldn't stifle the pain when I saw him with another woman. This seemed to happen often unexpectedly, in the local supermarket. The hope that I had been clinging to was dwindling. When I was on my own, I cried a lot. I felt empty and frozen on the inside. All I could do was keep occupied at work and busy at home and focus on my girls.

My daughter Anna's decision to leave home compounded my hidden emotions. She was eighteen and 'in love'; nothing could stop her. I felt sad about her going, and her decision to live with her boyfriend left me feeling like a failure. But at least I saw it coming and was able to resign myself to it.

The final significant blow came when Carmen decided to leave at the very same time as Anna. That, I did not handle well. I had no inkling that she would leave home at the tender age of sixteen. Carmen had her reasons, and, like Anna, nothing could stop her. I understood that she was unhappy at her school, and I could see that it made sense to go to a senior high school for the last two years. It even made sense to go to the selective school where her cousin John would attend because it was close to her dad's place in Sydney. But I wasn't ready for her to go.

Very alone and feeling no longer needed by anyone, disillusionment set in. At home and work, I continued as normal, but I felt numb, only half there. The few good friends I had were indispensable to my wellbeing. I was able to confide in them how I felt. I convinced myself that it was entirely my fault. My faith had not only driven Damian away; it had driven my girls away too. My friends encouraged me otherwise. Still, I couldn't help but feel disappointed with God for unanswered prayer. The empty nest and being let down by the man I loved left me completely consumed with the piercing question, 'What now?'

It wasn't long after that a timely answer came. In August 2003, a colleague invited me to a Reach-Out Conference in the Blue Mountains, west of Sydney. There I listened to people tell amazing stories about taking "time-out" to spend working in a foreign country. These people gave up their salaries, their time, and their creature comforts, all so they could help others.

What fascinated me most was that within such a diverse range of people, every one of them had one thing in common. They all related to me that by helping others, they had actually helped themselves. This struck a chord. It made me realise that I had been spending too much time focused on me. I knew I needed to step outside of myself. At the end of the two-day conference, I sought out a stall that represented South America, and I put my name down as being available. In less than a week, I received a letter from HCJB (Heralding Christ Jesus Blessings) Mission Ministry telling of a vacancy. It said that there was a desperate need for a midwife to cover a period of three months in a jungle hospital in Ecuador. This time the question in my mind was, 'Will you go?'

After making some enquiries, I felt that the position was tailor-made for me. I had the qualifications and experience in midwifery, I was fluent in Spanish, and I felt that three months was perfect; nobody would even miss me for that short period. The answer was easy, 'Yes, I will go.'

The biggest sacrifice was the financial outlay for the airfare and accommodation, plus the fact that I would have no income for three months. I had been a single mum for the past five years, so I knew how to make it happen: weekend night-shifts and double-shifts.

Another question closely followed. 'If you thought you weren't coming back, would you still go?' I couldn't answer. I tried to ignore the question, but like the hound from hell, it pursued me and troubled me. I knew it would not go away unsatisfied, so I began to think deeply. This question made me realise the enormity of leaving everything behind. Putting my life on hold for a short period was one thing, but the thought of never coming back – that was unimaginable and certainly not something I could do half-heartedly.

I started to think about my position at North Gosford Private Hospital, about my girls, my friends, my life as I knew it. The thought of leaving my lovely daughters was the hardest and hurt the most. At the time, Anna was nineteen, and Carmen was only seventeen.

I began to question my motives for going. I probably over-analysed them and became aware that everything I did was all about me; even my disappointment with God was because He hadn't given "me" what "I" wanted. I reflected on my life and saw an empty mechanical existence with no purpose, no goals – just nothingness. I struggled with the meaninglessness of life and decided that I could not bear to live another day without purpose, without something or someone to live for.

I came to terms with the question and discovered my real motives for leaving everything behind. It wasn't to help others just so that I could ultimately help myself. It was because I wanted my life to be meaningful, not just to me but also to others. I needed to love and to be loved. I needed my life to count for something, and I knew that living for me could never achieve that. With a mixture of fear and excitement, I approached this crossroad in my life and surrendered everything; my answer had to be, 'Yes! Yes, I would go, even if I thought I was not coming back!'

Once that decision was made, there was no turning back. I put my affairs in order, drew up my Will & Testament, and I was ready.

Chapter Six

CRUCIBLE OF FIRE

Journal Entry:
Lima, Peru
10th December 2003

The first thing I heard this morning was the sound of a muffled bring-bring...bring...bring. Realising it was the ringing of a telephone, I began to search the unfamiliar surroundings. The sound grew louder and louder; all my attention was drawn to the direction from where it came.

As I rummaged around the room frantically, the volume reached a deafening pitch beyond my tolerance level. I began to freak out. Anxiously I upturned cushions, scattering them around, and feverishly pulled out the drawers, emptying them; still, there was no phone to be found.

Becoming more and more stressed I urgently combed
through the items and clothes strewn around the room.
Still, the blasting echo continued. At the pinnacle of
my frenzy, I suddenly woke up.

The hassle-dream was over, but the irritating sound continued. I was momentarily disorientated before realising that the phone was real and ringing beside my bed. In a daze, I picked up and heard a voice babbling on the other end. I tried to gather my thoughts. Once I realised the babbling was in Spanish, I responded in Spanish, saying, 'I didn't understand, could you repeat that please.' The words became distinct. A very confident and clearly spoken male voice began an introduction, 'Soy Pastor Luis Alberto Guizada Díaz a su servicio (I am Pastor Luis Alberto Guizada Díaz at your service).'

Impressive as it sounded, I had no idea who this man was. He explained that he had recently spoken to my pastor in Ecuador and that Pastor Horacio and he were good friends. Reiterating their conversation, he said that he knew that I was a midwife, that I had just finished a short-term mission in Ecuador, and that I was praying about where God would place me. He knew that my purpose for being in Peru was to visit my sponsored child and that I was looking for cheap accommodation. He even knew my travel plans and how long I would be staying in Peru. I was stunned. It was apparent that this total stranger knew more about me than I was comfortable with. After a short time, I could only assume that confidentiality was not high on the list of mores for South American pastors.

Pastor Luis Diaz was a man of many words. Pausing only to draw breath, he said, 'There is something I want to show you.' Before I could open my mouth, he continued, 'Can I pick you up at 8.00 am from the foyer of your hotel?'

'Something to show me?' I repeated incredulously.

'I will explain when I get there; it's a little complicated over the phone', he said.

Giving it as much thought as one can in an instant, on the end of the phone, I found myself saying, 'OK.' Glancing at my watch, I realised that I only had twenty minutes. I quickly jumped out of bed and dressed in a mad panic. Reluctantly, I missed out on breakfast, not wanting to be late; a big sacrifice, I felt, as it was included in the tariff.

There I stood in the foyer, hollow in the stomach and a little frayed around the edges, but I was on time. I waited and waited. I occupied myself by focusing on the many questions I wanted to ask. They tumbled around in my mind as I converted them into Spanish, polishing the translation until it was perfect.

Thirty minutes later, a tall, lean man wearing a tailored jacket, white shirt and a classic red/white-striped tie showed up. Approaching me, he immediately repeated the same words he had used on the phone when he first introduced himself. Like a cracked record, there was no variation. He looked very typically Peruvian (except for his tall stature) with short black hair and a thin black moustache. His serious expression sullied his olive skin and dark features as he motioned to shake my hand. Though he acted in a professional manner, his speech was not indicative of a well-educated man. I responded by telling him my name as I shook his hand. I had barely finished speaking when he interrupted with a huge string of words all joined together. His speech was so fast; I missed it. The second time around was more comprehensible. He said, 'My car is double-parked on the main road outside.' He hastily ushered me towards the exit, talking and walking at the same time. I felt compelled to follow him. I also felt a little annoyed since, without even an apology for being late, he expected me to follow him blindly. I stopped behind him and asked insistently, 'Where are we going?' A deep furrow appeared between his eyes as he glared at me, as though irritated by my question. 'Te vas a ver (You'll see)', he replied with a frozen grin. Not satisfied, I stood my ground. This was my first encounter with the man, a complete stranger, and I wasn't comfortable with him. I didn't feel safe stepping into his car. I calmly insisted, 'I would like you to leave the address with the receptionist.'

He stopped and stared at me, smiling, but his pseudo smiles never successfully convinced me of his character. An awkward silence followed, then waving one hand in the air, he retorted, 'No hay problema (No problem).'

He walked back to the front desk and rapidly scribbled down the address on the scrappiest piece of paper, handing it to me. The words were barely legible. Instead of passing it on, I turned to the receptionist, asked for a piece of paper, and after writing my name on it, I asked the pastor to spell his name. As I wrote it down, I asked, 'How long might we be?'

'That depends on you', he responded, as if I was holding him up.

'Say, approximately one hour then', I replied.

'No, no, no', he churned out, shaking his head madly. 'It takes at least half an hour to get there.'

Like I would know, I thought!

'Let's say two hours then', I suggested, shooting in the dark. With an assertive, sharp nod of the head, he agreed. I wrote down the approximate time I would be away and then gave it to the receptionist. Finally, I followed him out the door. Though he didn't seem happy, the look of relief on his face relayed a nano-hint of appreciation.

Sure enough, his Kombi van was very badly parked right outside the main door, causing a major traffic problem. Bumper to bumper cars were impatiently blasting their horns, trying to get past, but the pastor took no heed at all. Unfazed, he casually opened the door for me and then hopped into the driver's seat and began to drive.

I was full of apprehension. He was silent. Not a word was spoken for some time, and I had so much I needed to ask. I broke the silence. For the next twenty minutes, I picked his brains with my numerous ques-tions. He was very polite and responded to all my questions. I understood from our conversation that he was taking me to a house in Surco, where he had placed twenty-six girls whom he had recently rescued from the streets of Lima. Surco is a suburb of Lima, which is only fifteen kilometres away, but traffic congestion was so bad it took thirty-five minutes to get there.

We arrived at a two-storey house in a quiet street. Instead of knocking on the front door, the pastor opened it with a key. As I walked behind him into the hallway, I asked myself, 'What can I possibly do here?'

The answer came as clear as a bell, in a small but very audible voice, 'Let me show you!'. My heart leapt with excitement, and the feelings of apprehension I had dissolved instantly.

Aware of a small group of girls approaching, I promptly dropped my guard as they crowded in around us. They began to speak all at the same time, greeting the pastor, 'Saludos, Pastor Luis.' They greeted me with words of welcome as they touched me on my hands, my shoulders, and my arms. I felt little hands deliberately investigating my fingernails one by one. My straight hair was patted and smoothed down by another inquisitive girl, and even the mole on my arm was probed. I felt strange like I was an alien-being under scrutiny. Such a surreal experience!

The girls were all mixed ages from seven to seventeen, and one tiny baby just a few months old. Soon the small group grew bigger as more girls gathered around. Pastor Luis seemed to fade into the background somewhere while the girls led me around the house, clinging on to both hands. The warmth and affection that radiated from these girls was unlike anything I had ever experienced. I felt God's presence was right there shining through them, using them to speak directly to me. More than just emotions, it was tangible, like my heart was being touched on the inside.

Two younger girls clung to my left arm and three to my right, each competing to hold my hand. They wanted hugs and kisses all the time for no reason. I think they just wanted to be seen. The older girls were more inquisitive and had lots of questions; they asked my name, where I was from, how long I would be staying, and lots more. They were all so in need of affirmation. The slightest attention I gave, even just eye contact, seemed somehow to satisfy their insatiable appetite to be noticed. Most of all, I recognised that the girls just wanted to feel valued and respected. In their short exposure to life, they had been robbed of all the natural feelings that make us human—they so desperately needed to be loved.

As the girls showed me their rooms, their only personal space, I was appalled. There were two bunk beds jam-packed into each tiny room, two or three girls to a bed. Such cramped conditions! The stained mattresses were bare, no sheets or pillows, with a single blanket hanging over the end.

I was upset when I found that a tiny space in the hallway was the place where the girl with the baby slept. Because the baby woke everyone up during the night, a makeshift partition was set up. It was made of thin plywood nailed to two uprights with a single foam mattress covering practically the entire floor space.

I spent the better part of that morning getting to know the girls and trying to remember their names. One girl was knitting, and this gave me an idea. I asked her for a piece of wool to play a string game. The younger girls watched intently as I tied a knot in the wool and placed it around my fingers. When I produced the "Eiffel Tower", squeals of delight went up harmoniously. After the "Irish Harp", one of the girls jumped to her feet with excitement, asking me for the wool. In no time, she was showing me what she could produce. This sparked off a major search for pieces of wool by the other girls. Before long, half a dozen girls were showing off their own impressive shapes with great glee. To my surprise, they knew many more tricks than I could even imagine, the most impressive one being Machu Picchu.

Pastor Luis suddenly appeared out of nowhere, and it was time to go. A farewell kiss and hug to each of the girls seemed to go on forever, and then I realised that some of the girls had come back a second time in hopes of another kiss and another hug. I didn't notice at first; it was only their cheeky smiles that gave them away. Far more than twenty-six kisses later, we finally got out the door.

It was an interesting ride back to the hotel, Pastor Luis no longer silent. Instead, he had much to say: 'The older girls are looking after the younger ones and, although there are some staff, I can't afford to employ them for a full day.' Speaking very plainly, he continued, 'Money is the biggest issue.' I listened, and he talked. He paused at times, but I said nothing. Finally, he paused and then asked, 'Would you consider taking on the role of live-in Housemother?' Before I could answer, he continued, 'It would have to be a voluntary position.'

Although I had felt extremely drawn towards the girls, I didn't share this with him straight away; I wanted to process the whole experience. I had reservations, and I really needed time to think about where exactly they were coming from. I held back and simply responded, 'I need to pray about it.'

'There's a small room available on the roof-top, and it's totally separate from the girls', he said enthusiastically. Pausing only for a moment, he continued, 'You could stay there now if you wish.'

I felt uncertain; he was far too keen, so I hesitated all the more.

'Then you could get to know the girls a little better', he added.

I found myself backing away and said, 'I have plans to visit my sponsor-child, which I am sure you already know about, so I will think and pray about everything over the next few days and let you know.' The disappointment was written all over his face; I felt like I had let him down. He thanked me anyhow and passed his card to me, offering to pick me up at any time if I wished.

I checked out of the hotel and moved to the Swiss

Mission Guesthouse; this was the place where Doctor Klaus and his family from Ecuador were staying. His wife had suggested that we could meet up there. I realised that it was the same place I had called the previous night. I took a taxi to get there. The ride was heart-stopping as the kamikaze driver dodged pedestrians and came within a hair-span of other vehicles. I flinched and gasped all the way, wondering if we would ever make it in one piece. The extremely poor condition of his vehicle only added to the intensity of the drive. Feeling ruffled and shaky, I stepped out of the taxi, extremely relieved to know that the ordeal was over. The one and only consolation was that the fare was very cheap.

I secured a room and met up with Doctor Klaus, Martina, and their three children. We shared a simple meal of cheese and German bread, luxuries that had been unavailable in Ecuador, and we talked at length. I learned that Klaus and Martina were in the initial phase of setting up a Mission Hospital for the Quechua Indians in Apurimac. Klaus was excited about the prospect of building a hospital in this region commonly known as the "Poorhouse of Peru". Both Martina and Klaus were animated when they showed me the floor plan of the modern building. The nurse's accommodation looked amazingly well-designed and well-resourced. Their enthusiasm spilled over onto me when they asked me to come on board and work in the maternity unit. I was quite persuaded, but I knew my heart was being steered in a different direction. The midwife in me, however, needed to weigh up all the possibilities, and I didn't want to dampen their enthusiasm. I said that I would certainly think and pray about it.

The next day after Klaus and family set off to Apurimac, I found the Swiss Mission Guesthouse a little quiet. My room was basic but very clean and inexpensive, so it was perfect. I felt relaxed and comfortable. In the solitude, I considered all that had transpired over the past few days. The debate in my mind flickered to and fro as I speculated on this new opportunity. I argued with myself, 'I am a midwife, and I do love my chosen profession.' My thoughts continued, 'I really need to keep my skills up.' Then negative thoughts of smoggy Lima with its noisy bumper-to-bumper traffic and its out-of-control crime rate continued to sway me towards Apurimac. Intuitively, my thoughts drifted beyond the smog, back to the girls in Surco. I remembered the warmth and affection of those girls, the overwhelming conviction that God had spoken directly to my heart. I remembered the still, small voice speaking those words, 'Let me show you', and again, magically, I felt my heart leap inside of me. All of a sudden, I realised what God was doing. God was planning my course just like I had asked. First, He had brought me to a place of total dependence on Him, in Ecuador, then to Peru to see the need, and finally to the children in the house in Surco.

I could see that the wheels were in motion for something that I wasn't in control of myself. The debate was over; God won, and I was left with no doubt to choose the girls in Surco.

Journal Entry:
Lima, Peru
11th December 2003

> *Feeling secure in my decision I rang Pastor Luis last night. I told him that I had been praying and that I was considering taking on the role as Housemother. He was delighted and without hesitation offered to pick me up straight away. He suggested that I could stay with the children that very night. Although keen to see the girls again, I had to decline as I had already made plans to visit Malinda, my sponsored child. I arranged to stay at the house with the girls today, so he's coming to pick me up later in the afternoon.*

Before visiting Malinda, I decided to go shopping. Motivated by the prospect of seeing the girls again afterwards, I wanted to buy something small to take to them. In the middle of Saga Falabela, one of the largest department stores in Mira Flores, surrounded by all kinds of decorations, I realised that Christmas was fast approaching. It had not even crossed my mind until that moment. Toys and treats, fairy lights, shimmering tinsel and colourful baubles; I was excited, but I felt like a kid in a lolly shop with no money. I strolled around the store, smelling, feeling, and touching, and all my senses were stirred. The aroma of chocolate and other delicious treats filled my nostrils, and the pretty dresses and rows of fashionable shoes grabbed my attention. I priced them, but they were all so very expensive. Even if I stayed at the girls' house, the money I would save wasn't enough to buy presents for all those girls. So many "things"; everything the girls needed was crowding in on me. It was so frustrating. I knew I couldn't buy any of them. A memory jolted to the days of our shopping sprees and visions of mum filling her bags. Then it dawned on me—this must have been how she felt.

My mother began stealing in Dublin out of necessity. By the time I reached my early teens in Manchester, a full-blown habit had developed, which went on for years. Stealing was my mother's only way of providing, at first, for all of our needs, but then, all of our wants! The focus on feeding hungry children became lost in the pride of wanting for the sake of wanting.

Mum developed a special relationship with Marks and Spencer, a big department store in Manchester, not unlike Saga Falabela. She discovered one day that their trademark bags were given in place of receipts. I remember when she stole a whole wad of them. Then she took my sisters and me with her on what she called "a shopping spree". Really, it was our initiation into the art of shoplifting; we observed while she took what she could. From ladies-wear to the shoe department, she progressed through the store until all the bags were full. A day or two later, mum gave us all a bag, each with explicit instructions and then sent us back to Marks and Spencer to return the goods for cash refunds. Later we met up at the Milkmaid Coffee shop in Piccadilly and were all rewarded with a Knickerbocker Glory ice-cream. We often had shopping sprees like that one. In fact, over the following year, "Uncle Marks" paid for a holiday to Ireland for all of us.

I must have been standing there for some time before the salesgirl approached me. 'Can I help you, Senora?' she asked. I gathered my thoughts and responded quietly, 'No, that's fine, I'm just browsing.' Continuing through the store, as if to haunt me, the harsh voice of my mother echoed in my ear, 'Necessity knows no law.' My heart began to pound. I knew I'd better get out of there, so I made a quick decision and headed for the check-out with a large tin of biscuits. It was the best I could do. I then made a speedy exit, glad to leave the temptation behind me.

I found a public phone booth and called Luisa, the sister of the person who helped me at the Cuban Embassy. She was expecting my call and knew all about me. Luisa was extremely friendly and quickly made it very clear that I was welcome to stay at her place in the spare room. During our conversation, I discovered that Luisa was a literacy teacher who had been working for Wycliffe Missions for the past twenty years. I told her about my plans to visit Malinda and about the pending visit to the "house" in Surco. We agreed that I would call her back in a couple of days.

After another gruelling taxi ride in the heat of the day, I stepped onto the street, wondering if there might be some other form of transport. I looked at the minibuses and Kombi vans and shuddered as I saw people's bodies rammed in and tightly packed together. 'Perhaps not', I thought. The heavy traffic crawling along at a snail's pace convinced me it would be quicker to walk. But the heat in the short stroll on that crowded street was unbearable.

I stepped into the poky office of my child-sponsor organisation; a lady introduced herself as Mercina and began to explain the plans for the day. I had also arranged to visit my friends' sponsor child, a little boy. Apparently, they were both located at a site not too far away. Mercina suggested taking a motor-taxi. Was this, perhaps, the alternative transport I was looking for? The small motorbike with a colourful two-seater carriage attached behind it resembled a rickshaw with a hard roof. I crouched into the carriage designed to accommodate the typically short stature of the Peruvian people. My head hit the roof every time we flew over a bump. The motor-taxi turned out to be as dangerous— if not worse—as the taxi ride. The young boy on the motorcycle managed to crash into every pothole on the road, and there were many. He had no idea of the trauma he put his passengers through, and he probably should have been at school. I doubt that he even had a licence.

MOTOTAXI - FIRST RIDE

Arriving a little dishevelled at the child-sponsor site, the first thing I saw was a huge banner. The colourfully painted letters read, "Welcome, Bridget". Instantly, I felt better; it was beautiful. The moment I walked into the classroom, all the children stood up and began to sing, 'Bien Venida, Bien Venida (Welcome, Very Welcome).' Their voices harmonized as if well-rehearsed. I was impressed, and I felt humbled that they had put so much effort into my visit. Malinda made a speech and presented me with a bunch of spectacular flowers. Though much more formal than I had expected, Malinda's words touched me, and I hardly knew how to respond. She was so very appreciative and sincerely thankful.

Taken by surprise, when she handed the microphone over to me, I blurted out words that seemed inadequate, then I choked up and handed back the microphone.

Later, we went to Malinda's home to meet her family. Apparently, her aunties and uncles, all her cousins, and her grandparents lived there. After being introduced to family on all three levels, we finally reached the top floor. Although it had walls, there was no roof. Obviously lived in by evidence of furniture and beds, I was curious. 'What about the rain?' I asked. 'In Lima, we have very little rainfall', Mercina said. 'The house will eventually have a roof when they can afford it.' Apparently, this was common, to share a dwelling, then to construct another level as the family grows. Everyone in the family contributes to the cost. Sometimes it takes several years to complete each level, depending on their means.

I was surprised that Malinda had a TV in her bedroom, and, in comparison to the house in Surco, I could see that this house was well furnished. Malinda's mother and father both had jobs, and they seemed to be reasonably comfortable.

In light of this, I talked to Mercina about the street kids and asked if their organisation could help. Apparently not, I was told. To be eligible for their aid, a child must have a fixed address and a responsible carer. I couldn't help but feel disappointed; it just didn't seem right. The fact that I, and others like me, had been sending our after-tax dollars and personal savings to families not truly on the edge of poverty made me feel

that this group was less than focused on helping those
who needed it most, those who were in abject poverty.

Later that day, Pastor Luis actually picked me up on
time. During the drive to the house in Surco, I
explained that my plans were to return to Australia and
spend a year fund-raising before returning to Peru to
take the position as Housemother. He seemed fine with
this and said he would explain this to the girls.

On arrival, he hastily greeted the girls, telling them
to be patient while he showed me to my room. He then
brought me out into the courtyard and up a spiral stair-
case, one that I hadn't noticed on my first visit. Three
older girls followed us up to the top floor, where a small
shed-like structure stood independently. Though there
was no roof on this level, I was relieved to see that the
shed had a roof. The walls around the larger perimeter
were unfinished, making it a dangerous place for children. I shuddered to think of a child falling from there.

Without entering the tiny room, Pastor Luis
handed me a set of sheets and instructed me, 'There are
no other staff until tomorrow; if you have any questions, just ring me.' He walked off saying, 'I must go
now, and you have my number.' In affirmation, I
nodded, but there were questions lurking in the back of
my mind. I was about to make the bed, but one of the
girls who followed insisted, 'We can do it.' I was
grateful and asked her name. 'Karina', she said, 'and this

is Ruby and Amelia.' After brief greetings, I handed Karina the sheets, thanked her, and quickly followed Pastor Luis down the stairs. He was hurriedly saying his goodbyes to the girls, so I waited. Catching him before he rushed out the door, I asked, 'Is it OK if I ask you a few questions?'

'I'm in a bit of a hurry', he said, 'but what is it?'

'I don't know where anything is, or the house routine, or the time the girls go to bed. Are there any instructions written down anywhere?'

'Just ask the girls!' he said. 'If it's an emergency, call me.' With that, he walked out.

There were twenty-six very excited girls, a tiny baby, and me – and the house was mayhem. Some girls were running around wildly screaming as they chased each other. Some were singing happily; others played a jumping game with elastics on the patio. The television was blaring, but nobody was watching it, so I discreetly turned it off. All the girls were too preoccupied to notice; that is all except my three vigilant shadows. They had finished making the bed, and they seemed to be following me everywhere, intensely watching my every move. I was learning that "personal space" was non-existent in Peruvian culture. I indicated to them by crossing my lips with one finger and a long, 'Shhhhh.' To my relief, they said nothing! The noise was deafening; girls were yelling above the din just to be heard. My second culture-shock was that anything making less noise than a live pop concert or military invasion was horribly unsettling to most Peruvians.

I found some teenagers in the kitchen preparing soup for the evening meal and asked if I could help, but they had it all under control. I began to chat with the eldest girl; she must have been around fifteen or sixteen. She was shy at first and lacked confidence, but she was happy to answer questions. The others listened quietly; they seemed to lack the ability to initiate a conversation, and when I addressed them, even to ask their name, they seemed anxious.

I discovered that the girls often had an elderly woman spend the morning with them, but at night they had no adult supervision. They seemed happy that I was staying over. One of the teenagers, Herleena, was curious enough to ask, 'How long will you be staying?'

'I really don't know', I responded. 'It depends on a lot of things.'

She didn't ask any more questions but didn't appear satisfied either. The rumble and clatter of noise grew louder in the other room, so I went to check what was going on. I was relieved. The chaos seemed to be, to some degree, under control, and I began to relax. I took my video camera out and casually started recording. The three watchful ones were immediately aware, but the others were all too busy in their own little worlds to notice anything. After recording, I showed some playback sections to Karina. Within a short space of time, one by one, the other girls became aware and wanted to see too. When they saw themselves on the screen, they reacted in different ways. Seeing their own image and hearing their voice was a new experience; some were horrified and ran away, while others were intrigued and glued to the mini screen.

After the evening meal, they all wanted to watch TV. The girls crowded on top of each other to get a seat on the sofa, but even with some spilling onto the arms and others sitting on laps, they couldn't all fit. Two girls stood up to offer me a seat; they sat on the floor, resting their backs against the sofa with the other girls. We sat huddled together, all peering at this tiny little box in the corner, but they were extremely happy. To my surprise, a movie was about to commence. Given that there was only one channel available, I was amazed that the movie just happened to be an Australian movie, *Matilda*. It was hilarious watching it dubbed in Spanish, and the kids loved Skippy.

Remembering the tin of biscuits, I tried to stand up, but the girls groaned with disappointment and pulled me back onto the sofa. They thought I was leaving! Their groans soon settled down when I told them about the biscuits, and they happily released me.

A chorus of sighs and gasps harmonized together once they saw the beautiful red tin with Santa and his reindeers etched into the lid. Their eyes widened when the lid came off as if something precious was within. Almost drooling with expectation, they were yet very well-mannered and waited patiently for their turn as the tin was passed around. They were indecisive and struggled to choose, overwhelmed by the variety of biscuits. They touched one after another and then changed their mind. After a couple of rounds, the tin

soon emptied, and when it did, they all claimed owner-
ship of it, each one pleading for the empty tin.

The only fair thing to do was to raffle the tin, but
they didn't understand what a raffle was. After explaining, they excitedly set about looking for some paper
and a pen to write down their names. This took some
time, as there seemed to be a scarcity of everything,
even scraps of paper. To me, their little antics and how
they grappled with each other were such fun to watch.
They were uninhibited and very natural, and it was
obvious that they relished just being noticed by me.

After settling them down again, I chose Meridian,
the youngest girl, to draw a name out of the tin. At the
sound of her name, Irmina, a very loud and excitable 8-
year-old, began to jump up and down as though she'd
won a trip to Disneyland. The other girls were also
animated and seemed happy for her; none of them
complained or begrudged Irmina for having the prize. I
was touched by this.

Although there didn't seem to be any routine as
such, I noticed Herleena putting a couple of younger
girls to bed, and Dionna, the 14-year-old mum, disappeared for a while. The rest remained, but they all
wanted to speak at the same time. It was pandemonium. I told them to quieten down as Dionna was
probably trying to settle her baby. After a momentary
hush, the noise reached peak level again, and I couldn't
hear what anyone was saying. With a stricter tone, I
told them that they had to wait their turn to speak, and
they could only ask one question at a time. The din

quietened, but not for long. I could hardly hear myself think. I picked up a big wooden spoon and began speaking into it, telling the girls that it was a "microphone". Slowly the voices dropped out one by one, and they began to settle down and listen. From then on, as if by magic, silence reigned. It seemed to work. If someone forgot and spoke out, I would say, 'I can't hear you!' and explain again: 'You can't speak until you have the microphone.' The girls would laugh hysterically each time this happened. Apart from intermittent uproars of laughter, the room was silent while one person spoke. At last, we could all listen and hear one another. I passed the spoon to the girls, and it, in turn, was passed around. Sanity returned, and endless questions were fired at me, but in a civilized manner, one by one. Where are you from? Are you married? Do you have children? Where are they now? What are their names? Do you work? Do you have any photos? What's your favourite colour?

Eventually, I grabbed the spoon and said it was my turn to ask the questions. As I looked at the sea of shiny, smiling faces, it became deadly quiet. I knew that they each had a story to tell. I didn't yet know all their names, so that was always my first question.

I chose one of the older girls, Amelia, whom I had at least talked to previously. She told me that she was fifteen years old and that she had only been living in the house for two months. My next question was, 'Where did you live before?' Her cheeks blushed with embarrassment as she shook her head in the negative.

An awkward silence followed. It lingered, but her lips were sealed; she didn't want to say. I said supportively, 'It's OK, you don't have to answer if you don't want to.' For just a moment, the silence continued, then Irmina cut in with a burning desire to tell all. Amelia quickly passed on the mic, and Irmina started speaking. Loud and excited, she clearly loved being in the spotlight.

Irmina casually shared how her father was drunk most of the time and how when he was drunk, he nearly always beat her and her mother severely. What followed was totally unexpected; she began to relive a painful experience which she described in great detail. 'When I was seven', Irmina said, 'I watched from behind the curtain.' As the story unfolded, her voice became softer and then suddenly, she became self-conscious and very emotional. The hurt and trauma she remembered became so real that she stopped speaking. After a moment of difficult silence, Irmina tried to compose herself. Again, barely able to speak, her voice almost inaudible, she said, 'My father beat her to death.' The repressed memory unleashed a look of terror on her face, and her eyes welled up with tears. Unconsciously lowering the spoon, she wept bitterly. I stood up and reached out to put my arms around her. The room became still while Irmina sobbed uncontrollably. Only the convulsive sound of her breath penetrated the silence for some time. Irmina fought hard to compose herself, and after a while, she slowly lifted the spoon. Between tears, she continued in a quivering high-pitched voice, 'I just ran away; I didn't help her.'

We were all dumbstruck. Some were in tears, while others remained detached and unaffected. Irmina's words revealed a deep sense of guilt. I once felt that same emotion of guilt when I was just a little girl. The memory flashed before me so clearly. It was late in the afternoon; I was with Carmel. We were playing "hand ball" in the back entry when our ball went over the high wall. A kind man appeared out of nowhere, offering to help us get the ball back. Innocently, we accepted. He picked me up by the waist and lifted me to lean over the high brick wall. As I looked for the ball, I felt his fingers slip under my briefs. For a moment, I forgot about the ball. I didn't know what to say or do, but I knew something was wrong. Time seemed to stand still. I felt awkward, then mortified, 'Put me down, put me down!' I screamed.

He did put me down, and in a panic, I grabbed Carmel by the hand and bolted, jerking her along frantically, saying, 'Run, run!' Without hesitation, we ran together; we ran so fast that my grip on her hand broke, but we just kept running until we were exhausted.

I carried the shame and the guilt for allowing that man to lift me up for many years. I didn't know it wasn't my fault until someone told me. As I hugged Irmina, I told her over and over; it wasn't her fault. When Irmina calmed down and I gained composure myself, I tried to bring back some normality. I took the spoon and softly smiled. 'Do you have any brothers or sisters?' I asked.

She wiped her eyes with the back of her hand and

her snotty nose along her sleeveless arm; there were no tissues to be found anywhere. Her mind was now in a different place; she became calm and said, 'I have an older brother who is seventeen.' In a more stable voice, she went on to describe their makeshift home situated in a shantytown just outside of Lima. 'In our house, there's no water or electricity', she said. Her voice became louder, 'But we always have plenty of food.' Everyone laughed. Irmina half-smiled, and her eyes began to dry. Her nose continued to run, so she pulled up the front of her T-shirt and crudely blew it – then she carried on, bearing her heart and soul into the mike but now in a much lighter way. The girls began to laugh. In some unexplainable way, the quasi-mike seemed to help. Irmina ended as strong as she began. With a furrowed brow, she told us that her dad was in prison. Her voice had a tone of bitterness as she stared at the floor, avoiding eye contact, when she said, 'I'm glad he's in prison!'

At this point, Dionna returned. She had finally managed to put her baby to sleep. I began to think of how hard my own experience of teenage pregnancy was, and I wondered how she coped with the trauma of childbirth at only thirteen.

At the age of fifteen, I dropped out of school because I fell pregnant with my first boyfriend, Paul. My mother was ashamed and suggested I have an abortion, but when I refused, she swore me to secrecy. She then brought me to the priest and told me to lie; she wanted a church wedding, and she was too proud to tell the truth. When she lied through her back teeth, I naively went along with the deception, but I felt so guilty.

Paul, only seventeen, had no chance against my mother; she was a force to be reckoned with. His parents didn't fare much better either, and we had a shotgun wedding before I began to show. It was a traditional wedding, at Uncle Marks's expense, as always. I felt like such a hypocrite wearing that white dress and deceiving all those people. I began to resent my mother's religion.

Five months later, an ultrasound showed that the baby was anencephalic (a type of neural tube defect). Given the choice of an induced delivery immediately or a deformed baby that may not live long, the decision was easy. But I was devastated. The next day I went to the hospital, and the induction began. Paul went to work; he didn't want to be there, but he promised to visit in the evening. The baby was born by the normal process of delivery, which stretched out long into the early hours. Finally, the pain, the tears, and the struggle gave way to silence. Only heavy rain hitting the window could be heard. I was told it was a boy, but I never got to see him. I tried to stifle deep emotions when Paul never showed up. Feeling very much alone and uncertain of the future, hot tears began to roll, and I was overcome with sadness. Through the veil of tears, I stared out the window, and then a nurse came to my bedside. 'Are you all right?' she asked softly. I couldn't speak. I was stoic. 'Silent tears', she said. 'That's OK, I understand.' She squeezed my hand gently and waited without saying a word for some time. Eventually, her gentle voice pierced the silence, 'Nobody in their right mind would come out on a night like tonight', she said. After another long pause, she whispered, 'Everything will be all right', then she left.

It wasn't long before Paul and I split; we thought we loved each other, but we were so young it was more like infatuation. Our decision to part was mutual but still painful. My mother wasn't happy; she dragged me along to the priest again, this time insisting I tell the truth. She wanted an annulment of the marriage, and she got what she wanted. It was granted on the basis that 'we were not fully mature enough to make it a marriage.'

My circumstances shifted radically from being a wife and an expectant mother to being single and living at home again, and all before my seventeenth birthday. Initially, I didn't handle it very well; I tried to drown myself in the bath, but that didn't work.

I wondered how Dionna coped with the trauma of childbirth. I wondered how she dealt with living on the streets and how she managed without the support of a mother, even a mother like mine.

There was no need for the mike anymore; the girls

were half-stunned into silence. I explained to Dionna about the mike and that we were getting to know each other a little by telling something about ourselves and asked her if she could tell us something about herself. Shaking her head reluctantly, she said, 'I don't know what to say.'

I responded, 'What if I ask you some questions?' Silence followed. Trying to coax her, I said, 'I'm a midwife, and if it's OK, I would love to hear about the birth of your baby.' She indicated with an affirmative nod, so I handed her the mike after asking the first question. 'Where was your baby born?' Dionna began to share her story. In a softly spoken voice, she said, 'I didn't even know that I was pregnant for a long time; I had no idea until this big bump came, and I felt something moving inside.'

'So, you didn't have any ante-natal care?' I interjected.

'Nada de nada (No nothing)', she replied, blushing. 'I was by myself, and I didn't know anything about that.' Then, with a huge smile and still blushing, she said, 'I was so embarrassed. I thought I wet myself.' She began to giggle. Wide-eyed, the girls laughed with her; they were riveted. As Dionna continued speaking, she stroked her abdomen with one hand as if feeling the pain and said, 'The pains started very suddenly, and I could hardly walk.' Her voice became heavy but not overly emotional as she went on, 'I managed to reach a derelict building nearby and sat on the dirty floor. I was in agony. The pains got worse and worse, and I thought

I was going to die. I screamed and screamed', she said, mimicking some stifled screams, which made the girls laugh again. 'But no one could hear me. Then, all of a sudden, I heard the cry of a baby, and the pains stopped.'

After a huge sigh of relief, she continued, 'I looked on the ground and saw my baby crying.' Now with an air of excitement and arms waving, she exclaimed, 'The baby's arms were jerking, and her legs were kicking, and she cried so ferociously. I thought it was a miracle!' With a pensive look on her face, she continued, 'I was scared to touch her at first, but I picked her up and wiped her face in my skirt, and it wasn't that bad. The worst thing', she went on to say, 'was that the cord was still hanging from my private parts, and I didn't know what to do.' Blushing again, she continued, 'I just got up and walked all the way to a clinic with the baby still attached.'

Journal Entry:
Surco, Peru
13th December 2003

> *We talked late into the night until sleepy eyes were hardly able to stay open. Little by little, the group seemed to diminish as the girls sporadically excused themselves to go to bed. Down to only five girls, I began to feel tired myself and suggested that we all go to bed.*

Reluctantly they groaned and tried to persuade me to continue chatting, but 'No!' I insisted, 'Enough is enough, we must go to bed!'

I checked on the girls that were asleep, stunned to find that most of them were sleeping in their clothes. Despite the heat and the cramped conditions, they appeared to be sleeping soundly.

As for me, I'm not sure whether it was the intensity of the stories or the strong stench of old-dry urine reeking from the thin foam mattress beneath me that kept me awake. The putrid odour triggered the recall of my childhood monsters and the memory of how they turned into malodorous demons when I started bed-wetting. They accompanied the painfully shy girl to school each morning to make sure that she struggled with inferiority.

I hardly slept a wink; instead, our earlier conversations, mingled with childhood memories, rolled around my head all through the early hours. The night seemed to stretch out forever, and because there was a notice-able drop in temperature, I just hankered for first light to appear so that I could jump out of that awful bed.

At the first opportunity, without disturbing anyone, I quietly tip-toed off to the shower. I badly wanted to get rid of that dreadful smell, but I couldn't find any soap. I couldn't find a towel either. In desperation, I woke up Karina and discreetly whispered, 'Where do you keep the towels?'

'Que (What)', she said loudly, with squinting eyes,

still half asleep. After repeating the question a little louder, she responded in a softer voice, 'We use our dirty clothes to dry ourselves.'

'So there are no towels anywhere?' I affirmed in disbelief. She shook her head with a definite, 'No.'

I was so disappointed but determined to have a shower; nothing could deter me. My tiny micro-fibre face-washer would do. The slow trickle of water that dribbled pathetically out of the showerhead was freezing cold—having no hot water, no soap, and no towel made for a bad experience. When I discovered that my body was covered with bright-red spots, I was really cranky. 'Flea bites!' I knew them well! I told myself to stay positive, and my next thought was, 'It can only get better from here.' I continued to dry myself and thought, 'At least my face-washer is effective!'

Returning to the roof-top, I found that the sun was up. A single beam of sunshine managed to seep through the shadows of taller buildings, and I stood for a while just basking in it. Feeling a little more human with the sun warming my back, I told myself not to be discouraged and went in search of breakfast.

I discovered that some girls were up and roaming around the house. Their warm greetings melted away my frustrations, and their keenness to give kisses and hugs made me feel better. Then I opened the kitchen cupboards. They were completely bare. Trying to hide my negativity, I calmly asked Karina, 'What do you normally eat for breakfast?'

'We wait to see if the pastor brings anything', was her reply.

The cog wheels in my mind began to turn, and an idea popped into my head, 'Pancakes!' With that thought, I asked two of the older girls, Karina and Kari, if there were any shops nearby.

Soon the three of us set off to buy the ingredients for pancakes, while Herleena stayed behind to watch the rest of the girls. On the way, my thoughts about the practicality of making pancakes for so many conflicted with the fun that we might have, then the thought of ice-cream... 'Pancakes and ice-cream, hmmm! That would be perfect.'

I asked Karina, 'Does your fridge have a freezer box?' She looked at me a little weird and said, 'What fridge?'

'Whaaat! How can you not have a fridge!' I exclaimed. How could I not have noticed that they didn't have a fridge? I was so angry with myself. I tried to calm down and thought, 'OK, OK, it's not the end of the world; it just means no ice-cream.'

We walked in silence for a while as I processed the situation, and then another aspect of "poverty" began to dawn on me. Poverty means not having the basics. When we returned and began to make the pancakes, I realised that poverty was the friend of frustration in the shape of frying pans with no handles. It was also the master of improvisation when there are very limited utensils, not even a spatula. Oddly, there seemed to be heaps of tablespoons but no forks and only three knives.

What could have been a fun activity became a real challenge. Although I felt a sense of helplessness, the girls seemed to be resigned to not having the things they needed, and they remained positive. They were happy simply being involved in the process and being able to help.

We had three frying pans going all at once, with one girl responsible for each pan. Half a dozen others looked on. The younger girls were happy to set the table and chop up the lemons. Beating the mixture with a spoon was difficult, but our biggest test was flipping those pancakes with no panhandles. Not easy, we had to turn the pancakes over with a spoon; the tossing competition was out! Still, we had incredible fun just talking about pancake-tossing rather than actually doing it.

Twenty eggs, a can of condensed milk (diluted with water), six large cups of flour, and a cup of sugar later, the pancakes were finally done. After two full hours of slaving in the kitchen, we had a mountain of pancakes keeping warm in the oven. At last, we sat down to an Irish breakfast of delicious, hot pancakes dripping with melted butter, sprinkled with sugar, and topped with a squeeze of lemon.

We crammed around two tables, and I had to take a turn on each table to keep the girls happy as both groups begged and pleaded with me to sit with them. What seemed like a huge stack of pancakes quickly disappeared before our eyes, enough only to have one and a half pancakes each. I'm sure the girls could have eaten twice as much, but they didn't complain.

Complete silence ensued while all their little mouths were occupied. When they were finished, Marcia unashamedly licked her fingers one by one, and all the little ones copied her. I looked around the table, observing the girls closely as they laughed and giggled. The joy on their faces was incredible. It struck me that despite their sadness, this was a happy moment where they were able to forget the past and enjoy this present experience.

THE PANCAKE EXPERIENCE IN SURCO!

I had questioned whether I could really make any difference to these spirited kids, but now I could see that just being there was enough. Just sharing what little I had seemed to make a difference. They were so easily pleased and so easily distracted from the pain they harboured. In my heart of hearts, I wanted to stay with the girls. I really wanted to help them, but at the same time, I wanted to run a mile. In my mind, I questioned, 'Could I manage? Could I live with fleas again?'

I needed to escape to clear my head and get some space. I explained to the girls that I was going to make a phone call. 'No te vayas (Don't go)', Irmina said as she latched onto my arm. I continued walking towards the front door, almost dragging her along with me, when Alexia followed and grabbed my other arm. More girls swarmed around trying to hold me back, 'Will you return?' Irmina's voice shrieked.

Even before I had a chance to respond, Karina insisted, 'When will you be back?' I found their questions demanding and became irritated. Responding firmly, in a most determined way, I told them, 'I will definitely be back, but remember I'm only visiting Peru and I will soon be returning to Australia; but right now, I'm just going to make a phone call.' Karina insisted that she would show me the way to the phone box, but I gruffly refused. My words seemed harsh, but their pestering stopped instantly. They sensed my annoyance and reluctantly loosened their grip.

I tried to cover my true feelings with a smile as I

looked back at the girls through the front door. Trying to assure them in a softer voice, I said, 'I will be back soon', but they knew I was upset. The look on their faces caused me to draw a deep breath. I felt so bad!

The itchiness all over my body became unbearable, and I scratched till it hurt. I couldn't stop scratching, but the discomfort somehow justified my abruptness with the girls. Leaving the girls alone just didn't seem right to me, but all I wanted to do was to get away and be left alone. I'd had enough! It was time to call Luisa Pinto.

As I walked to the phone box, I felt troubled. Then, bizarre as it may seem, I pictured a scene from the movie *The Sound of Music*. It was a carefree scene where the main character, Maria, sang "My Favourite Things". How different was my reality? The nurturing, angelic Maria was so patient with all the children. 'I never really wanted to be Maria anyhow', I sniggered. I began to laugh at myself, which put me in a much better frame of mind.

The public phone box was easy to find. Luisa answered with enthusiasm; she immediately recognised my voice. I asked if I could stay at her place for the night.

Her spontaneous reply, 'You can arrive at any time and make yourself at home', made me feel much better. Luisa explained that the spare room was ready for me, but she didn't finish work until 5.00 pm and would leave the key with her father, who lived in the down-stairs apartment. Our conversation ended with a huge sigh of relief on my part; I couldn't wait to have a decent shower and some time to myself.

The quiet walk back gave me time to reflect on my stay at the house. It had been a kaleidoscope of pathos mingled with joy; the pancake experience had somehow been burned into my consciousness, yet I was deeply disturbed by the thought of living with so many constantly demanding girls and in such poor conditions. The conflict I was feeling within began to magnify when I reached the house with another dilemma raging.

Journal Entry:
Surco, Lima
13th December 2003

> *Arriving back at the house, I knocked on the door. I could hear what sounded like a herd of elephants stampeding down the hallway. The sound of pushing and shoving was evident as if the girls were frantically tackling each other to see who would get there first.*

> *The door opened, and the brawl spilled out into the street recklessly. Loud and noisy squeals, like caged-up stir-crazy puppies, they were beside themselves. So desperate was their need for adult company, I think they would have been just as keen to see almost anyone!*

I had only been gone for a few minutes; I guess they didn't really believe that I would be back.

While mingling with the girls, I eagerly waited for a staff member to arrive. That's when I noticed that one of the girls was limping badly. She saw me staring at her and quickly looked away, blushing. She was so painfully shy that we had not yet exchanged any words. I continued looking at her, and again she glanced over; she didn't look away this time. Without breaking eye contact, I began to approach her, but again she looked away. I asked her what her name was. Avoiding eye contact, she timidly responded, 'Yaani.' Her speech was awkward, but she continued, 'Are you really a nurse?'

I responded, 'Well, I'm a midwife, but yes, I am a nurse too.' She began nervously biting her fingernails as she stared down to the ground. I realised that she had been staring at her foot, probably hoping I would notice it. After a short pause, I said, 'Can I look at your sore foot.' Yaani nodded her head. On closer inspection, it was in a terrible state. The swelling was so great that her skin had erupted. She was wearing thongs (flip-flops). The plastic septum had sunk deep between her toes, almost disappearing into a weeping crack that oozed with puss. I tried not to embarrass her, but the sight of it made me feel nauseous: it was revolting. Her foot was so infected; I wondered how she could even walk on it.

I asked her why she hadn't told someone before it got that bad. She looked up at me and blushed in a silent moment of hesitation, and then she blurted out, 'Who could I tell?' She continued in a softer tone, 'I was too embarrassed to tell the pastor and', a short pause followed before she mumbled, 'no one cares anyhow!' I was about to speak when she quietly interjected, 'I did tell Ruby.'

Yaani showed me a grubby-looking blister pack of antibiotics which Ruby had been given months ago for a bladder infection. It seemed logical to Yaani to take the leftover antibiotics to fix her infection. She had been taking them for some time, but the infection had only worsened. First, I thought the antibiotics must be expired, and I checked the date, but they were still current. Then, looking at the severity of the infection, I realised that it must be a fungal infection. I know that antibiotics actually aggravate fungal infections, and I strongly suggested that she stop

taking the tablets.

Removing the thong caused too much pain; it was stuck and needed to be soaked off. I asked if I could bathe her foot, and she agreed. A couple of girls went to find a bucket or a basin, but like everything else, nothing could be found. I got all the girls to search the house, looking for something that might do. Eventually, a wide, shallow basin was found. It wasn't very practical, but I had to improvise by using a very small amount of water. I headed towards the kitchen table where Yaani was sitting. 'Qué vergüenza (How embarrassing)', she said as I approached with the water sloshing and spilling over. Yaani seemed humiliated. At first, she didn't want to put her foot into the water; she refused. I had to hide the basin under the table out of sight and then coax her until finally, she agreed to soak her foot. To cover her foot, I had to add more water with a pot from the kitchen.

Eventually, after a good soak, I eased the thong out of the wound and off her foot and told her not to wear those awful thongs again. After changing the frothy water, she returned her foot to the basin, but this time her relief seemed to overrule her embarrassment, and she began to relax.

Some girls joined us around the table, and we began chatting. To my utter surprise, the girls shared their stories in incredible detail. Yaani's wound became the catalyst to the telling of stories never told before. Hidden scars were exposed for viewing, and talk of all the bad things that ever happened to them flowed spontaneously out of their mouths. It was as if they were trying to outdo one another with the most awful scar or the worst injury. It was like opening Pandora's Box! The lid came off, and out flew tales of cruel bashings, anger and rage, bitterness and hate, sickness and even murder. I wanted to slam the lid closed, but it was too late: the girls were unstoppable.

In front of all the girls, Herleena, a well-endowed 14-year-old, without inhibition, pulled up her T-shirt to bare all. I was taken aback as she wasn't wearing a bra, but the others sitting around the table never flinched an eyelid. Herleena was concerned about her nipple. It was red and inflamed with a nasty weeping split across the centre. It was definitely infected and looked very sore, probably another fungal infection.

Karina asked if she could speak to me in private. We went out to the patio, and she told me she wanted to show me her scar, but she was too embarrassed to let anyone else see it. She hesitated; 'I'm ashamed of it', she said as she smoothed her long black hair over her ear. I tried to engage her in conversation about how she got the scar, but she said it happened a long time ago and that she couldn't remember. 'So why are you ashamed of it?' I asked.

'It's so ugly', she said, pulling a face. She covered the side of her head with one hand as if to make sure the scar wasn't visible. She had a side-parting with the thick section of her hair combed over to conceal the scar completely. Again, she hesitated. I looked at her and said casually, 'You don't have to show me, but I'm a nurse, and I've seen many scars: it won't bother me.'

Karina stepped forward. She slowly moved her hair out of the way and, trembling, revealed her secret. Her left ear was completely missing. I put my hand on her neck and leaned over for a closer look. There were no stitch marks, just a jagged scar where her ear once was. The inner ear appeared to be normal. My inspection was interrupted by Karina as she turned her head to look me in the eye. Still silent and trembling, her facial expression was very tense, but she seemed relieved. Even before I said anything, Karina sensed that it wasn't that hideous.

In a faint whisper, I asked, 'Can you hear me?' She nodded affirmatively, saying, 'Yes.'

'Your hearing is good', I responded with a reassuring smile. 'It's really not that bad.' I continued, 'The most important thing is your hearing.' Her shoulders dropped with a sigh of relief, and she began to smile too. I gave Karina a big hug and felt a deep connection with her. I told her I was glad that she confided in me.

Just then, interrupted by two girls screaming at each other, our time was brought to an abrupt end. I wanted to say more to Karina, but the escalating commotion compelled me to go and prevent the two from killing each other.

Talia, a 10-year-old, was running around with Yaani's disgusting thongs on her feet. Yaani, with feet still dripping wet, trailing behind her. The thought of that puss-oozing wound spreading infectious material all around the room made me feel sick.

Trying to get control of the situation, I raised my voice, but the girls couldn't hear above their own screams. I grabbed Talia by the arm as she flew past me; it was the only way to get her attention. It turned out that Talia had loaned her thongs to Yaani and was claiming them back. I sat them both down, and turning to Talia, I asked, 'Do you want a sore foot like Yaani's?'

'Eeww no', she said. The gleeful look dropped off her face, and she couldn't get those thongs off quick enough. Looking to Yaani, I exclaimed, 'Do you know that you're doing a great job at spreading a very contagious infection around?' She immediately blurted out, 'I don't have any other shoes.'

'Good! Then you can't spread the infection', I responded impulsively. I asked Yaani to sit down and dry her foot.

She said, 'There's nothing to dry it with.' She was right; no tissues, no towel, nothing but dirty clothes. The wound looked much better after soaking, but it had picked up a lot of dust and was still very moist. I walked Yaani out to the patio, poured clean water over the wound, and made her sit in the sun until it was dry.

An elderly woman finally arrived just as I was measuring my foot against Yaani's for size. After a brief greeting, we discussed wound care. She had no idea that Yaani's foot was even sore, let alone how to treat it. I tried to give her instructions, but the girls kept grabbing her attention, and she wasn't listening. We talked intermittently about flea-infested heads, ringworm, itchy skin from heat rashes and dust mites, but she dismissed them all, 'These are all just normal things here in Peru!' She said.

Stopping only to pick up some Nopusid (flea-rid shampoo) at the pharmacy, I set out to find Luisa's house. After two long, jerky bus rides and a lengthy walk, I finally arrived in the late afternoon. Sure enough, Luisa was still at work, but, as promised, the key was passed on to me by her father. He was an elderly man who seemed friendly and unobtrusive. He showed me around Luisa's place. After briefly telling me to make myself at home, he left for his own apartment downstairs.

I made myself a cup of tea and sat looking around this lovely clean home. It was so blissfully peaceful after the rowdiness of the girls. Funny how in the quiet, we become acutely aware of our own needs. Suddenly I felt itchy and dirty all over. All I could think of was a hot shower, but I felt it was a bit of a liberty to take a shower without asking. I sat a little while and waited in the comfortable surroundings, but I just couldn't stand the itches any longer. I convinced myself that I would be in and out of the shower before Luisa got back. After laying out some clean clothes on the bed, I made my way to the bathroom. Almost as soon as I stepped into the lovely hot water, I heard movement and voices in the adjacent room. It seemed that Luisa had returned! I had to rush like crazy to get my hair washed before leaving the shower. How embarrassed I felt coming out of that bathroom wearing Luisa's towels, one wrapped around my head like a turban, the other about my torso. To compound my humiliation, Luisa had a guest with her. I was mortified; I just wanted the ground to swallow me up. Nervously, I tried to explain about the fleas and the awful bed and the cold water, but the stunned look on their faces said it all. Luisa and her friend were a little shell-shocked. They tried to convey some understanding by silently nodding simultaneously, but it was obvious that they needed time to process; not a word was spoken before I disappeared into the bedroom.

That evening, like old friends catching up, Luisa and I talked and talked for hours. I couldn't believe that we had only just met for the first time. I sensed a real affinity towards her which I felt was reciprocated. Luisa had cooked a Peruvian meal of beef heart on skewers, which to my surprise, I enjoyed very much. Most of all I enjoyed Luisa's company. We related well and felt at ease with each other. Luisa had to work the next day, and I was exhausted, so we didn't stay up very late.

That night, I relaxed back on the soft, thick mattress and slipped into the fresh-smelling sheets, feeling clean all over. It was like heaven; I counted my blessings and began to fade away, then suddenly I remembered Yaani's foot. I had to investigate my first-aid kit before I fell asleep, so I jumped out of bed. Delighted to find a full tube of broad-spectrum anti-fungal cream and some sterile gauze swabs, I got back to bed and my thoughts began to drift again. Amazed that I had packed just the right things, but then I remembered Yaani's need for a pair of shoes. Money was so tight, 'How am I ever going to get her a pair of shoes?' I asked myself.

I had made sure that I set aside a certain amount of money to cover the cost of food and to offer something to each of my hosts, but now, very little cash remained. As much as I wanted to, I couldn't really afford to buy shoes. Refusing to worry, I closed my eyes and tried to get some sleep. Instead, I just lay awake, toying with the idea and trying to figure out how to make it happen. It seemed impossible. It just didn't work out. I was so tired, so I handed it over and prayed for the provision of a pair of shoes. Then a thought instantly popped into my mind, 'You could skip a meal or two.' This sparked an internal dialogue of thoughts: 'What about the other girls, wouldn't they feel put out?' I questioned. 'The others already have shoes', was the response. 'I can't even buy them a small thing', I insisted. 'That's OK. You don't have to.'

I accepted that I couldn't buy something for everyone, but I could buy shoes for Yaani by skipping a meal or two. No more argument, no more thoughts; I rolled over and drifted off into a sound and peaceful sleep.

The next morning, I woke to the pleasant smell of a cooked breakfast. I quickly dressed and found Luisa in the kitchen; we sat together briefly and shared a wholesome feast, then she left for work. In the quiet ambience of her comfy home, with no noise and no demands, it was wonderfully refreshing. I had the freedom to do whatever I wanted. I picked up my favourite book and began to read. In it, Matthew, the tax collector, told me not to worry about my life, or what I will eat or drink, or about my body, what I will wear. He said life is more than food and the body more than clothes. I read on and felt reassured that all I had to do was to put God first, and then everything else would fall into place. Could it really be that simple?

Feeling very much at peace, I decided not to worry about the cost and enthusiastically headed off to the local markets. I soon found a pair of shoes and managed to barter the price down to thirteen nuevo soles. That was very cheap. They were open-toe shoes, wide fitting and adjustable around the instep by a strap and buckle. The quality wasn't brilliant, but they were better than nothing. The shoes measured just a little smaller than my foot, so I guessed that they would fit.

When I arrived at the house, the air was filled with excitement, and the girls were all hyperactive. Immediately they crowded around me, desperate to tell me that it was someone's birthday and they had a birthday cake. When I inquired as to whose birthday it was, the girls, wanting to surprise me, told me to close my eyes and then led me along by both hands straight to the birthday girl. I opened my eyes to see Yaani! She was seated with her foot soaking in the basin, looking serious and a little helpless. I handed her the plastic bag with the shoes and wished her a happy birthday. She peeked into the bag, and in an instant, her face lit up. This shy girl jumped to her feet and flung her arms around me, one foot still in the basin. I nearly cried when she gave me the biggest hug. I hugged her back misty-eyed and whispered in her ear, 'God really loves you, Yaani.'

The days passed quickly, and before long, it was time for our final goodbyes. The air was heavy, and the fun and smiles ended, but I was determined to remain calm and relaxed. I knew I was coming back, but for the girls, a year was a lifetime. Still, I hoped that they would mirror my emotions and stay calm. Waiting in turn for a kiss and a hug, the mood became more emotional by the minute. It was Irmina's turn, and in her usual demonstrative way, she flung her skinny little arms around me and, prolonging our embrace, nearly crushed me. With each of her stuttering deep breaths, I could hear her silently screaming on the inside as she held tight. Irmina had no understanding of my return; she only knew that I was leaving. Before it became unbearable, I patted her on the shoulders and confidently said, 'I'll be back before you know it.'

It was painful to see her this way; I had to blink my tears away and gulp down the emotion. 'I promise I will send you a photo of us together to remind you that I will be back', I said, but my voice cracked when I spoke. Even so, Irmina was comforted; I felt the tension in her body begin to relax. I continued in a whisper, 'I will be thinking of you, and we will see each other again.' Irmina loosened her grip and gradually broke free. I then asked her if she would draw a picture for me and send it to Australia. This seemed to help to lighten the mood, and whenever one of the girls became emotional, I asked them to promise they would send a drawing too. The girls were at least hopeful, and the goodbyes, painful as they were, became more bearable.

Chapter Seven

MACHU PICCHU

Journal Entry:
Luisa's Place, Lima, Peru
16th December 2003

> *The last few days I've spent most of my time with the girls but I have to admit, each night I was eager to escape the noise and the chaos. Luisa's place is so peaceful and it has much more to offer in the way of creature comforts. It's good to have someone to talk to besides kids. Luisa always seems keen to hear about the girls, she's a good listener but she's often shocked about the lack of help and resources at the house. I find our times together refreshing, very enjoyable and some of Luisa's suggestions were very helpful too.*

It turned out that Luisa is not only qualified in secondary education, but she has a B.A. in Christian Education and is an expert in literacy and bilingual education. Luisa is working on the revision of a book for teaching Castellano as a second language to the indigenous-speaking people of Peru. I found this fascinating, especially since she is from Spanish stock.

One morning while Pastor Luis was driving me to the house in Surco, he asked if I was going to visit 'MAPI' while in Peru. Not knowing what or where MAPI was, I simply said, 'No, why?' His eyebrows arched, and his eyes widened in surprise.

'MAPI! Haven't you heard of it?' he exclaimed. He became quite disturbed that I had no idea what he was talking about. He explained, eyes bulging, 'MAPI is the colloquial term for Machu Picchu, "The Lost City of the Incas"', he cried. With exasperation in his voice, he continued, 'It's one of the Great Wonders of the World! Everyone should know this!'

Instantly I wanted to know more. When he informed me that it was one of the world's most famous archaeological sites ever, I became quite excited. That is, until I discovered that MAPI was in Cuzco, a good distance away; in fact, a plane ride away. Knowing that plane tickets are not cheap, my enthusiasm dampened. I informed Pastor Luis, 'I can't go because I can't afford it.' He shook his head negatively and remained silent for a while.

My thoughts had wandered on to new horizons when suddenly, Pastor Luis, still driving, turned to me, taking his attention off the busy road, and blurted out, 'You can't come all the way from Australia and not go to MAPI.' He was frowning while at the same time grinning; then, he remained silent. To my relief, he turned back to the steering wheel. I didn't say anything for fear of distracting him. After a couple of kilometres of silence, he blurted out again, 'What if I could arrange free accommodation and cheap travel? Would you go then?'

His confident attitude started me thinking. He conveyed a definite sense of knowing; perhaps he had done this before, perhaps for the last tourist, I wasn't sure. 'I am interested, but I still may not be able to afford it; it depends', I told him. Over the next few minutes, we discussed the possibility. It turned out that Pastor Luis had connections. He suggested that I stay with a host family whom he knew, and he could purchase low-cost flight and train tickets on 'Peruvian Economy Class.' It sounded a bit dodgy, so I investigated further to see if it was above board.

I found that Pastor Luis was originally from Cuzco and that he was involved with a school there. 'La Directora of that school', he said, 'is a close friend of mine.' He went on to explain that accommodation within the school was provided for the teachers, and apparently, there was always a spare bed. He explained that Peruvian-class tickets are really meant for Peruvians, but, 'If you're not too proud and don't mind travelling in this way, it's quite legal.' He was so convincing that by the end of our conversation I decided I would at least give it a try.

Before long, I found myself checking in at Lima Airport for an early flight to Cuzco. I carried only a small backpack, which passed as hand luggage. My intention was to stay for just a few days in Cuzco. I wasn't sure whether or not I would make it all the way to MAPI, but it really didn't matter. I was motivated enough to have a cultural experience travelling with the locals, Peruvian style!

Still determined to continue with my original plans, I set apart the money needed for the rest of my trip and left it at Luisa's apartment, so I couldn't spend it in Cuzco.

In spite of being very early that morning, the bus was crowded, and the traffic was heavy. The trip from Luisa's place to Lima Airport took forty-five minutes, and I had to stand up all the way. I wondered whether I might have to stand on the plane too? Astonishingly, it turned out that the flight was shorter, and no, I didn't have to stand. Despite curious looks from the ground crew, there were no questions asked. I was happy.

With no bags to collect, I was the first person out the door at Cuzco Airport, but this proved to be disastrous as I became the only target for a mob of desperate taxi drivers. They harassed me so much that I had to turn on my heel back to the sanctuary of the airport just to escape them. Pastor Luis had given me a contact number, for which I was grateful. I rang from the airport. A female voice at the end of the phone introduced herself as Luz. She immediately made me feel at ease when she confirmed that she had spoken to the pastor. I managed to check the address, but just as she was explaining how to get there, we were cut off mid-conversation. I had no more coins to ring back and decided I would have to find my own way.

The people in Cuzco were well-used to tourists and were very helpful. When they realised I could speak the language, they were more than enthusiastic about chatting. The bus terminal was just outside the airport, and with some assistance, I found the right bus.

Eventually, I arrived; the ride, an hour and a half out of Cuzco, was reasonably pleasant. My destination, Colegio Mi Familia in Leon de San Jeronimo, turned out to be a private Christian school. The Directora, Luz, was in her tiny but very busy office. It was like Central Station, inundated with students, teachers, parents, cousins, and family, continually traipsing in and out of her office. I stood back for a while, observing until Luz eventually noticed me. She stopped just for a moment to welcome me then instructed a student to show me around the school while she attended the multitudes.

Brought to a very basic dwelling within the school grounds, I was advised that this was the teacher's quarters where I could leave my backpack. After a brief look at the kitchen and dorm, I realised that it must be where I was going to stay. This old, run-down portion of the building was also where Luz lived, and it was shared by her mother, her sisters, and various other teachers.

The tour continued around the classrooms, which were archaic. Blackboards and chalk for the teachers, old desks and chairs, scattered around on concrete slabs, were chipped and carved with graffiti. Apart from these things, the classrooms were bare, completely empty of any resources. Within a short time, it started raining heavily and suddenly became very cold, not at all like Lima. More like a cold winter's day in England, I was freezing. I asked the student to take me back to where I had left my jacket tucked away in my backpack.

A delicious aroma of home cooking filled my senses as I walked through the door, and the room was warm and cosy. Luz's mother, Juana, was stirring a large pot on the stove; she offered me a bowl of soup. There were two young people already sitting at the table eating. Not wanting to intrude, I remained standing and declined, but within minutes a bowl of soup was pressed gently into my hands by Juana, insisting I sit and join them. She must have known I was hungry. Right from the start, I felt very much at ease with Juana. She radiated a calm presence. There was something special about her ways. I loved how she made it so easy for me to accept her amazing hospitality.

The people in Cuzco had a warmth about them and a way of making one feel very welcome. Despite their modest surroundings and obvious poverty, I could see that they were big-hearted people. Food was top on the list of priorities for them. Following the bowl of hearty soup, I was handed a plate of rice with some chicken and fries, more food than I could possibly eat.

Many young people were coming and going; they were obviously teachers, and it was their lunch break. After the meal, friendly conversation flowed easily. Juana was curious and asked lots of questions about my plans; the others wanted to know more about Australian life and politics. There was no awkwardness or silence. I felt comfortable and was able to blend in quite naturally. It was a good feeling. Juana shared photos taken in Machu Picchu of people who had stayed with her from all over the world. I also had some postcards and photos of Sydney and passed them around too.

Early in the evening, we again sat around the table, this time to a lighter meal. After eating, Juana promptly cleared the table. With no living room, I realised that life happened around the kitchen table. As we conversed, the inevitable question came up about Machu Picchu. When I told them, 'I probably won't be going', they were dismayed. Stunned looks and a chorus of sighs went up with a prolonged 'Porqueeeee (Why)?' expressed almost unanimously.

'I can't afford to go', I said. 'Not all Gringos are as wealthy as you might think', I assured them. I could see the look of scepticism on their faces. 'I didn't expect to get this far', I explained and then told them a little more about my situation. After convincing them that I truly was strapped for cash, the room became very quiet. In the stillness, I noticed a look passed around the table from one to the other. 'Did they know something that I didn't?' For the first time, I felt uneasy. Juana smiled and broke the silence, 'There is a way', she said, 'but it's not first class.'

Intrigued to hear more, I nodded in affirmation, 'That's OK! I've never travelled first class.' With that, the others interjected, all speaking at once. I listened with amazement to their excitement as they explained just how it was possible. They had contacts everywhere (so it seemed): cousins, brothers, friends, and even friends of a friend. They knew the cheapest way to get to MAPI; they had it all worked out and were more than keen to share it with me. 'Forget the usual route by tourist coach and train', Juana said, 'that's much too expensive.'

I was told that I needed to get to Ollantaytambo by catching the local bus, which departed from the terminal in Cuzco. A train would take me from Ollantaytambo to Aguas Calientes, but the Peruvian section, the very last carriage, was only a fraction of the cost of the tourist carriages. Aguas Calientes was apparently the closest location to the actual ruins of Machu Picchu. From there, the ruins were only a short coach ride a way, served exclusively by special tourist coaches. The amazing feature about Aguas Calientes is the fact that there is only one single road which leads to the ruins. All roads end at the Hydroelectric train station, which is fifteen kilometres away. The only way in, is by train, helicopter, or hiking from the Hydroelectric station in Santa Maria.

In Aguas Calientes lived Luz's husband, who owned a Hostel, and Juana's second cousin, Jaime, who just happened to be one of the Machu Picchu Tourist coach drivers. The instructions, once in Aguas Caliente, were to catch the very first coach departing at 5.00 am and say to the driver, 'Luz me envió (Luz sent me).' This, I was told, was the password for free passage.

The Hostel owned by Juana's husband was safe and clean, and he would only charge me $10.00 per night if I told him that Juana sent me. I felt very much part of the family by the time they finished explaining. Although I wasn't entirely comfortable with all their suggestions, I was comfortable in their company and decided to trust them. Suddenly, I couldn't stop yawning and felt exhausted. Juana was quick to notice. 'You probably need a rest because the air is very thin', she said as she began to make a pot of tea. Within minutes, she handed me a hot cuppa made from raw coca leaves. 'Drink as much as you can to prevent headaches', she said persuasively as she left the teapot nearby. Soon Juana ushered me beyond the curtain, which hung in place of a door, and suggested that I lie down for a while.

The room on the other side of the curtain was long and very narrow, more like a wide hallway. With barely enough space between the wall and the three bunk beds lined up end-to-end along the opposite wall, I made my way to the very last bunk, the one assigned to me.

Carrying my backpack, I awkwardly sidestepped my way past others to reach my bunk. Fully dressed, I lay down on the bottom bunk, just to try it out, but then immediately I crashed. I was out to the world.

Woken up by the sound of an alarm clock coming from behind the curtain, I gazed around the room. It was dark, with just a dull glow seeping through the thin fabric. I could barely see, but I could hear the sounds of heavy breathing and snoring. The glow cast shadows, and I could just make out a lump in each bed. With no windows, I wasn't sure whether it was day or night. I glanced at my watch, but my eyes strained to see the numbers; it was too dark. Reluctant to disturb anyone, I remained silent for a while until I could hear some stirring, then I felt safe to get up and navigate my way past the other beds. Drawn towards the glow beyond the curtain, I could now see my watch – it was 5.00 am. I couldn't believe I had slept for ten hours without stirring!

Since there was only one bathroom, I thought I'd be smart and grab a shower before the rush. Compared to Lima, the air was extremely cold, and the water was icy. I let it run for a while, hoping it would warm up, but no. I could barely tolerate the freezing water when it came to washing my hair; rinsing the shampoo out was torture. It took some time for my shivering body to recover, and my hair felt like it might ice over.

I sat alone at the table for a while, but very soon, every place was full. Breakfast was consumed quickly as people stood around waiting to jump into a space at the table as soon as it became available. Juana served a satis-fying breakfast of porridge and churros with hot choco-late. Conversation was short as people sat down, politely introduced themselves, ate in a rush, and then ran.

My comment about the cold water raised a few eyebrows, then Juana said, 'Nobody ever showers that early in the morning; it's far too cold.' Those hearing couldn't help giggling. Apparently, they simply had a wash at the sink.

Soon, everyone disappeared, and it was quiet again. After the hustle and bustle of breakfast, the silence was truly delightful, so I began to journal. With time on my hands, I began to rethink the possibility of going to Machu Picchu, and I looked more closely at my budget. I calculated that the trip to MAPI, including the train and bus tickets plus food and two nights' accommodation, all came to $70.00. My budget for the week in Cuzco was $100.00. It was tight, but it was definitely possible.

Cuzco, noted for its crazy extremes, made the weather difficult to predict. With no time to lose, I wrapped myself up in warm clothing and set off to the city centre to investigate. It turned out to be a scorching hot day. After rushing around in the heat and the activity of the crowded streets, I was feeling breath-less. Cuzco is 3,500 meters above sea level, even higher than Machu Picchu itself. Even while sitting at rest, without exerting a muscle, it's possible to suffer (soroche) or altitude sickness. I remembered Juana's advice and went in search of some coca tea but couldn't find it anywhere. Instead, I purchased a bottle of water and sat for a while in the Plaza de Armas. I looked around to see some tourists who, like me, had the same idea. Trying to avoid dehydration and soroche, we occupied the park benches under the blazing sun while swigging from a bottle of water.

The city hummed with excitement as the tourists darted around the many places of interest. There were ancient buildings, many hotels, restaurants, tacky souvenir shops, cathedrals, and churches. In the crowds, I saw a cosmopolitan mix of olive-skinned Spaniard and dark-skinned Quechua bloodlines mingled with that of tall, fair, blue-eyed Scandinavians.

After a short time, I was pressured by a number of fast-talking peddlers offering a variety of goods from finger puppets to food. Then the artistic types approached, desperate to sell their works. They showed me some amazing paintings of high quality. Even the most courteous of campesinos (farmers), bearing sheaves of wheat and fine embroidery approached in the hope of a sale. I sadly had to decline them all.

The biting sun made my skin feel as though it was literally burning; I wondered how the others could tolerate it. My head began to pound, and the excitement turned into annoyance. Even the once delightful rhythm of the harpist from the nearby Pacha Papa restaurant became irritating. The din of competing noises became unbearable. I couldn't sit there a moment longer.

Walking around in the noisy ambience, I sought refuge somewhere, anywhere away from the maddening crowd. I headed for my place of escape, where sanity and restoration are found. In the cool and quiet solace of the public library, I was able to think again. I made some enquiries; then I headed back out into the furnace. Before returning, I managed to purchase a local-bus ticket to Ollantaytambo and a train ticket to Aguas Calientes for the next day.

Journal Entry:
Aguas Calientes, Peru
18th December 2003

> *Still dark, I found my way to the bus terminal at Avenida Grau in the centre of Cuzco where I located the bus stop to Ollantaytambo. The first bus arrived at 4.30 am, a little Kombi van, but incredibly, it was already full. I could barely see any standing room. I knew it was a two-and-a-half-hour trip so I was surprised that the ticket collector tried to usher me onto the bus. Without hesitation I said, 'No thanks.' He tried to convince me to get on, but I flatly refused. As the bus pulled away, he stared at me long and hard with a puzzled look on his face.*

Before long, the bus terminal became crowded with locals everywhere, with scores more arriving by the minute. Soon another bus for Ollantaytambo arrived, and it was empty this time. Before I knew it, even before the wheels became stationary, the masses lunged forward, crowding around the closed doors. They shuffled along with the vehicle as if magnetized to it. When the doors opened, they immediately crowded on board, and within minutes the bus was full to the max. I watched with astonishment. The ticket collector observed the gob-smacked Gringo standing in front of him, and again I was ushered onto the crammed bus. The passengers were so tightly packed that I couldn't see where I could possibly fit. 'There's no room!' I exclaimed.

'Plenty of room on the steps', the ticket man responded. The bus began slowly rolling into motion. 'Quick, quick', he yelled out persuasively. 'All the buses are the same. We don't shut the doors. Quick, get on!' he yelled. As the bus slowly picked up speed, with no time for indecision, I hopped on.

I shared the lower step with two others, and despite being pressed hard against other bodies, I was bulging out of the doorway. I gripped onto the bars for dear life when the bus frenetically jerked around the corners. I told myself I must be mad. Feeling like my life was in danger, I wanted to get off. The ticket man just wanted his money and pressured me for the fare. I told him that I wanted to get off. He refused to stop the bus and told me there would be a seat soon. Not convinced at all and afraid to let go of the bars, I insisted that I would pay him when I got a seat. With that, he started collecting fares from the other passengers and left me alone. It was a scary ride. My rash decision was a bad one, but sure enough, a seat soon became available. So relieved to feel safe again, I was happy to pay the five soles.

I began to relax and stared through the distant window as miles upon miles of green fields floated by. The fields cultivated with a variety of sugar cane, corn, and other crops against the backdrop of beautiful snow-capped mountains and blue sky were breathtaking. All the stress and tension began to melt away, and I felt triumphant – I'd survived!

Finally, we arrived at the last stop, Ollantaytambo, where the whole bus emptied out. Many people poured into the terminal from other buses and coaches, all arriving at the same time. An extremely large crowd formed, and crammed tightly together, they shuffled along in the same direction. It would have been impossible to do anything else without getting trampled. I didn't have a clue where I was going; I just got carried along with the flow of the crowd. After a few minutes, I noticed a number of high-quality backpacks bobbing up and down in the crowd. 'Tourists', I thought and was reassured. Speaking in Spanish, I casually asked the girl walking next to me, 'Are you headed for the train station.' She responded in English with a broad German accent, 'I think we are.'

Smiling, I remarked, 'Wow! We're all like sheep.' She nodded with a sombre look on her face and tried to pick up her pace, not that she got anywhere fast as the crowd dictated the pace. After a brisk ten-minute walk, we arrived at the train station. A train with its doors closed waited on an empty platform. It was labelled Aguas Calientes. As we all spilled onto the long plat-form, the crowd spread enough that I could squeeze through a little more freely, so I headed for the back inferior carriage. While waiting for the doors to open, I felt conspicuous and a little taller, standing next to all the Peruvians. I tried to look shorter by bending my knees and wondered if some official might spot me and usher me to the tourist carriages. When the doors opened, I stepped into the very basic carriage, relieved that no one approached me.

The locals were much friendlier than the German girl; without hesitation, the young woman sitting oppo-site me began to chat. At first, she attempted to speak English, but her accent was so bad that we soon reverted to Spanish. Straight away, the other passengers nearby joined in the conversation, which initially was good, but they never stopped chatting all the way to the end of the line. That was two hours of constant talk. There was no sign of any ticket inspector, so my ten-soles ticket not only bought me a ride, it even bought me a seat all the way. I felt celebratory and so relieved. Getting off that train and outside the station, I experi-enced a great feeling of escape.

Nearby, in the main square of Aguas Calientes, a line of approximately twelve people were waiting. They held up placards with the names of hotels and hostels. People crowded around them and began to barter. I walked up and down the line, but the hostel that I was looking for wasn't there. I asked the first person in the line what their tariff was. Fifteen U.S. dollars a night, I was told. When I declined, the price dropped, but not enough, so I moved along the line. Finally, I agreed to fifteen soles and was immediately taken to the hostel.

It was an uphill walk for some distance, a long way from the square. The room was basic but clean, so I stayed there for the first night and found the hostel recommended by Juana on the second night. The only difference was the location; Juana's recommendation was more central to everything. Both had a shared bathroom, and both had cold showers.

After dropping my backpack, I walked around the quaint little township of Aguas Calientes. The air was clean and fresh. I loved the fact that there were no roads, so no cars anywhere, only cobble-stoned pedestrian areas. The narrow streets were packed with people and the occasional alpacas! The one and only road was the one leading up to the ruins themselves, which could only be accessed by tourist coaches.

Such friendly and talkative people! I experienced a different reality from the world I came from, with people here striking up conversations with strangers as if they already knew each other. A cultural norm in Peru, I was learning and loving.

Unfortunately, the tourists outnumbered the locals by far, and it seemed that the American tourists were the main ones being catered for. Burgers and French fries everywhere! I craved some authentic Peruvian food, even a simple bowl of lentils, but apart from expensive al-la-carte dining, with Cui (guinea pig) being the only Peruvian option on the menu, I couldn't find anything.

I got talking to a young man who turned out to be a tour guide. He knew all the best places to eat. He told me about Cantina Chelita, a well-concealed canteen that catered for the locals where I could get a great Peruvian feed for a very low price. The risk of food poisoning was always a problem in the small cantinas, but he guaranteed that I would not get sick after eating there.

As the evening grew colder, the plate of Matasca was very warming. This dish was the house special at Cantina Chelita: it comprised of a combination of lamb, potatoes, carrots, and peas in a soup-like sauce with rice, and it was delicious. While eating, I planned a big day ahead: starting with the 5.00 am coach, spending the full day at Machu Picchu, and returning on the last coach back. I decided an early night would be good.

The next day I woke refreshed after a comfortable sleep with no ill effect from the food. Arriving in the dark, around 4.30 am, I was surprised to see a short queue already waiting at the coach terminal. Half an hour later, the coach opened its doors, and we all hopped on. Sure enough, when I mentioned the magic words, 'Juana sent me', the driver (presumably Jaime) beamed a smile and, without hesitation, ushered me to take a seat. Apart from the magic words, we never spoke again! The exit door was at the back of the coach, and I couldn't even thank him; I felt very strange like I was a spy or something. Or maybe it was a pang of conscience. But I justified my actions, as we sometimes do.

Because our coach was the first to arrive, there were no crowds to contend with. The heavy mist not only covered the tall peaks of the ruins, but it also came down to the ground to envelop everything.

As I stepped off the coach into the thick haze, visibility was so poor that the others just seemed to disappear like ghostly figures into the fog. Their audible voices reassured me that I wasn't alone; however, once through the main gate, the little cluster of people dispersed, and I could no longer hear or see anything. It was so quiet; I felt totally alone.

A strange eerie feeling crept over me, like something bad was about to happen. I couldn't believe I had made it all the way to Machu Picchu for this. It was disappointing, definitely not what I had anticipated.

It began to drizzle lightly. 'It can't get any worse', I thought. Then the drizzle turned into rain, and the rain turned into a storm. With a loud clap of thunder, the heavens opened, and the rain poured down heavily.

I couldn't see anything, and not knowing which way to run, I urgently scanned the immediate vicinity around me. In the wall of the ruins, I spotted a dry patch on the ground sheltered by an overhanging rock. It was low down, but I managed to scramble into the hollow.

It receded back more than at first appeared, and I was able to sit upright. I felt cold and damp, but I was glad to be protected from the wind and the storm. The wind howled, and thunderbolts blasted loud enough to hurt my ears, but I felt safe in this dry nook.

I began to marvel at the sight of horizontal rain. The sunlight barely breaking through the haze resulted in a display of sparkling drops dancing in defiance of gravity.

After a time, the rain began to ease, and the haze began to clear. Like a mystical apparition, the ruins appeared before my eyes. I sat enchanted as I gazed out through the opening.

I could see a stone image in front of me, El Templo (The Sun Temple), its walls of stone intricately woven together in the most refined style of architecture.

Fascinated, I wondered how the Incas ever managed to do this back in the fifteenth century without the use of mortar, metal tools, or the wheel? I could see that these large, boulder-like granite blocks had been finely chiselled to fit into place with such precision that they locked together like a complicated puzzle.

After all these years, through earthquakes and wars, this engineering marvel remains standing.

I observed a small sparrow landing on the lower wall of the ruins and quietly crawled out of my cave. It felt good to stretch the legs. Pulling out my notebook, the sparrow remained, and I decided to sketch it.

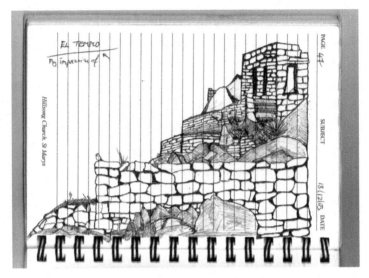

THE RUINS & THE SPARROW

While standing there sketching, I saw beams of sunlight shining through the mist, dispersing it even further, and then the lush green terraces below slowly began revealing themselves. I could hardly believe my eyes. I gasped as I looked down from the top of the grassy ridge where I stood. The terraces interlaced this complex series of ruins, which was cradled in the heart of a valley and surrounded by layers upon layers of rugged mountains as far as the eye could see. Standing before this stunning ancient city in admiration, I felt total respect. Even now, as I relive the memory, I can still feel the power of that intensely spiritual place. Machu Picchu's mysterious origins only add to its appeal. It's no wonder that thousands of visitors are drawn to it every day. Awe-inspiring!

MACHU PICCHU AND THE MYSTICAL MIST

Slowly, people appeared emerging from their hidden shelters, and voices could be heard everywhere. A group of schoolchildren approached and crowded around me; one girl very courteously asked if she could see my sketch. I showed it, and the others also wanted to see it. A boy with a camera asked if he could take a photo of us. They hung around for a while exchanging words and smiles and some laughter; they even sang the national anthem for me, very harmoniously too. But then they left. When they were gone, it was so silent. The consuming quiet engulfed me again, like the fog, and suddenly I felt very much alone. I longed for a friend or even an acquaintance to share the magic. Since there was no one, I penned my feelings and wrote these words:

Never Alone

I have a friend, closer than a brother
His company superior to any other
He knows my beginnings, and He knows my end
He knows me far more than any friend
Always, He watches over me
Only the very best will be
Content in His love, His mercy,
His grace until I see Him face to face.

I recalled a promise from Scripture, 'I will never leave you. I am with you always, even to the end', and I realised that I was no longer alone. Reminded of the warmth and hospitality of the past few days, I felt privileged, and as swiftly as it came, the loneliness left. A smile crept onto my face, and I felt comforted. I knew that the Peruvian people were far from perfect, especially the taxi drivers, but in truth, they had made a big impact on me, and I began to embrace them.

Journal Entry:
Cuzco, Peru
20th December 2003
Peru v Brazil: The South American Cup

I skipped breakfast to make the 5.45 am train from

Aguas Calientes back to Ollantaytambo, and from there I caught the bus to Cuzco. After many hours of travelling in very cramped conditions, it was good to stretch my legs and take a stroll around this charming city. The more I walked, the more Cuzco seemed to expose itself. There were many interesting places I hadn't yet seen.

As always, the crowded city exuded excitement. The multitude of local peddlers, the cosmopolitan mix of tourists, and the constant activity created a magical atmosphere. I felt energized on this cool day. Juana wasn't expecting me back until late, so I had the whole day ahead of me. With no plan and no time restraints, everything seemed to be in my favour.

Cuzco had a myriad of things to see and do. I was happy to have the time to stroll down the steep, narrow cobblestone streets in a leisurely rhythm of discovery. Passing by the remarkable old buildings in the area of San Blass, I became aware of how well the streets had been planned with their many parks and public squares.

I came across the underground Archaeological Museum with its mummies, textiles, and ancient sacred idols, the Santo Domingo Convent, and then the remains of the Golden Temple and the Cathedral, which date as far back as 1560. I could only look from outside. I heard the locals speaking in their Quechua language, no doubt direct descendants of the Incas. Some were dressed in traditional clothing, while others had llamas in tow. The richness of it all was fascinating.

I walked around the city, returning once again to the massive Inca walls lining the street of Hatun Rumiyoc. I stood taking a closer look at the walls when interrupted by a young boy dressed in traditional clothing. He asked, 'Have you discovered the Twelve Angled Stone?'

'Not yet', I said.

'I can show you for only one dollar', he quickly responded.

I declined, saying, 'I think I can find it myself.' I thanked him, and eventually, I did find the special stone. A group of loud American tourists made a big fuss as they excitedly crowded around the stone, pointing to it. That was the end of the boy's earnings for a time.

The enormous centrepiece slab was carefully chiselled to create twelve tightly interlocking angles like a jigsaw puzzle. It was this rock that was so special. It had twelve huge slabs of thick stone slotted into each angle around it. The large stones were bound together only by their interlocking. The highly polished centrepiece was so smooth that I instinctively went to feel the surface.

As I motioned to touch the stone, a loud, intimidating official bellowed out, 'Don't touch.' I almost jumped out of my skin, automatically jerking my hand back in an instant. I dared not touch the stone and risk his harsh voice yelling out at me again. I guessed it was smooth as a result of being touched so many times over the past five hundred years.

I found a place to sit near the temple and began to

read a pamphlet about the history. I read that similar walls were the foundations for many of the more modern buildings. The Spanish colonists demolished the Golden Temple, named Quri-Kancha in Quechuan, and used its foundations to build the Convent of Santo Domingo.

Likewise, all of the Catholic monasteries were built on what used to be the ancient sun temples of the Incas, thereby cementing the apparently superior culture of the Spanish. As if to prove differently, major earthquakes had severely damaged the recent buildings, but the original foundational stones remained unscathed.

Amazingly, these enormous stones were laid without cement. With such sophisticated methods of stone masonry so many thousands of years ago, the Incas were hardly inferior!

I read that once the Spanish conquistadors set foot within Cuzco, they could see the temple glowing in the distance. The impressive temple of Quri-Kancha was illuminated by the sun reflecting off many layers of pure gold. The gold totally covered its entire structure, including the floors. Even the adjacent courtyard and the city streets were decorated with gold and silver statues of gods and idols. Shocked and impressed by the wealth and beauty of the city, the Spaniards claimed it for themselves.

There I was, sitting on a bench in the middle of this amazing place, the irony being that I only had seventeen soles to my name. So very limited by my purse strings, I thought about it for some time; what to do and how to make the most of what little I had. I noticed that close to where I was sitting, some sort of construction was happening.

I made enquiries and found that it was to be a huge cinema screen. Apparently, a live broadcast of the grand-final match between teams from Peru and Brazil was in store. Even though it was not for another seven hours, people were already gathering for this big event.

I never had much of an interest in football despite growing up in Manchester, but with no money and nothing else to do, I thought I might stick around to watch.

To kill a little time, I walked around the Artesanian (Hand Craft) Markets, which were filled with so many lovely things. Handmade tablecloths, artistic wall hangings, Alpaca jumpers, and souvenirs of all kinds.

Normally I only use my credit card in emergencies, but this was an exceptional time, 'I may never get this opportunity again', I told myself convincingly. After carefully and painstakingly choosing something special, I attempted the purchase.

It didn't work! Another frustration in Peru: foreign credit cards just don't function. 'Maybe it's for the best', I thought and consoled myself by giving in to my hunger.

I took a risk by purchasing something off the street vendor; stuffed potatoes, which were delicious!

ARTESANIAN MARKETS

With still five hours left, I decided to take a closer look at the architecture of the Santo Domingo Convent. While I was in the courtyard near the entrance, a large group of German tourists swarmed around me to look at the huge doorway. As they moved through, I was virtually carried along, almost involuntarily, through the open doors. Once inside, as the group moved on, I was left standing alone very conspicuously. I looked around, half expecting the officials to jump on me, but surprisingly nobody had noticed. For a moment, I stood puzzled, but then, surrounded by interesting artefacts and amazing paintings, I felt excited. A wave of guilt tried to dampen my eager curiosity. I reasoned, 'Forgive me, Lord, I can't waste it.' Then I thought that perhaps He had even orchestrated my grand entry. Relief replaced the guilt, and I was grateful for small mercies.

I hadn't been inside a Catholic church for decades. Everything about it reminded me of the religion that once enslaved me. Candles burning at the foot of statues kindled old memories of how I used to light them, not understanding why I did it. The confusion that reigned in my adolescent years was brought to life by the sight of the wooden confessional box standing in the corner. As I studied the intricate woodcarvings, I remembered how I lied, unwilling to bear my soul to the invisible man behind the curtain. Those awful, oppressive feelings of condemnation were unbearable; I felt like such a hypocrite back then.

It dawned on me that I had moved from religion to relationship. My relationship with God made me feel taller, stronger, and more powerful. A euphoric feeling! I was so, so grateful that I was no longer "the blind following the blind".

The ornate interior design fascinated me, and the exquisite paintings, as well as the life-size statues, were all so magnificent. One painting did puzzle me—it was called Asunción de la Virgen (The Ascension of the Virgin). I had never read any biblical reference to the Virgin Mary rising into heaven.

My attention turned to the history of the last Inca Emperor, Atahualpa. Like most invaders, the Spanish had little time for honour or compassion. The deceitful Spaniard, Francisco Pizarro, lured Atahualpa and his men to a feast, supposedly in the emperor's honour: he then opened fire on the unarmed men, massacring them. Capturing Atahualpa, he sentenced him to death by burning him at the stake. Because the Incas regarded cremation as a sin, Atahualpa, in order to commute his sentence to strangulation, was compelled to convert to Catholicism. He was hung once he was baptised.

Time was ticking by, and the match was soon to commence. I made my way back to the already packed plaza. All the benches were chocker-block full, hundreds and hundreds of people were standing around, and the atmosphere was electric. The big screen showed the Ciencianos, a Peruvian team, running onto the soccer field, and outcries of praise roared. This excited the crowd immensely. The Ciencianos were the home team from Cuzco. The entire population of Cuzco and their dogs were there; dogs were literally everywhere. The game hadn't even started, and people continued to pour into the square by the hordes; soon, there was no standing room, and the crowds firmed up against each other. I was fearful when they began to push against each other. Those around me, afraid of being crushed, began to scream. That same dreadful feeling I had previously experienced on the bus returned. I wanted to get out, but it was impossible!

The family sitting on the bench next to me, pressed by the crowds, clambered to their feet, crouching on the seat and leaning on the backrest, hanging on tightly with both hands. I heard the man suggest, 'We should make room for the Gringo.' I made eye contact with him, looking mournful. He ushered me to hop into a tiny space between his two young daughters standing on the bench. Without hesitation, I hopped on and sat on the backrest alongside them. Hanging on anxiously, I thanked him profusely. The crowd swept by involuntarily.

From the higher vantage point, I felt a little safer, that is, until I peered into the massive crowd. Looking full-circle all around, I was stunned by the enormity of the multitude, and my heart sank. 'Oh!... Good!... God!' was my shocked thought; a feeling of impending doom swept over me as thoughts of hysteria and panic erupting caused my imagination to run riot. 'We could all be crushed to death by this crowd. They're such an excitable people', I told myself, and I was stuck in the very nucleus. There was no escape!

In the endless sea of dark-haired people bobbing around were men, women, and children. Some kids sat on shoulders, and some were only babes in arms. 'Reassuring signs', I told myself, 'at least it's not a crowd of soccer hooligans.' The game started, and the crowds began to settle. The family on the bench informed me that it was a very important game because only two other Peruvian teams had ever made it to the South American Cup Final, and neither of them had won.

Both teams were so desperate to win, and both were equally skill-matched; they fought hard to defend their goalposts. Even I was riveted. With only four minutes to full-time, the score remained nil, nil. Tension mounted every time the ball went anywhere near the nets. Time was almost up, and then Carlos Lugo from the home team had a free-kick. Miraculously, he scored, and what a goal it was. Absolute uproar and pandemonium broke out. People were screaming, cheering, even crying as they jumped up and down, arms raised in adoration of their team. The noise level was absolutely insane, with air horns blasting, firecrackers and bangers exploding, and a brass band booming through loud speakers all around the square. A display of colour filled the air as hundreds of balloons and confetti were thrown down from the crowds standing on the balconies all around the square; it floated down, landing on the jet-black heads below. I had never seen anything like it.

I couldn't comprehend how a football match could invoke such emotions, such passion. 'It's just a game!' I thought as I watched groups of young men dancing around in a frenzy while madly chanting, 'Umpha! Umpha! Umpha!' Women were cheering while freneti-cally waving flags. Some were blowing elongated black bugles while others were whistling with their fingers or singing expressively. I couldn't help but think what a zealous lot they are!

Although I was in the centre of the excitement, I didn't really feel a part of it. I wasn't as emotionally affected as the rest appeared to be. Just then, the crowd started pushing and shoving again. They pressed hard against us, but we hung onto the bench with such tenacity that our knuckles turned white. The bench, securely fixed into the cement, became an anchor in a swirling sea of people unwittingly dragged off into a rip of panic.

Victory chants turned into screams of terror, and the smiling faces became sombre. The terrified young girl next to me started crying; her tears provoked her father to yell ferociously at the crowd. The stressful situation was bringing out the worst in people. 'No le impuje! No le impuje! (Stop pushing! Stop pushing!)', he repeatedly cried as he violently pushed back at the crowd. His daughter, seeing the rage in her father, only became more and more distressed. Even with all his strength, it was impossible; he couldn't budge the solid wall of people. At this stage, I was concerned that the bench would be ripped out of the ground; I closed my eyes and began to pray. I acknowledged that God was in control and asked Him to help us. I asked Him for "calm" to fall on us and for protection.

When I opened my eyes, some people looked like they had insufficient room even to breathe properly. It was an extremely tense situation; they were so hard-pressed that they could have lifted their feet off the ground and remained suspended by the crowd. Then, unexpectedly, a deafening sound like a bomb explosion went off, and overhead the sky lit up with colour; it was fireworks. Astonishingly, this had a profound effect on the crowd. Momentarily distracted, they gazed upwards in unison at the sky. Suddenly, the pushing and the shoving eased off, and the panic gradually abated. The crowds began to spill out of the plaza from every angle, and a semblance of order returned.

I waited for some time before it seemed safe enough to step off the bench into the mob. Once I left the safety of the bench, I was compelled to walk in the direction of the masses until their numbers thinned out towards the perimeter of the square. Outside the main square, I was relieved to see large numbers of buses arriving in succession. Within no time, each bus filled beyond normal capacity, but there were so many people that they didn't seem to make an impact on the queues. The queues formed quicker than the buses could cart them away.

After much waiting in incredibly long lines, I finally managed to squeeze onto one of the crowded buses. Arriving at Juana's place in the early hours, everyone was in bed asleep. I flopped into bed, relieved to have survived yet another narrow escape. Exhausted and emotionally drained, I crashed instantly.

PLAZA DE ARMAS, CUSCO

Chapter Eight

DOUBTING GOD'S CALLING

(Philippians 3:10-15)

Journal Entry:
Leon de San Jeronimo, Cuzco, Peru
21st December 2003

The blisters on my right foot combined with my upset stomach are painful reminders of yesterday's adventure in Cuzco. Eating food from a street vendor really isn't a good idea, but I knew that!

As a result of all the rain in Machu Picchu my leaking sports shoes are about ready to drop off, but I have to make them last until I return home. It's a pleasant, dry day today and the sun is shining, but all I want to do is stay inside and nurse my wounds. I feel like I've been hit by a bus!

A pile of washing begged for my attention, so I begrudgingly filled the sink designed for midgets and began to hand-wash. After a short time, my back was aching. Feeling sorry for myself, I stopped to stretch and then went outside. Juana's place overlooked a deserted playground, which was quiet and peaceful, and the warm rays seemed to soothe my aches and pains. I decided to forget the washing and go easy on myself. Even dragging the wooden chair outside was a huge effort, but the thought of resting with my favourite book in the warmth of the sun and peaceful ambience was worth the struggle.

Less than halfway down the page, the golden silence was shattered by an army of uniformed kids pouring into the yard with buckets of water and scrubbing brushes—the sound of rowdy children dragging desks and chairs over the rough concrete surface grated on my brain. The noise irritated my mild headache, and my head began to pound. 'No rest for the wicked', I thought. Within minutes, the playground was full of industrious kids yelling and screaming as they busily scrubbed the graffiti off their furniture. Even the small children got right into the job. My attention, no longer on reading, was completely taken up by the busy spectacle. As I observed, I saw one boy splashing a group of girls, who instantly retaliated by drenching him with an entire bucket of water. The frantic laughter and girly screams spread contagiously to the other children, and when the boy went for back-up, they became embroiled in a massive water fight. The excitement spread like wildfire, and they all ended up soaked to the skin. I watched them with a sense of envy and wondered if their world was really so carefree. Could childhood be so magical? I wondered what it was like for them at home.

Interrupted, Juana approached, asking me with much enthusiasm to accompany her to the markets. I didn't feel like going but compelled by her persuasive insistence, I pushed past my "self" and went.

Shopping in San Jeronimo wasn't like the usual trip to the local supermarket back home; it turned out to be quite a cultural experience. The dead chickens lay out in the open sun on a wooden slab with swarms of flies buzzing around their rigid feet poking up into the air. Juana requested a fresh chicken, and the vendor brought out a live one and immediately chopped its head off right there in front of us. The loud squawking came to an abrupt silence as its head rolled into the basket below, where several other heads lay. The blood-splattered as its body continued twitching and squirming. My uneasy stomach churned dangerously.

We walked in the blazing sun as there were no shaded areas anywhere. A herd of sheep led by a boy crossed our path, then minutes later, we side-stepped a cow outside the bakery before it sauntered off down the middle of the street. Before long, Juana's bulging shopping bag was full of yuka (root vegetables) and chancho (pork) as well as the chicken. The shopping bag looked heavy, and I offered to carry it. After a short time, it was a challenge even for me to manage. I was amazed that Juana normally did the shopping by herself. She was obviously accustomed to hard work.

As we walked down narrow cobbled streets lined with tiny run-down houses, I commented on how small they were. Juana explained that the houses were mainly one-bedroom and were occupied by families of four or five children. Reminded of the tiny, terraced house I grew up in, I was curious to know if they had a bathroom, or could Leon de San Jeronimo possibly have a public washhouse like the one in Manchester? Juana told me that they had no such luxury as running water, let alone a washhouse! Water was purchased (when they could afford it) and delivered by trucks that filled the moderate-size plastic barrels sitting outside the front of the houses. Juana explained that all of life was experienced in the same room, comprising a sink, a table, and some chairs scattered around. The houses had no electricity. Hot water and gas were non-existent, and most people used coal for cooking. Basic things such as a bath, shower or toilet were luxuries. Washing was done at the sink or using a basin in the bedroom. Outside and behind the house was a hole in the ground delegated for a lavatory. I learned that the bigger houses with two or more bedrooms were shared by several families, and the rent on average was fifty soles a month, the equivalent to AUD $20 per month.

Returning to Juana's place at the school, I realised it was quite a luxury in comparison. That evening, several of us sat around the table, as usual, enjoying a great meal and talking comfortably. Again, I felt acceptance and nothing but a genuine sense of caring. It was a good feeling. In a sense, it seemed that these people were rich in spite of their poverty. Rich in ways that we lacked back home in Australia. I realised that the cold water or the dodgy toilet seats had little significance. What really mattered was how the people cared for one another and accepted one another.

After dinner, everyone was busily getting ready to go to the youth group at the local church. Luz ran the group with the help of a pastor named Pastor Americo and his wife. I was content to stay home with Juana. We enjoyed talking whilst listening to some Peruvian worship music playing in the background. Our conversation about faith was intriguing. Juana was a person whose words and actions reflected the very character of God. I loved being in her company; I wanted to be like her, and I hoped that somehow her patience and grace would rub off onto me. I knew that I had many rough edges that needed to be chiselled away, and I prayed that God would do just that, but also that it wouldn't be too painful. I especially prayed for more patience.

The days passed very quickly, and it was time to return to Lima. I had accepted the offer of a lift to the airport from Pastor Americo and his wife. We set off an hour earlier than was necessary, which good because the car he drove was an old bomb, and I wasn't too confident in it. I couldn't afford to miss my plane. When Pastor Americo announced that he wanted to show me a project of his on the way, I was a little concerned. The project was near the top of a mountain, close to the airport, he assured me. As we drew closer to the distant mountain, it became bigger, and as we began to ascend, it became steeper and steeper. The earth beneath the wheels was sodden from the heavy rain the night before, and the car really struggled through the mud. Slipping and sliding along the dirt track, I felt unsafe. Some of the corners were nerve-wracking. Halfway up the mountain, the car began to labour, and before long, steam rose up from under the bonnet. When we stopped the car, the wheels sank deeper into the mud.

I would have been happier to walk. I was furious, but I remembered how, just the night before, I had prayed for patience! Trying not to panic, I said nothing and waited quietly as Pastor Americo lifted the bonnet. He said optimistically, 'It's OK, just needs a little water.'

That's the amazing thing about the Peruvians: they are always ever hopeful! After much pushing and grunting, and with the help of a few tree branches under the wheels, the car was running again. We lost a fair amount of time, but Pastor Americo continued heading uphill, determined to show his project. Looking intently at my watch, with as much grace as I could muster, I calmly expressed my concerns about missing the plane again. 'Just two minutes around the corner', he said. I had no choice but to continue.

He was correct, we arrived promptly, and I listened carefully as he explained all about the project. He showed me the foundations of a building and some adobe mud bricks laying out to dry, describing in great detail how the bricks were made. He went on and on until, finally, I interrupted him by tapping on my watch. He assured me that we would make it to the airport and then carried on talking. I interrupted again. 'The car is not very reliable', I said, 'so we really should go.'

'Don't worry', he insisted. 'It's downhill; we'll get there much quicker.' He continued talking, and the more he talked, the more frustrated I became. I began to realise just how impatient I was.

Time in Peru is one of those cultural differences that visitors often discuss. Peruvians appear careless, even contemptuous, of the need to be on time. I have had it calmly said by many different Peruvians that, '*Whatever time one leaves, the journey will still take as long as it takes, and a twelve-hour working day will still be a twelve-hour working day no matter what.*' I still don't get the meaning of this statement! Peruvians think that foreigners are anal about time. They think it unhealthy to be neurotically attached to the movement of a pointer on a dial attached to your wrist. They really don't worry about time and believe that their perspective makes life less stressful and more balanced. To the uninitiated foreigner, this is nothing less than maddening.

Finally, we were back on the muddy road going down the mountain. At a flattish area, the car came to a halt; this time, it was leaking oil as well as being overheated. We had to get out and push until we reached the top of the next gradient and then jump back in and free-wheel the rest of the way. Tricky! Predictably, at the next flat section, we slowed down to a standstill. Stopping and starting in this fashion most of the way took much longer than anticipated.

By the time we reached the airport, I was devoid of all patience and grace. I grabbed my bags, barely said goodbye, and ran to the check-in desk. The lady at the counter quickly issued my boarding pass and told me, 'Gate sixteen, run.' Running all the way to the furthest departure gate in the airport was like one of those "hassle" dreams where you never quite make it. Unlike the dream, I did make it! But only by the skin of my teeth! I sat on the plane feeling quite unnerved and shaky, and I wondered how on earth the Peruvians ever imagined that their concept of time made life less stressful.

Journal Entry:
Lima, Peru
22nd December 2003

Even before I stepped outside the airport, everything felt so familiar. I no longer felt intimidated by the onslaught of taxi drivers; instead, I walked with a purpose right through them, smiling and nodding as I ignored their demands. I knew my way around, where to catch the bus, which bus to catch and what the fare was to Luisa's place.

I hopped on a bus and enjoyed the familiar sights that flashed by the window. I observed the street peddlers, the shoe-shine boys, and the ladies with their many layers of colourful skirts. The sound of the ticket collector yelling out the names of suburbs while hanging from the open doorway no longer baffled me. I recognised the names, and I even knew their location. When I stepped off the bus, it was like "coming home"!

'Coming home…' I wrestled with that thought. 'This is not my home', I affirmed to myself. My mind drifted to that distant sun-burnt land of Australia, to fond memories of times spent with my own girls; I felt a longing to see Anna and Carmen again. 'Home is where they are', I confirmed, afraid to admit that I was beginning to feel at home in Peru. 'I'm a midwife, not a babysitter!' I told myself. Even more convincingly, I reminded myself, 'I have strived to get my qualifications, and I have worked hard to reach a level of expertise in my profession.' The conflict in my mind refused to go away. I struggled to reconcile the calling of God to the reality of my own yearnings to be with my daughters. My heartstrings were tugged in opposite directions, at times, each pulling stronger than the other. A physical pain in my chest left me feeling crushed, almost to the point of paralysis.

I got off the bus and made my way to Luisa's place

instinctively and tried hard not to think anymore, but I felt troubled. Miguel opened the door; he had been waiting to greet me. With his familiar smile and his warm manner, he welcomed me, and after a brief chat, he handed me the key and disappeared down the stairs.

Luisa was at work as usual and wouldn't be back until after 6.00 pm, so I had full run of the place to myself. The first thing I did was have a hot shower. After Cuzco, Luisa's shower was amazing; I must have stayed under the incredibly hot, steamy water for a long time. The luxury of brushing my teeth at a sink with a mirror and having enough light to see my reflection was pleasant. Sitting on a toilet seat instead of the cold porcelain felt good too. The simple comforts in life that I had previously taken for granted now seemed like absolute luxuries.

I put the kettle on, sat in the comfy armchair, and looked around the room. With only the sound of the kettle boiling, it seemed unusually quiet. I started to make a cup of tea when a shiver ran up my spine; I had made this cup of tea and had this shower before. The peculiar feeling of dèjá vu came over me. It was the weirdest thing. 'How odd', I thought. I went out to the patio, tea in hand, and sat in the warm sunshine. After a moment, I relaxed back into the chair and closed my eyes to soak up the heat of the sun. In the still, calm ambience, the warmth on my face was glorious. All my concerns seemed diminished. 'I do love this climate', I reflected.

My thoughts drifted to the house in Surco not so

far away, to the patio where the girls played with their elastic bands. 'They are probably playing right now in the sunshine', I mused. I was half-tempted to visit again, but instantly I thought, 'No.' We had said our goodbyes, and that was painful enough; no way was I going to go through that again. 'What would it achieve anyhow?' After a pensive silence, I had no answers.

In the silence, I recalled those familiar words, 'Let me show you.' My heart leapt in the same way as when I had first heard that still small voice. I was filled with inexplicable joy. Dèjá vu again. But my critical mind questioned, 'Was it really God speaking?'

I remembered how the devil had so subtly tempted Eve by saying to her, 'Did God really say, "You must not eat from any tree in the garden"?' (Genesis 3:1, NIV). Instantly, I felt ashamed that I doubted God's calling, but then I became acutely aware of the sun warming my face, and I knew that God really was speaking to me. The experience was eerily the same as when God had spoken directly to my heart in the hallway of the house at Surco. Again, it was more than just a feeling: it was a tangible presence. It was like being touched on the inside.

The shame dissolved, and an overwhelming sense of love and acceptance inundated my soul. This time I stood firm, and I dared to believe. I believed with my whole heart that, 'Yes! God spoke to me.' My heart pounded, and my mind was stopped from making excuses.

I was sure that God had a plan and a purpose and

that He would take care of everything. My faith grew stronger, and the apprehensions about leaving my girls grew fainter. All of the conflict and confusion waned into nothing. An overwhelming sense of peace touched the very core of my being and left me with no doubt that I would return to the girls. They were now my focus, my calling, my life!

Chapter Nine

A LOVE STORY

Journal Entry:
Quito, Ecuador
Late December 2003

Goodbyes were sad this morning as I left Luisa's place, but Miguel lightened things up a little by taking photos of Luisa and I. Even up to our last evening together, Luisa shared her home-cooking and we enjoyed long conversations. I am left with fond memories and hope to keep in contact with Luisa, she and her family have been so good to me.

The guesthouse in Quito, Ecuador has become my base. I can come and go from here and safely leave some of my luggage, allowing me to travel light. It's a comfortable place run by a retired American couple who very graciously host volunteers from Hospital Vozandes.

On the flight back to Ecuador, I had lots of time to reflect on my stay in Peru. I thought about Malinda, my purpose for going to Peru in the first place, but so much more had happened. It was all beyond belief: Luisa, Doctor Klaus, the girls in Surco, Juana and family in Cuzco, the crazy taxi drivers, Peruvian-class travel, the excitement of the South American Cup Final, and the unexpected pleasure of Machu Picchu. It blew my mind!

Catching the bus from Quito Airport to the guesthouse seemed anything but familiar. I carefully noted the bus route for the next day when I was due to catch a flight back out again, this time to Cali, Columbia. I felt reasonably confident of finding my way back to the airport, and at least I knew to catch the bus at that same stop as I got off.

Early the next morning, I sat on the last remaining seat at the back of the bus. At every stop, more and more people piled on until there were so many people crammed in the aisle that I couldn't see out the window. I had no clue where I was! I tried to recall how long the trip had taken the day before, but I wasn't sure. I didn't want to ask anyone because from past experience, I have found that when a Gringo asks a question, everyone within ear-shot wants to answer it. I didn't want the fuss, so I waited to ask the ticket collector. It took forever for him to make his way down to the back of the bus, but finally, he reached me, and I was able to discreetly ask if we were close to the airport.

'You are way past the airport!' he exclaimed loudly and then yelled to the driver, 'Stop the bus!' The bus came to a screeching halt and waited while I painstakingly pushed my way past the standing passengers. The ticket collector said, 'You just have to cross the road and go back.' Feeling flushed with embarrassment, I thanked him and hopped off the bus. The bus pulled away, revealing a busy four-lane highway with a frenzy of traffic speeding past. There didn't seem to be a crossing anywhere. I stood shakily, my heart in my mouth, feeling like a fearful child. Somehow, sometime later, I made it to the other side. I then jumped straight back onto another crowded bus moving in the opposite direction.

This time, I stood close to the doorway of the bus and asked the driver to indicate when we arrived at the airport. Determined not to get shoved to the back of the bus, when other passengers boarded, I didn't budge. They had to brush past me. Sometimes my plans just don't go smoothly, and I wondered why. I pondered on this for a while and reflected, 'It's like my walk with God. There have been some unexpected rough patches, but nonetheless, the journey is exciting.' I decided to accept all the hiccups that came along as just another aspect of the adventure. No dramas! Even if I missed my plane, it was not the end of the world. A pleasant calmness flooded over me, and I relaxed.

I made the flight to Cali, Columbia, and I had the pleasure of going to the Ekklesia Church and praying on The Mountain of Prayer, where Dr Ruth Ruibal and her husband began the overnight prayer meetings. I went to the Estadio Pasqual Herrero, the Football Stadium where thousands gathered to pray, and their prayers had had such an impact on the crime rate that even government leaders acknowledged the amazing improvement to the chaos and general breakdown of that society. My Christmas day was celebrated with an invitation to a Pastor's home amongst thought-provoking Columbians, and after a hurried flight to Cuba, I spent New Year's Eve watching a ballet perfor-mance in the Gran Teatro de Havana.

Listening to Cuban music, watching the salsa dancers with such rhythm spill out onto the streets of Havana, and discovering more about the culture, were the highlights. Cuba, with its complex mixture of multi-ethnic people, its different religious beliefs, and its politics and propaganda, left impressions that will remain with me for life.

Journal Entry:
Sydney, Australia
8th January 2004

> *While in transit from Cuba to Australia, waiting at gate nine in the departure lounge of El Salvador International Airport, an elegant looking flight attendant approached me and asked for my passport and boarding-pass. She then walked off with both*

documents in hand. After a moment, with no flight attendant in sight, I had thoughts of being stranded in El Salvador with no passport. I was about to panic and run to the counter, when she suddenly reappeared. On return, she handed me my passport with a new boarding pass and said, 'Your seat has been upgraded to first class, madam, compliments of Taca Airline.' I smiled and thanked her. My smile grew wider at the irony of travelling first class and yet I didn't have enough money to buy a coffee! God surely has a sense of humour.

With plenty of leg room and wide armrests on the comfortable seats, I felt thoroughly indulged. Being served champagne and a delicious three-course meal in oven-baked dishes made me feel somehow *precious*; I didn't enjoy it.

I was so excited when the plane touched down in Sydney; I could hardly wait to see Anna and Carmen. I felt proud of my girls; I had missed them so much, and all I wanted to do was to hug them long and hard.

It was so good to see their faces and speak in person. They seemed so grown up. We greeted and hugged, but both Anna and Carmen seemed a little restrained, even uncomfortable when we hugged. Perhaps my extended hug was too much; I felt compelled to let go sooner than I was ready. I became acutely aware of how inhibited our culture really is when it comes to any show of affection. The conversation was easy and flowed well as we walked out of the airport, then suddenly Anna stopped to pause at a stretched limousine. With a big smile, she said, 'This is your transport home, mum!'

'Yeh, right', I responded cynically and carried on walking, but they stopped, and the chauffeur began to load my luggage into the boot. This just didn't compute with me. I felt uncomfortable; it seemed like such an extravagant waste of money, but I tried to receive it gracefully. Really, all I wanted was a big, long, drawn-out hug. I felt sad. But this was their display of affection, and I didn't want to disappoint them.

The interior space was immaculate, the leather seat felt soft, and the mirrored bar with crystal decanters and glasses was just over the top. We spread out with ample room for even more people. A flash-back of how I'd squashed into the back of a small taxi with six or seven Peruvian girls tightly packed in made me feel worse. Anna offered me a choice of different chocolate bars. I remembered that I'd mentioned in an email how I had craved for Cadbury's chocolate; I was touched by the thought. I felt very self-indulged.

After the scarcity I'd experienced in South America, the excess was all too much. I couldn't help but think about the cost of everything. I found myself calculating soles for dollars and working out how many pairs of shoes or how many days' supply of food all this expense could have bought. Something had changed in me: none of this material stuff mattered anymore. After eating the chocolate, I felt sick. I didn't know if it was the richness of the chocolate or the abundance that made my stomach churn.

My perspective had changed. I realised that I, too, had been guilty of undervaluing the small things in life; the hugs and the kisses, the thoughtful words, and acts of kindness. Even worse, I had taught my children to do the same. Like a chain that can't be broken, our cultural norms seem to pass from one generation to another. I tried to blame my culture, but truly I could only blame myself.

The drive home was so smooth; no potholes, no blasting horns, no gridlocks, no road rage, no head-banging reggae-ton music. The drivers on the road stayed within their lanes and courteously gave way to each other. They used their indicators and even stopped at red lights. All the way home, I never heard even one car horn. It was all so quietly civilized, and we could actually hear ourselves speak. We glided through the surreal suburbs with their pristine streets, well-kept houses with manicured lawns, and kids in straw hats and spotless uniforms. Yet, I felt uneasy; as much as I tried, I just couldn't enjoy it. I felt a kind of tension, one I had never felt before.

Remembering how Paul said that he knew what it was like to be in need and he knew what it was like to have plenty,[1] I realised that I needed to learn this secret of being content in any and every situation because the joy was being sucked out of this wonderful homecoming. I made a

conscious decision right then that this "lucky country" was God's blessing to us. I had to accept the blessing and endeavour to be happy with it. I stopped calculating the cost of everything and began to enjoy the precious moments spent with my girls.

Carmen, in the last year of high school, was busy studying for the HSC, and her weekends were often filled with socializing. I had a burning desire to speak with Anna and Carmen in-depth about Peru and to see how they felt about me going back for an extended period, but the weeks passed without us ever getting together. When we did, it was usually short and sweet. The difficulty was that Carmen lived in Sydney, a two-hour drive away. Anna was closer, at least geographically, but a young man named Ben had become Anna's shadow, and in between her job, he occupied her every waking hour. She was besotted with him too.

My girls no longer needed me. On the one hand, it was good, a healthy milestone in life. Both Anna and Carmen were living full lives and were completely independent of me. On the other hand, I was left with feelings of sadness and loss. I exercised a lot of positive self-talk at that time. 'Their separation from me is a normal fact of life', I told myself, but in reality, letting go was painful. I told myself that I should be happy for them, that they are well-adjusted young adults. If they were needy and insecure, I could never have gone. Only when I handed them over to God, trusting and believing that He would take care of them, could I go to Peru.

I tried to take every opportunity to talk with Anna

and Carmen on the subject of Peru, but with their busy lives, I hardly got a "look-in". On fleeting visits with Carmen, she seemed all-consumed with school life. Our conversations were superficial; rarely did we get into deep and meaningful heart-to-heart talks. Carmen happily encouraged me regarding Peru; she never expressed any apprehensions about me going, and she seemed happy living with her dad.

Often, after talking with Anna, I felt that maybe I was a bit of a drama queen; it was no big deal in her eyes. She would say, 'If it's what you want, mum, then you should do it.' In truth, I felt those words showed that Anna really didn't understand. In her mind, God never came into the equation. She felt it was something I wanted to do for myself.

I felt that the time was slipping away fast, and I needed to prepare Anna and Carmen for our time of separation. As a result, I came up with an idea. I invited Anna and Carmen to come to live with me for that final year. In retrospect, I can see that this was a big ask and an unrealistic expectation. Anna was happily living with Ben; she could not be persuaded and blankly refused.

Carmen was completing her final year of high school, and the only way I could get her to agree to live with me was to move back to Sydney. This was something I swore I would never do. However, I relented, and we found a comfortable apartment in Parramatta. It was the halfway point between Sydney and the

Central Coast where Anna lived, and it was reasonably close to Carmen's school.

The plan was for Carmen and me to spend that year together. The following year, Carmen would either go to university or take some time off to travel. In regards to Anna, it seemed that she felt I was overly involved with her life and that I needed to let her live it. She expressed once, 'You should get a life, mum.' Consequently, we saw each other only on occasions.

Going to Peru for the long term seemed like madness to most of my family and friends. The common questions were, 'What will you do there?' and, 'What about your own children?' The answer to the latter question was the hardest to grapple with. To the believer, I responded, 'I'm trusting God with my girls. If He has called me, He will take care of them.' They were not as judgemental as those outside of church. It was more difficult for those who didn't have faith; they just didn't understand. Their condemning accusations saddened me, 'How could you leave your own children to look after someone else's?' In my heart, the answer was clear, but it was not always easy to communicate. I responded, 'My children are no longer children. They're young adults, and they are mature enough to take care of themselves.'

I was encouraged by those closest to me and by my church family because they knew that I loved my children. They understood how hard it was for me to leave them, and they knew that it was my faith that enabled me to do it. The most important thing in my mind was a promise that God had given me many years earlier, that He would save both Anna and Carmen. I felt that I had failed in leading them to Christ, and now it was time for me to relinquish all rights. I had to get out of God's way so that He could bring them into the fold.

My own experience has led me to believe that we all have a "God-shaped void" in our hearts. I somehow managed to fill the void for over thirty years, but whatever I tried was only a temporary fix. Whether it was new possessions, work, study, men, overseas trips, a home, a husband, children, or even religion, the void returned.

Whether you or I believe in God is irrelevant to His existence. What is relevant is that the void remains until we seek Him for ourselves.

Journal Entry:
Gosford, Central Coast, Australia
2nd March 2004

> *Within the small sphere of my hometown in the Central Coast, everything seems to have remained the same. The people I know appear to be living in humdrum lives, existing only to work, to pay bills, and to watch a lot of television. It's as if theirs is another reality, one that I am afraid of being drawn back into. I feel that I have broken free from that trap, that I have discovered another radical reality, one with*

purpose, and I do not want to go back.

The direction of my life was changing, and I was glad. I committed myself, heart and soul, to God's calling, determined to focus all my efforts on preparing myself mentally and physically for the task. I needed to raise funds for the girls in Peru, but I also needed to pay my own way.

Although I found employment, my perspective on life had changed dramatically. Work was not the be-all and end-all of everything; it was a means to an end. The local hospital provided plenty of work on a casual basis. Although I never did like casual work, as I found it difficult to be constantly moving from one area to another, the upside was that I could choose when to work and when not to work. This became all-important and suited my needs at that time.

Later, when I moved to Parramatta with Carmen, I found full-time employment as a phlebotomist with the Red Cross Blood Bank. It was a contract for the complete year and just walking distance from our new apartment.

It was perfect. I especially loved the opportunity to meet people from all walks of life, and I really enjoyed the challenge of getting the nervous first-time donors to relax. The downside was that the work was quite repetitive and boring, but at least that meant I could be efficient without too much effort.

Although I never tried, I think I could have inserted the needle with my eyes closed! Often, I had plenty of headspace to plan events, organise my presentations, and even make the occasional phone call in between donors.

It slowly began to sink in that I would soon spend some years in a different culture, away from the creature comforts of home. I set to the task of adapting, first by sharing with just about everyone I knew all about Peru.

Then with some trepidation, I talked to my pastors, Paul and Sandra Piefke. They were open to overseas missions and were very encouraging. We prayed together, and they organised a time slot during the Sunday service for me to give a video presentation.

The anticipation of my talk was truly a roller coaster of emotions. Over the next few days, every fibre in my being underwent a rise in both excitement and apprehension. I had visions of accomplishing great things as well as visions of being a complete failure.

The presentation went well, and the positive response was overwhelming. I was very much encouraged by many who demonstrated their support by sponsoring one of the girls in Peru. Others came on board with fundraising ideas, and together we created a sponsorship program.

Lilian Aldering created sponsorship cards, with brief details and photos of each girl, on her computer. Fini Kuipers partnered with me in prayer on a regular basis, and many other individuals helped with all the logistics.

PRESENTATION AT HOME CHURCH BRIDGET, ANNA
& CARMEN

I followed Pastor Paul's advice to join a mission organisation and soon commenced the application process with Pioneer Missions. Advised to reach optimum health before going to Peru, I undertook some physical preparation. While in the Central Coast, this involved walking in Kincumber Mountain; it was a great stomping ground to pick up some fitness. When I moved to Sydney, I walked all around Parramatta Park on a regular basis. Apart from work and exercise, the application process with Pioneer as well as fundraising occupied most of my waking hours.

I became involved in raising funds for three projects, and the results were very poor. My endeavours to help both Pastor Americo's project and the school in Cuzco were competing with the needs of the girls in Lima. I realised that trying to raise funds for all the projects was nothing more than foolishness; I was spreading myself too thin. From then on, I fully focused on raising funds exclusively for the girls in Lima.

In the meantime, I was corresponding with Pastor Luis, who sent information and photos of each girl as well as prayer requests regarding the needs and hardships that the girls were facing. Each month, a significant amount of funds collected by my church from sponsors and other individuals was sent to Pastor Luis. He, in turn, provided copies of receipts for substantiation of the funds used. The funds at this stage were for the daily needs of the girls: school supplies, uniforms, medical care.

I continued to give talks and presentations to anyone and everyone who would listen, which was mainly the local churches and a couple of schools in the area. Raising funds for such a project outside my home church was a slow, arduous process. I could never keep up with the needs of the girls in Peru; it seemed like the more funds raised, the more they needed. Then the situation became worse when Pastor Luis informed us that the municipality had given him a period of two months to vacate the rented house in Surco. Apparently, the neighbours had complained bitterly about the noise level.

Pastor Luis told us that he was 'stepping out in faith' and had sold his home to buy a block of land for the construction of a girl's refuge. He assured us that he and his family had a place to live at the manse of his church. My home church responded by going above and beyond my expectations. Our whole church prayed together, and then a special offering was collected towards the construction of a new home for the girls.

The urgency of the need ignited a passion in me to try harder in my fundraising efforts. Despite my utmost efforts, I felt like my tiny voice was lost in a whirlwind of thousands of other competing voices. It seemed that there were many, many individuals all trying to gain awareness and support for their own particular projects. It seemed impossible to make any headway. I began to feel a sense of desperation as time was running out for the girls. After much prayer, I felt that I could do something, though it was a little radical; I put my house up for sale. The economy in Peru is such that the cost of my house would be almost sufficient to construct a refuge.

In 2004, the real estate market in Australia was thriving; real estate agents were virtually dancing in the streets. There were buyers everywhere and not enough homes on the market. It was the perfect time to sell. Inexplicably though, my house didn't sell. The weeks passed, and still, no sale. I felt completely helpless. I prayed earnestly for the sale of my house. More weeks passed. I prayed again. Nothing! Over those weeks, God helped me to realise that instead of relying on Him, I had been relying on my own means. This was one of the most difficult lessons for me to learn. I repented and took the house off the market. This began the long road of learning to truly rely on God. I'm still learning today!

Journal Entry:
Parramatta, Sydney, Australia
12th March 2004

> *Today my path crossed with a certain person named Greg Bonner. He, persuaded by his son Patrick, decided, for the very first time, to give blood at the busy branch of the Red Cross Blood Bank in Parramatta.*
>
> *Greg was just a typical first-time donor, nervous but willing and brave enough to shed his life's blood for someone else. The one difference with this donor was that he listened attentively to everything I said. Our conversation flowed well, and we instantly had a most unusual rapport with one another.*

Greg just happened to end up in the cubicle where I was working that morning. On reading his registration form, I noted that he had just returned from Nepal. Restrictions with taking blood from certain countries

meant more questioning. I asked Greg the usual questions about the nature of his visit, how long he had
stayed, and if he had visited any remote areas in Nepal.
I listened with curiosity; intrigued by his work with
Rotary International, I asked far more questions than
was necessary for the paperwork. When he mentioned
that his rotary club had raised all the funds for the
extension of a hospital in Nepal, my antenna immediately went up.

On passing the requirement for donating blood, I
began to palpate his veins and clean the skin with
alcohol wipes. New donors are always very anxious, but
instead of calmly talking him through the process, I
found myself sharing about my time in Peru, about the
desperate needs of the girls and how I was finding it so
difficult to raise funds. I was about to puncture his arm
with a big nineteen-gauge needle, but he was so
absorbed in the conversation that he was oblivious of
the needle even going in; he never as much as flinched.
I was a little taken aback when this total stranger asked,
'Do you think you could prepare a presentation for my
rotary club?' I had never done any public speaking in
my life, but I confidently said, 'Yes, definitely. When?'

Months later, after the exchange of a few emails,
Greg was to introduce me as the guest speaker at Castle
Hill Rotary Club. The night of the presentation arrived;
the room was crowded with men, some sitting, some
milling around, others just standing whilst in conversation. Looking around the room, I could see that the
members were mainly crusty old men in formal black

suits. I felt very intimidated. The only females there were the ones who came with me. When I saw the numerous grey-haired gentlemen, all the ties, and even some dickie bows, I became extremely nervous. I looked around the room for Greg, but I couldn't really remember what he looked like. When I couldn't see him anywhere, I wondered if I would even recognise him.

A man who spoke the "Queen's English" approached me and showed my group to a table in the large room and me. There were numerous tables set tastefully and with name place cards at each setting. Everyone in my group found their name cards, but my name wasn't there. This made me more anxious. Not knowing if my USB was compatible with the projector or if I'd even recognise Greg added to the tension I was feeling. Then, through the crowd, I noted a younger man approaching me with a glass of "red" in each hand. I knew instantly it was Greg. 'To help you relax', he said, smiling. I was relieved but a little embarrassed that he had perceived my nervousness. 'Is it that obvious?' I responded. I took the glass readily and smiled back as I sipped. The wine must have helped as we managed to figure out the high-tech equipment even though neither of us was tech-savvy. From then on, I began to calm down and enjoy Greg's company.

Before the presentation, a request over the loud-speaker was made to take our seats; dinner was about to be served. In front of all the other tables was a long table, on which I found my name card placed next to

Greg's. I felt a little strange sitting next to him, as I had expected to sit with my family and friends. But it was sharing a meal at that table when I first started to see Greg in a different way.

After dinner, when introduced by Greg to do my presentation, before commencing, I felt it appropriate to ask if we could bow our heads in prayer. I had no idea about Rotarian rules at the time, but no one complained; instead, the men all respectfully bowed their heads. I followed this with a power-point presentation, which included a video I had taken of the girls on the day of the pancake experience. In all, it went well. Many showed interest in the project by their encouraging comments, but it wasn't until some weeks later that I learned just how successful it had been. I received a very excited phone call from Greg. In one evening, more funds were raised by the Rotarians than by the churches I had approached over the previous four months combined. Greg suggested that I should look for more openings in other Rotary clubs, and he offered to write the letters of introduction for me—I agreed enthusiastically.

I explained to my pastors about Greg's idea to approach more rotary clubs; they not only approved but also agreed to have the funds pass through the House of Praise Church for accountability and for ease of transfer to Peru.

Once Greg constructed a letter, he suggested that we could perhaps get our children to help with the mail-out over a BBQ at his house. We did exactly that and invited Anna and Carmen as well as Greg's two youngest children, Nick and his sister Sarah.

They all responded positively to the invitation. On the day of the BBQ, Anna, Carmen and I arrived at his place a little nervous; it was our first time in unknown territory, and the girls had never met Greg or his kids before. The girls had only ever heard the name Greg Bonner in connection with fundraising for Peru. All three girls were in their late teens, and Nick was twenty. They seemed to speak the same language, and before long, were joking around and making witty comments. As only youth can, they out-smarted us with their sarcasm, so there were lots of laughs. It turned out to be a fun and productive day. As a result of the mail-out, further engagements were booked at different rotary clubs over the following months.

Greg and I began to email each other, initially to organise the equipment and the transport, but then we found ourselves discussing other interesting topics. The months passed, and we continued emailing regularly. I knew from his emails that Greg was quite distant from God. At each presentation, over a glass of wine, we got to know each other a little more. I became very fond of Greg, but because of his non-existent faith, I kept our relationship strictly business-like and kept my feelings to myself.

The funds kept coming in at a much better rate than before, and along with the money collected from my home church, enough money was raised to commence the construction of a girls' refuge in Lima.

The money, sent to Pastor Luis each month, covered the daily living expenses of the girls as well as the costs of the construction materials for the new girls' refuge. He provided informative letters keeping us updated with the progress of both the girls and the new building. I translated his letters into English for our church, and together we created and managed the sponsorship program.

In an email one day, Greg asked me to go out with him. I could have been tempted if he was a man of faith, but I knew from past experience that it would only end in disaster. This made it easier for me to decline. Greg persisted, but I simply kept saying, 'No.'

Finally, another email came from Greg asking, 'Why not?'

'Because you are an uncircumcised Philistine',[2] I responded and added, 'The last thing I want is a relationship with an uncircumcised Philistine!'

His response, 'What the #*#*#.......' showed that he had no idea what I was talking about. I think he was thrown into a spin and totally confused, even a little offended. In my next email, I tried to explain, but he still didn't understand. He wasn't happy but, although somewhat reluctant, he did agree to continue with our email relationship.

I knew that to be unequally yoked with an unbeliever could only end badly. Alarm bells told me loud and clear, 'Don't go there!' Dealing with the hurt from my marriage breakdown and still clinging on to the possibility of reconciliation, there was no room for another man in my life. Also, I was fully aware of my own fragility, and I didn't want to risk being broken all over again. Consequently, I fought hard against all of Greg's attempts to start a relationship. I continued to put him off and push him away.

Fini, a strong-minded widow in her seventies and my prayer partner and friend, at that time was one of the pillars in our church. She couldn't understand why I would do such a thing.

'He's an unbeliever, Fini!' I automatically responded. Surprisingly she still advised me, in her broad Dutch accent, 'Bridget, just go.' I was shocked that she would give such advice and blurted out with great emphasis, 'But Fini, he's an unbeliever!'

'Ahh!' she said, shaking her head negatively, 'You're going vor a coffee, Bridget. You don't have to jump into bed vit him!'

At that, I snapped at her, 'What if Greg is the enemy in disguise, sent to distract me from going to Peru.'

'Ahh! Vat if, vat if… don't be silly, Bridget', was her response.

I remained uncertain but continued our internet conversations. I found that Greg and I were able to connect at a much deeper level than I would have ever imagined possible via email. We talked about faith and shared our innermost thoughts. I did so enjoy his intriguing responses. I discovered that our conversations were the culmination of a long search, which Greg had begun in Nepal many years before our paths had ever crossed. Gradually, Greg began to share his desire to know God; then, one evening, he asked if I could go and pray with him. This seemed a little unusual, and I was suspicious. I felt I needed to talk to him, so I picked up the phone and, for the first time, I called him. After a short conversation, Greg said, 'I have finally surrendered to God.' His tone of voice was very serious, even emotional. We arranged a meeting; I was to go around to Greg's place after work the following evening. That night, I called Carmel and made myself accountable to her by telling her of my plans and giving her Greg's phone number. (No mobile phones back then.) I asked Carmel to ring at 9.00 pm to prompt me to return home safely.

Bringing my Bible and a worship CD with me, I arrived at Greg's place not knowing what to expect. He seemed thoughtful but happy to see me. He offered something to eat, over which we talked about his experience, with a cup of coffee in hand instead of a glass of wine.

Greg talked, and I listened. I knew by the tone of his voice and the emotion behind it that Greg was sincerely seeking God. After a light meal, Greg told of the previous night when he had prayed for the first time. I asked if he would mind playing the CD so that we could enter into prayer together with some music first. We stood in his living room as we quietly listened to the worship music. I closed my eyes, and I could clearly sense God's presence in the room. I felt moved and drawn into the worship music; I raised my hands and began to sing along softly. Before I even began to pray, I heard Greg sobbing. I kept my eyes closed and continued to worship. His weeping continued, then I heard the sound of a thud to the floor. I opened my eyes to see Greg on his knees. I stopped singing. Through his tears, he began to speak out a simple but calm prayer. His words acknowledged his desire for God. But as he spoke, his trembling voice began to break up, and he wept uncontrollably. Greg was deeply touched and overcome by intense emotion. Closing my eyes again, I began to pray for him silently. He tried so hard to keep it together, but he couldn't. God was at work and speaking into his heart; it was all too much. By the end of that night, Greg was no longer the uncircumcised Philistine. When I returned home as planned, I called Carmel to let her know I was home. Then I was overjoyed to find this email in my inbox...

From: Greg Bonner <gregbonner@optusnet.com.au>
Sent: Friday, 1 October 2004 10:37:13pm
To: Bridget Geraghty < yeost_1@hotmail.com>

Bridget,
        Had no intention to email tonight at all...no need. But in the end wanted to share this... (Actually, would have liked to talk till dawn).
        I was so determined... I mean so determined... not to lose my composure... not to be like those who (I thought) act out some kind... born-again role... you know shaking and

speaking in tongues or whatever... that's for fools I told myself... that's for the ones that spring up and then wither in the heat... no, not for me, I'm too strong!

...And what happened? ...I asked God to take away my self-awareness and I've become... like a child unable to control myself... unable to disassociate... hyperventilating but without the effect... Tears streaming (and snot) ... really fighting to regain control... Yet unable... prayed 'give me a break' is all this necessary? ...came to an understanding that to fill the clay pot I must let go of all the other stuff, whatever that is...so, Fine! ...I'll do that... get rid of my "self"... and prayed 'take my "self"'... still it goes on... then... calm and peace.

We talked and shared a simple meal and then you had to go.

Stood outside for a while...a dream? ...No! ... Fooling myself? ...test it! ..."I was fooling myself." (Repeated three times)

...Thought of Jesus our Lord... became aware of tears in my heart... No dream; no delusion; this is it! ...but now aware something is out to get me... Tell that something to forget it! ... I have the protection of the Lord and of God... At peace now!

Now I reread this it seems melodramatic... a little all about me again... and yet I know I know

my life has changed now (better or worse) and I
will not/cannot go back!

God Bless you,

Greg

Touched by what had happened and fully
convinced by the emails that followed, I began to
believe that Greg was the "real deal". I felt so privileged
to be a part of Greg's salvation. With no more excuses,
our courtship began with a memorable trek in the Blue
Mountains. We spent the whole day walking and talking, clambering up enormous boulders and sharing
lunch. It was a gourmet lunch prepared by Greg, and
we found a magical location to share it at the top of
Ruined Castle. It was the beginning of a God-ordained
relationship that, over the next few months, grew
stronger and stronger. We both fell hopelessly in love
with each other, but more importantly, God was in the
centre of it. Greg diligently read from the scriptures,
gave up smoking, and his faith grew stronger every day.

I loved the way Greg and I could pray together and
the way we actually listened to each other. I discovered
that Greg was secretly a romantic at heart, and the way
he looked at me made me feel so very special, often
leaving me quite euphoric. Emotions, euphoria, and
chemistry all left me feeling no different from when I
was a 17-year-old teenager. The struggle to keep our
relationship holy was not easy. Greg was passionate and
manly, but in spite of wanting to be strong, I was weak
and let myself down at times. It was a real struggle, but

my writing of the poem below helped me to overcome the struggle.

Love or Lust

The spirit, the flesh at war in me.
Interludes of ecstasy,
Longing for intimacy.

The battle rages, the fight goes on,
Round one…defeated…the magic's gone.
How weak the flesh, but feels so good,
A true expression of our love.

Fooling myself, falling for sin.
Surely, I know the truth within.
Naïve, deceived; let's rationalize,
Or maybe…just open my eyes.

'Have mercy on me O God,
Blot out my sin.
Wash away all my iniquity,
And cleanse me from within.
Create in me a pure heart, O God,
And renew a steadfast spirit in me.'

Great compassion His love remains,
Forgiveness sweet…strong again.
My needs are met, He makes me whole,
Secure in Him I'll reach my goal.

Round two…so hard…just can't be strong,
Get wise; realise where you're going wrong.
Build meaningful bonds that last eternal
Instead of castles in the sand destined to crumble.

Round three, can't you see, is set for disaster.
Before it's too late, seek the Master.
His wisdom is yours if you so choose,
Free will He gives, it's your move.

So, make a choice, what will it be?
Slippery slope of me, me, me,
Or pleasing the master as you submit.
You'll find, without doubt, it's definitely worth it.

Round four, at last, the victory,
You and I together will be.
Forever committed, prepared to wait,
Peace abounds, what a blissful state.
The battle is over the pressure has gone,
We now united by bonds eternally strong.

The wheels were set in motion for me to go back to Peru, and I knew that inevitably Greg and I would be apart. Confirming with Greg that I would remain steadfast in my commitment for a period of four years overseas, as planned, he simply said, 'Four years, that's only 1,461 days!' Greg then asked me to marry him. He said, 'Sooner or later, it doesn't really matter.' He seemed secure in his decision and his commitment to me. I was won. It was so easy to say yes.

BLUE MTS. FIRST DATE

After much prayer and thoughtful consideration, we agreed that I would continue with my plans to go to Peru; Greg would follow later, once he had tied up a few loose ends, and God willing, we would get married in Peru on Valentine's Day the following year. I was close to completing the long, drawn-out process of application through the Pioneer Missions Agency. The application form required a written autobiography from birth to present and a brief account of my testimony (how I became a Christian), which I had completed. I had attended the orientation weekend, as well as the various other weekend courses. I had also begun fundraising and partnership development workshops, as well as undertaken a medical exam and a psychological exam. I was up to the stage where my photo card was being designed and almost ready for printing. The whole process had been a mammoth task, but having jumped through all the hoops, I was glad to be at the end of it! Then I introduced Greg to the Pioneer Missions Team. Greg was interviewed, and the team was happy to have him on board. However, due to stringent rules, we were told that we would have to be married for at least one year before we could go and that Greg would have to commence the application process from the very beginning. That meant a delay of two years, and the rules were none negotiable.

After praying with Paul and Sandra, our pastors, they supported us in our decision to follow God's calling, and we felt encouraged to step out in faith and fully trust in Him. The House of Praise became our commissioning church and our spiritual covering.

The year 2004 was a culmination of both ironic and extraordinary experiences: the conflict to reconcile abundance and poverty, the challenge of letting go of Anna and Carmen, the amazing relationship I had not sought after, and the struggle to keep it holy. Even the minor challenges of public speaking and fundraising had all combined to prepare me for the next phase in God's plan. I was ready for the journey of a lifetime.

Chapter Ten

A LIGHT IN THE DARK

Journal Entry: In transit
11th April 2005

> *It's time to go! The plans and preparations of the past year will finally culminate in Sydney Airport tomorrow. My heart pounds with excitement yet I feel like bawling when I think of Anna and Carmen. I hate leaving them. I wish they could come with me, but I know that's selfish. I remember not to trust my feelings. I hold the turmoil in and sometimes I feel like I don't know what I'm doing, but I trust that God does!*

I'm not sure I said goodbye well. Anna and Carmen were quiet, which made it even harder for me. I wanted to be strong, and I felt that perhaps they both wanted to be strong too. We kept the mood light to make it easier. The people around us were a welcome distraction by doing the same, but it wasn't easy.

Once seated on the Boeing 747, tears slipped down my cheeks and my eyes became like fountains; I let it all out and almost lost it. It was the whisper of Greg's parting words echoing in my ear, 'I love you', that somehow strengthened me, and I managed to compose myself. After a few moments, my thoughts drifted back to the airport coffee shop where family and friends had gathered to see me off. The vision of pastors Paul and Sandra eating crispy cream doughnuts warmed my heart and brought a smile to my face. Fini was there to pray with me. Others turned up unexpectedly to offer support. Then I recalled the tense moment when my baggage was overweight by 20kg! The deadly silence lingered, but I said nothing and waited. Amazingly, I was allowed through with no extra charge.

SYDNEY AIRPORT – DESTINATION PERU – FAMILY &
HOUSE OF PRAISE SUPPORTERS

My fleeting thoughts carried me all the way to Singapore, where I had a connecting flight to Frankfurt. After sitting a few minutes in the transit lounge, I looked at my watch. It was an hour before my flight, and time seemed to be standing still. Then suddenly, I was aware that my name was being called over the loud-speaker: 'Bridget Geraghty, Bridget Geraghty, please go to the information desk.' I thought I was hearing things, but then the announcement was repeated. I made my way to the desk, and to my amazement, there stood my niece Linzy. I had no idea that she just happened to be in transit too. Having coffee in Singapore with Linzy was surreal! Our conversation was like a healing balm to me. My melancholy mood vanished as the time passed quickly.

The twelve-hour flight from Singapore to Frankfurt was a sleepless one, partly because my mind wouldn't stop racing, but also because my seat was on the last row and didn't recline. The next flight from Frankfurt to Manchester was uneventful, but Manchester itself was full of surprises. I had a few days to spend there before the flight to Peru.

I caught up with old friends from my early nursing years at the Salford School of Nursing. It had been over fifteen years since I had seen them. We spent hours reminiscing over old photos, recalling fun stories that even their husbands enjoyed. They were all interested to hear about Peru, and I was really impressed that my friend Mary wanted to sponsor one of the girls from the refuge.

The most unforgettable experience was the time spent with my eldest sister, Mary. Mary is twelve years older than me and had left home when I was around six years old, so we didn't grow up together, and consequently, we were never really close. On the last Sunday, Mary asked me to go with her to the Catholic mass at St. Chad's Church. I hesitated at first, and then I remembered it was the church we once attended over thirty-five years ago, and it was where I was married as a teenager, so I agreed to go with her.

The moment I set foot inside the church, I had the strangest sinister feeling. A shiver ran up my spine. After all those years, the ornate statues still stood in the exact same spot, but they didn't look the same. They were smaller than I remembered and much less intimidating. I noticed that the statue of the Virgin Mary stood in a position raised high above the smaller crucifix, which hung below. I hadn't noticed this before, nor had I been aware that there was no representation of the risen Lord anywhere. Only Him dying on a cross, in several places. It seemed that the Virgin Mary was the highly exalted one while Jesus was the sorrowful one, being crucified.

Distracted by the numerous flickering candles casting shadows on the confessional boxes in the corner, their dancing silhouettes brought back childhood memories that made me cringe: memories of condemnation and guilt and all the bad things I used to feel. The priest would dish out his ten Hail Marys, ten Hail Holy Queens, and ten of the Lord's Prayer, but no amount of penance ever seemed to relieve my guilt. I had no sense of forgiveness at all back then.

I used to think that God was confined within those church walls. It's no wonder I never found Him; I was looking in the wrong place. In that big old church, nothing had changed – only I had changed.

My thoughts were interrupted as Mary genuflected at the end of the pew and made the sign of the cross. I followed her into the pew and noted a look of disapproval when I didn't do the same. I sat quietly beside her, then she whispered, 'I want to swap places with you.'

'Why?' I whispered curiously.

'I intend to go to communion', she said.

'I'm going to communion too', I clarified quietly.

Suddenly, in a raised voice, Mary said, 'You can't go to communion, you're not a Cat-lic anymore, and besides', she said with a furious frown, 'sure-ye haven't even been te confession!'

Aware of people all around us, I was embarrassed by her loud accusing voice, but I tried to stay calm as I whispered, 'God is no respecter of denominations, Mary.' She became even more furious, and she was about to open her mouth when I motioned, 'Shhhh', as I crossed my lips with my finger.

I could see that she was angry as she tried to maintain a whisper and retorted, 'If you go to communion, den, I'm not going!'

'That's OK', I whispered. 'It's between you and God, but I'm still going.'

With that, Mary stood up abruptly, pushed past me in a rage, and stormed out. I was flabbergasted by her response.

Complying with the ceremonial mass, I stood up, I sat down, and I kneeled, but when the priest requested that we all express the sign of peace (a handshake to those around us), I felt very uncomfortable. There I stood, in a Catholic church, making peace with strangers while my sister was outside very upset. She was the one that I was there for in the first place. I became quite confused and thought, 'What am I doing here?' I found myself praying earnestly for Mary; I prayed that God would set her free as he had done for me so many years ago. Then the congregation dutifully sat in unison, myself included, and the priest began a Bible reading from John chapter 10.

'John 10:3: The gatekeeper opens the gate for him, and the sheep listen to his voice. He calls his own sheep by name and leads them out' (NIV). I ceased trying to understand and prayed that Mary would return. When communion began, I hesitated and waited as long as I could, hoping Mary would return, but she didn't. I went forward anyhow. Walking down that long aisle to the front of the church brought back a memory. It seemed like a lifetime ago when I walked down the very same aisle all dressed in white. Eery emotions flooded in.

Deep in thought, I stood waiting for a place to kneel at the altar. A tapping on my shoulder brought me back to reality. I turned around to see Mary standing there; her eyes filled with tears as she extended her hand to give me the "sign of peace". I took her hand and gently drew her close to hug her. I quietly murmured, 'I love you, Mary.' She clung to me tightly and sobbed like a baby as she tried to verbalize those same words.

Though her words were muffled and barely audible, I heard her say, 'I'm sorry.' Her sincerity broke the floodgates in me, and I responded, 'I'm sorry too.' We just cried together, embraced in beautiful understanding, and I knew that God was at work. We then knelt together side by side at the altar, received communion and were reconciled.

I left the U.K. feeling very encouraged and closer to Mary than ever before. I felt that she knew God more and was moving into a closer relationship with Him. I thanked God for our time together.

The next step in my journey was Peru, and I felt ready for anything.

Journal Entry:
San Juan de Lurigancho, Peru
13th April 2005

> *All international flights land in Lima late at night, so I arrived when it was dark and dangerous, once again.*
>
> *Pastor Luis's familiar face was reassuring. He looked*

very tired and drawn, and after minimal courtesies he explained, 'It's late! You will be staying at my place with my wife and children, and in the morning, we will be going to CEDES.' He was friendly. He just wanted to get going and I was tired too; I agreed happily. We both seemed to be exhausted, so it was a silent taxi ride to his house in Surco.

I met Pilar, Pastor Luis's wife, early the next morning. They had three children, all girls, whom I didn't get to meet as it was very early. Pilar was a happy, gracious lady who showed an interest in Australia and had many questions. She prepared a wholesome breakfast, and without much delay, we set off. Soon we were outside in a busy street; he was negotiating for a cheap fare with a taxi driver. The taxi drove off, and Pastor Luis flagged another, then started negotiating all over again. Finally, we were headed for CEDES, the name given by Pastor Luis to the newly constructed girls refuge. CEDES is an anagram representing the words Casa de Educación y Desarrollo Espiritual y Sicosocial (House of Educational, Spiritual, and Psychosocial Development).

The roads just outside of Lima became rougher and rougher. The traffic lights were fewer and fewer, and the buildings became more and more inferior. Everything looked so rundown and depressing. Pastor Luis was silent, so I peered out the window most of the time. The further out we drove, the deeper my heart sank. After an hour on the road, the taxi abruptly stopped, and Pastor Luis got out without saying a word. I thought we had arrived, but no, we just had to change to another taxi. This taxi was an old, rusty bomb of a car with a gaping hole in the floor directly beneath me. Curious to know why we had changed into a much worse taxi, I enquired of Pastor Luis. He said, 'The road gets a bit rough, and not all taxis will go that far.'

The hole in the floor, through which I could literally see the road zooming past at an exaggerated speed between my feet, kept drawing my attention. I was careful not to drop anything, and when my foot was at rest, I felt the vibrations drawing it towards the crumbling rusty edge. I was in fear of losing my foot, and I remained on maximum alert. The car, with no air conditioner, was hot and sticky in thirty-two degrees' heat. I was definitely out of my comfort zone. Gridlocks replaced traffic lights, and I found myself flinching at every intersection after the first two near-accidents. The many intersections with cars constantly tooting horns while trying to push their way into the traffic made for a harrowing trip. I was on edge.

We drove over dusty, bumpy, pot-holed roads for miles through even poorer townships with very little infrastructure. There were no paved sidewalks; instead, the dirt ground was piled high with garbage lining each side of the road. Stray, rabid dogs scavenged and scattered the trash around. The air was so dry I could taste the dust in my mouth, but it was too hot to close the window.

The further we drove, the worse it became until eventually, we reached a mountainous landscape with meagre homes spread around the base. Speckled in the distance higher up the mountains were numerous tiny little boxes on the steep slopes. They were constructed of thin wood or cane, or even cardboard, many with no lids!

'What are those box-like constructions for?' I enquired of Pastor Luis.

'People live in those boxes', he responded.

In disbelief, I said, 'But a lot of them don't have a roof. What do they do when it rains?'

'It rarely rains here, so it's not a problem', he assured me.

He went on to explain how the shanty towns in San Juan de Lurigancho developed. 'These days', he said, 'the people from the country flood into Lima hoping to find work. When they can't, they end up sitting in the dark because they can't afford to pay their electricity bill.' He continued to inform that, instead of a better life, they find themselves in appalling conditions, unable to provide even the basic needs for their children. Some families split up and, in desperation, single parents leave their children abandoned on the streets; others band together in large numbers and come to invade these hills. The authorities show little interest and ignore the "invasions", and the government ignores the need for infrastructure. The "invaders", mainly uneducated, illiterate indigenous people, end up living like this, with no water, no sewerage, no electricity, and with very little food. This, combined with poor social networks and no village ties to provide some structure for life, has caused an increase in crime as well as drug and alcohol problems.

As Pastor Luis explained, I listened with interest and felt sad for the Peruvian people; life seemed so unfair. Apparently, San Juan de Lurigancho was supposed to be one of the more developed areas, yet, without electricity, running water, or sewerage and, CEDES was located smack in the middle. There were no telephone lines, no garbage collection, nor any postal services.

The taxi came to an abrupt stop when only dirt and large rocks lay ahead of us. The bumpy road had come to an end. I gazed all around me in disbelief; it was like landing on Mars. The little boxes were much closer, and I could see that they really were dwellings. Washing lines were strung up, and small water drums stood out in the front. People were milling around, with children playing in the dirt – and there were dogs, lots and lots of feral dogs. The tiny homes spread over the hills right up towards the peaks, where they disappeared into the hazy mist at the top. The mist, I later realised, was not mist at all; it was the pollution blown in from Lima caused by all the numerous run-down cars and Kombi vans. In the distance, hovering over the city of Lima, was a dark, ugly cloud of smog. The dark-grey colours seemed to dilute into lighter shades of grey, which eventually formed the dull, murky sky above us.

Conscious of the two men babbling louder and louder, I listened and realised that we weren't there yet. The taxi driver didn't want to go any further, but Pastor

Luis continued insisting. After some persuasion and extra cash in hand, the driver changed his mind. With three kilometres to go and sixty kilos of luggage, I was grateful.

Back in the car, Pastor Luis was soon pointing to an ugly, spooky-looking building that stood like a haunted house on the top of a hill. It was a much larger construction than any other around it. 'That's CEDES!' he said.

'No way!' I thought. Then I saw some girls running down the hill towards the big wooden gate and realised that he was serious.

CEDES HAUNTED HOUSE

Several girls painstakingly tried to jerk the gate open; it kept catching on the uneven ground as the hinges weren't supporting it sufficiently. They finally succeeded, and as the driver drove in, they came sprinting towards the taxi, chanting, 'Hermana Brijeet, Hermana Brijeet (Sister Bridget, Sister Bridget).' As we slowly drove approximately twenty meters to the end of the property, the girls caught up and jogged along each side of the taxi, chanting breathlessly with voices full of anticipation and enthusiasm.

I recognised Irmina first, and then Kari and Karina, along with some other familiar faces. There were lots of faces that I didn't recognise, but even they were caught up in the excitement. Stepping out of the taxi, the girls crowded around, trying to hug me all at the same time. I was dumbfounded.

After many hugs and kisses from the girls, I was briefly introduced to Jahnique, the tutor. Jahnique was short and well-built, probably from Indian stock. She had curly black, shoulder-length hair and her bubbly character and smiling face were welcoming. She seemed very positive, but she was hard to understand. Her words spilled out of her mouth fast and continuously until she became breathless and incoherent. If she could breathe and talk at the same time, I'm sure she would have. But then, she would never stop talking. Literally, she laughed a lot, sometimes nervously, and when she did, I kept thinking I'd missed something because I wasn't sure why she was laughing.

Pastor Luis showed me to my room; all the girls trailed closely behind. He began to give me instructions, but the commotion of the girls pushing and shoving as they crammed around my doorway made it difficult to concentrate. He totally ignored the girls, desperate to get a peek into my room, and simply raised his voice a few syllables higher. Above the ruckus, he reeled off a few names and mentioned a few things and then plunged a large bunch of keys into my hand and said, 'I have to go now; the taxi is waiting.' I didn't take it all in. Feeling a little bewildered, I asked, 'What's the routine here?'

'Just ask Jahnique; she'll tell you.' He said as he scurried past the crowd of girls around the doorway. I rushed after him trying to keep up with his fast pace, and I blurted out. 'But, who's in charge?'

'You are', he responded.

In disbelief, I continued the chase. 'What if I need help?' I stammered. But the door of the taxi slammed shut as I spoke. He wound down the window as the vehicle began to move and yelled, 'Jahnique, just ask Jahnique; she knows everything.' Then in an instant, he was gone.

The girls closed in on me, so it took a while even to break free and find Jahnique. Finally, in the laundry, I found her reprimanding a couple of girls. She was telling them to pick up all the washing off the ground. They didn't show much interest or respect and just ignored her. Jahnique seemed a little embarrassed but said nothing; then, she offered to show me around. As we walked around the house, I began what seemed like an interrogation with so many questions. She nodded in a positive, helpful way, but Jahnique talked at machine-gun speed, and I found her hard to under-stand. Her answers were long, and I only caught a small portion of what she said, so I began to ask very short, simple questions.

'How many girls are there?'

'It was twenty-six at the last count', she said with a big smile and a nervous laugh.

'Is there a list of names anywhere?' I asked.

'No, Hermana, the girls come and go all the time; there's no list', she said.

'But surely there must be a file or some information about each girl', I responded.

'The files and all the paperwork are kept in the Pastor's office at his house. Ha ha ha!' Jahnique explained with her unusual nervous laughter.'

'So, there's no procedure manuals, no routine sheet or health information on the girls, nothing at all?' I insisted.

'No, we don't have any particular routine; every day is different, ha, ha, ha!' She replied.

A deep sense of frustration began to rise in me, and I stopped asking questions. Unable to get any real answers from Jahnique, I realised that she was as much in the dark as I was. The information that I did manage to get was that supermarkets and shops were far away, so we did our food shopping in the nearest markets only twenty minutes by bus. The nearest telephone was in the same place, and only some mobiles had reception in the area. Also, that Jahnique's hours of work were 2.00 pm to 6.00 pm Monday, Tuesday and Thursday.

All around the property, I could see spectacular steep mountains rising as tall as 2,000 meters. They were close by, very dry and dusty, and much like a dull grey desert with no trees.

The house comprised of two main buildings, which were cleverly built into the steep slope of the foothills. The main building had three levels with very high ceilings. On the top level, there were ten bedrooms and a balcony which looked down into the living room. The balcony had no railing, and with a two-meter drop down to ground level, it was an instant concern to me. I asked Jahnique, 'Has anyone ever fallen off?'

'Apparently not', she responded with a hearty laugh, as though that was funny.

The living room was a huge, split-level room with an open fireplace. It was sparsely furnished with a lonely TV and a video recorder sitting on the empty tiled floor space. From one end of the living room were a few steps leading down to more bedrooms and a bathroom on the lower level.

I tried not to notice the stench of urine as Jahnique walked me through the toilets at the end of the corridor. The four showers were positioned at a right angle to the three toilets, and there were no shower screens or toilet doors; instead, nylon curtains hung in their place. I was told that although plumbing was in place, the girls were instructed not to flush the toilets because water was expensive. Instead, they bucketed the grey water from the clothes washing to flush the toilets. A door led from the toilets to the outside of the house, where a laundry with many sinks and clothes lines stood. There were no pegs, and most of the washing was strewn around the dusty ground.

From the other end of the living room, the front door led outside, where there were stairs going up the steep slope to the dining room. The stairs, constructed of uneven stones, were very deep and difficult to negotiate. The dining area at the top of the stairs stood independently. On entering, I saw three smallish tables and one large table with many chairs around them. The dining area was separated from the kitchen by a serving counter with a sliding glass window almost the full length of the wall, with a door at one end. The window was open and on the other side was a serving bench. In the kitchen stood the cooker, fridge, and a double sink.

Jahnique introduced me to a petite young girl, also standing behind the bench, whom initially I assumed was one of the adolescent girls. She was introduced as 'Raisa the cook.' She was from Quechua background and had two small boys, but she looked far too young to be a worker, let alone a mother of two. Raisa evidently cooked lunch and dinner and took care of the shopping, and her shift was finished once the evening meal was served around 6.00 pm. Her mornings were free so that she could take care of her own children.

Her husband, Eddy, who was nowhere to be seen, apparently was the master builder who did all the maintenance around the house. I was told that Eddy was available all day until the evening meal and that he knocked off around 6.00 pm after starting the generator.

Raisa remained very quiet the whole time while Jahnique showed me around the kitchen. The kitchen seemed bare of resources; even food supplies were low. A few unusual products lay around, one being a bowl of pasty, gooey substance that sat at the sink. I was told this was Ayudin, used for washing up.

In the middle of the kitchen stood a huge 5-horse-power generator, which Jahnique explained was normally turned on at night by Eddy. I had no idea how to use a generator, so I asked Jahnique if she could show me how it worked. 'I don't know how to switch it on', she said, 'because I'm gone before it's needed; and Eddy is responsible for that, so you don't have to worry.'

When we finished the kitchen tour, Raisa said in a soft sheepish voice, 'Hermana, can I have permission to finish work early tonight.' I felt uneasy. Why is she asking me, I thought? It really hadn't sunk in that I was in charge. I wondered who would cook the evening meal if she left early. Hesitantly, I looked at Jahnique for backup. There was a moment of awkward silence, then Raisa timidly interjected, 'I've made dinner, and the girls can serve it', she blushed. 'I have to go to a parent's meeting at the school', she said pleadingly. Jahnique remained unusually quiet.

After another moment of silence, 'Of course', I said, 'no hay problema (no problem).'

Soon Jahnique's shift finished, and after she left, I decided to explore the house for myself. Walking around the place to orientate myself, I was dismayed at the numerous safety issues; it would never have passed Australian safety standards. There was cracked and broken glass in some windows. The glass was such poor quality, much too thin for windows. One window had shards of very fine glass hanging precariously, about to drop out. What really concerned me were the electrical cables wired to the motor. They didn't look safe, and they hung too low down across the yard outside. Bizarre as it might seem, there was an empty concrete swimming pool in the middle of the massive yard. 'Who in their right mind would build a swimming pool when water is so expensive?' I questioned. Standing on the flat area in between the kitchen and the main building was a tiny shed-like storage room full of broken furniture, and directly in front of it was a construction site with a pile of rubble in the centre. It looked like the foundations of a small house had been laid and left unfinished. Sharp reinforcing steel protruded out of the concrete slab. 'How dangerous', I thought: just then, an unbearably loud thumping noise shocked my ear-drums. It was so loud that I had to cover my ears with my hands. I followed the sound into the kitchen, where it became deafening. When the girls talked, it looked like they were miming. Black, noxious fumes bellowed out of the exhaust pipe of the generator, and I didn't know whether to cover my mouth or my ears. Even when yelling at each other, it was impossible to hear. The din was only enhanced by the sound of salsa music blaring at full volume in the background. This apparently was meant to drown out the noise of the generator! It was insane. If we didn't all go crazy, we would surely go deaf. That's if we survived the fumes!

Journal Entry:
San Juan de Lurigancho, Peru
14th April 2005

> *Last night, just before dinner, without warning the lights went out and the nightmare began. Alarmed by the sudden pitch blackness all around us, everything fell into complete stillness. But only for an instant, then Irmina pierced the silence with a bloodcurdling scream. Fear at once spread like wildfire and the other girls followed suit, their combined screams reaching a frenzied level. Deafened by the high-pitched squeals I could hardly gather my thoughts.*

When the generator dropped out, the sheer contrast from the loud music, the hollering, and the pounding of the motor, combined with a sudden silence and dark nothingness, sent the girls into a spin. When Irmina shrieked out her terrifying cry, everyone panicked and entered the terror by screaming. Even I yelled out in an attempt to quiet them, 'Tranquilas, tranquilas (Calm down, calm down)'. But my voice was drowned in the deafening chaos. It garnered no response at all. Unprepared and not knowing where anything was, my confidence started to wane. Then I remembered the matches in the kitchen I had used to light the stove earlier.

Groping in the dark with outstretched arms, frequently bumping into chairs and stumbling over objects, I made my way towards the kitchen. The terrifying screams in the darkness invoked emotions of stress, even in me. Feeling my way along the surface of the kitchen bench, I suddenly felt a slimy sensation between my fingers – I squirmed, and my stomach churned, but then to my relief, I realised it was only the Ayudin. With a sigh of composure, I continued to feel my way along until finally, I found a box of matches— it was like finding gold.

I struck a match, and its tiny flame lit up the small space around me. One step at a time, the light bubble enabled me to see what was immediately in front of me. In this way, I made my way back to the dining area. Like moths to a flame, all twenty-six girls gathered around me; their screams continued but a little less intense. The little ones clung on tight to my waist while the older ones grabbed my arms and shoulders. I could feel their fear behind every grip. Controlled and very softly, I said, 'Calmate, calmate, todo esta bien (Calm down, calm down, everything is all right)', as I patted their hands.

The screams slowly died down, waning into complete quietness, but then the match dimmed and went out. Sharp intakes of breath with a sense of panic could be heard. For an instant, fear was floating in the air as I quickly fiddled to relight another match. The light bubble revived before the terror took hold again, and I calmly asked, 'Does anyone know if there are any candles in the house?'

Karina volunteered to go and get some, but only if she could take the matches with her. We had just one box, so I took a few matches out and gave her the box. The flame from the match in my hand began to dwindle again. Just in time, I lit a second match from the first and told Karina to be quick. She disappeared into the shadows with a lighted match in hand.

Rapidly lighting one match after the other, I was fast approaching my last match, and Karina was nowhere to be seen. Anticipating the imminent darkness, I forewarned the girls as calmly as possible. 'The next match is the last one', I said softly and quickly continued, 'but there's no need to panic because I'm going to tell you a story in the dark.' The match dimmed, and I quickly managed to say, 'You're not allowed to scream because you won't hear the story if you do.' No sooner had I spoken when the match went out.

Abrupt blackness weighed heavy all around us, and I could hear some groans and whimpers. 'Why are you so afraid?' I asked uncomprehendingly. No verbal responses came back; instead, their little arms tightened around my waist, and even the older girls' grip grew stronger. They couldn't see me, but they made sure they could feel me, and I, unmistakably, could feel the tension in their grasping hands. I didn't understand why they were so afraid. I could only imagine their misty blind eyes wide as plates, seeing only blackness, and I could most definitely feel their grip of fear.

Without really thinking about what I was saying, the words just poured out of my mouth, 'Don't you know that God's angels are here with us?' I said, but the silence continued. 'I know they are because Jesus said so, and I believe Him.' Complete silence persisted, and after a short pause, I continued softly, 'Even though we can't see the angels, they are here with us, all around us. Even in the dark. That's why we don't have to be afraid.'

Only the sound of our breathing could be heard in the deadly silence; I longed to see the expressions on their little faces, but the darkness made it impossible. My words continued, 'Did you know that God commands His angels to look after us?' Just then, a tiny light drew closer and brighter, the glow dispelling the darkness as the light grew bigger. We could see it was Karina with her candle. Their cheers broke the silence, and the mood was changed. Karina had brought several small candles in her arms, and the girls instantly made a grab for them.

How quickly the girls resumed their normal poise and chatter as we set the candles up in strategic places around the room. The dining room now softly glowed with flickering candlelight, and with the absence of noise from the generator, a much warmer atmosphere of calm reigned. The older girls were able to finish serving the evening meal, while the younger ones helped to set the tables and pour the water into plastic cups.

The storytelling moment was lost, but it didn't matter because the good feelings that remained were all the better. I took a look at the motor to see if I could get it started again; Karina and Herleena followed me. They seemed interested in my every move and so willing to help. I sensed that they were looking out for me. It felt good. Herleena offered to pull the chord; she said that she had managed to start it once before. I watched her pull the chord; she tried again and again, trying so hard but with no result. Then I tried, but no, it just would not start. I persisted until I became hot and bothered but, nothing. It was impossible; the motor was completely dead.

Resigned to spending the rest of the night in the dim candlelight, we returned to the dining room, where most of the girls sat around two large tables waiting for supper. One of the older girls served the hot soup out of a large pot into the bowls which they had laid out on the kitchen bench; each girl collected a bowl and took it to the table. I could hardly see the contents of my bowl, but seeing the girls' faces and their smiles shining in the glow melted my heart. Drifting deep into thought, I remembered how, (as a child) even in the midst of turmoil, a dish of hot soup made me feel settled and satisfied. That's the beauty of a child, their resilience and their innocence. I remembered how easily frightened I sometimes was, and yet how easily comforted too.

The trauma passed. I was happy, and I knew that they were happy, at least for now! After we cleared the tables, we all huddled around the larger table. It was quite a squash, but the girls didn't seem to mind. Being close up and cosy was always good for them. They loved it. The older girls relished the opportunity to nurse the younger ones, who would gladly sit on their laps to enjoy the attention they craved. I found it quite lovely to observe one of the girls fiddling with another's hair. She curled it round and round her finger as the girl on the receiving end happily lapped up the attention. How easy it is to please a child. Their world is so uncomplicated.

The girls, back to their normal selves, were noisy and excitable. Picking up from where I left off in the dark wasn't easy. I tried a new tactic to hush them up. All I did was stand up and silently wave my arms around, and somehow, magically, it worked! Later I discovered that once they were accustomed to this, it didn't work so well.

In the momentary silence I could speak, and suggested that each one could introduce themselves to me and tell me their age. Scarlet interjected, saying that she wanted to hear about the angels. I paused and smiled at her, and then another soft little voice affirmed that she too wanted to hear about the angels. How lovely and how blessed I felt with such an opportunity as this.

Although I wanted to find out more about the girls, the rest of the evening was dominated by warm, fuzzy stories of angels. We tried to imagine what angels might look like. We impersonated them and talked about what they did, how beautiful their voices might be, whether they had wings and how they especially loved children. The discussion and the impressions of the angels continued for a while until I noticed one of the younger girls fading in and out of sleep. She looked so comfortable in the warmth of the loving arms wrapped around her. I pondered that, perhaps to her, these arms were just as comforting as those of her absent mother, and all that really mattered to her was that she had someone's arms around her to comfort her.

We were all exhausted, and it was late – even so, the girls protested when I suggested it was time for bed. With some authority, I stood up, and as I blew out one of the candles, I insisted we must go to bed, now! Thankfully Karina followed by blowing out another candle, then Kari did the same, and all the girls began to move into the dorm downstairs.

Several girls stumbled down those uneven steps; it was no small task in the dark with just a candle. I noticed that the temperature dropped quite dramatically at nightfall, and it was much cooler. The girls slept, mostly two to a bed in their clothes as usual, on bare mattresses with no pillows and just one blanket. They didn't seem to have any idea of personal hygiene; none of them brushed their teeth, and I wasn't about to search the house for toothpaste and brushes.

What seemed like a long day had finally come to a close. I was exhausted and lay down, but sleep eluded me. It wasn't the wooden slats I felt beneath the thin foam mattress that kept me awake. It was my incessant mind ticking over at lightning speed. My thoughts meandered from one question to another: How did the girls ever get the generator started in the past without Eddy? Surely, with no electricity, they were accustomed to the dark before? Had they perhaps had prior bad experiences in the dark? Why such an overwhelming response? This question, in particular, lingered for a while as I thought about their uncontrollable, unmanageable fear. I had never experienced anything like it before, and I never wanted to again. I imagined that their insecurities overcame them because of some past horror, but I really didn't know.

This set my mind thinking on the Salem Witch Trials, in which I had read about mass hysteria. All at once, I felt my body relax as I realised that this was definitely a case of mass hysteria. Satisfied with this conclusion, my mind was able to rest.

I knew that something greater than I had kept me from being drawn into the hysteria, and I closed my eyes to pray. I saw in my mind's eye the girl who was sleeping comfortably in the warmth of those loving arms and reflected on my belief that blood is thicker than water. But I wasn't sure anymore!

This was the beginning of the end of all my preconceived ideas. The children were having a profound impact on my life, and my understanding of the world was shifting, my sense of self and others with it.

Chapter Eleven

A FLAG FLYING HIGH

Journal Entry:
San Juan de Lurigancho, Peru
15th April 2005

> *I woke up to the commotion of girls chatting loudly and the resonance of what sounded like furniture being dragged across the ceiling. The chatting escalated into yelling and screaming and then to what sounded like a cat fight. I jumped out of bed and grabbed my watch wondering if any other adult had arrived. 6.15am, unlikely; from the sound of it, they were pulling each other apart. I snatched my dressing gown and rushed to see.*

I found a group of girls crowded around, watching and goading two girls in a grid lock who were snarling at each other with fists full of hair. They were loud, but I could still hear a voice echoing above them, 'La Hermana viene, la Hermana viene (The Sister is coming, the Sister is coming)', as I approached.

The noise petered out as I cried, 'Chicas, chicas (Girls, girls)', reaching out to the two girls fighting. They loosened their grip on each other, and their shrieks died down to nothing.

Turning to me, they broke out into a verbal hulla-baloo, speaking at the same time, trying to justify their actions. Both girls talked at supersonic speed; I didn't understand a thing. Kari, the 14-year-old, tried to slow her speech, but still, it was way beyond my compre-hension.

Not wanting to take sides, I spoke harshly to both girls saying, 'There is no excuse for two beautiful young ladies behaving like feral cats.' The girls around me burst into laughter, and their chuckles spread rapidly to all the others. Before long, everyone was laughing. I wasn't sure why, but it didn't matter, the contagious laughter diffused the whole situation, and I could only laugh with them.

I couldn't remember who or what time the next staff member was due, so I quickly gathered my clothes to have a shower. Walking down the corridor towards the open-plan bathroom, I could hear some girls pushing and shoving each other. The three sinks oppo-site the showers were occupied by a bunch of younger girls competing for the dribble of water trickling out of the taps. Suddenly, they all stopped dead. 'Buenos dais, Hermana (Good morning, Sister)', they beamed harmoniously. I didn't know all their names but responded cheerfully, 'Good morning, girls.'

Looking around, I could see that there was nowhere to strip off, and although the girls had their backs to me, there was a big mirror in front of them, so there was no privacy. A little uncomfortable with this, I stepped behind the shower curtain fully clad in my dressing gown and pyjamas and pulled the curtain across.

Even though the sun was up, it was dark and dingy behind the blue curtain, and I could hear the girls giggling on the other side. I felt very exposed. The curtains barely fitted, there was a space at each end, and they just didn't provide the privacy I was accustomed to.

When I took my dressing gown off, there was nowhere to hang it, and the floor was wet. I rolled it up and reached outside the curtain to feel for a dry spot on the ground, but that too was wet; the girls giggled louder as they watched me struggle. From behind the curtain, I asked them, 'Where do you normally put your clothes?'

'We don't use the showers, Hermana', they said, 'it's too cold!' I knew that the water was cold, but since the alternative was no shower, I decided I'd just have to get used to it. I put my small bundle on the wet ground and continued to undress, placing my other items on top of the dressing gown.

Each time, after I reached outside the curtain, I would carefully check both sides of the curtain, trying to close the gaps, and each time the girls would chuckle. The room temperature was cold, and I expected the water to be really cold, so I stood back from the shower head to avoid the spray. Turning on the tap, only a continuous drip of freezing cold water slowly oozed out. I lingered in the hope that the volume would increase, and maybe somehow, it would get just a fraction warmer. Instead, the water seemed to get colder as it began to splutter and spit out at me. Finally, a steady stream of chilly water flowed, and I had to make the plunge. It wasn't easy. I had to focus on something besides the water because I didn't want the girls to hear me groan. A song came to mind, and I began to sing. Knowing the girls were listening, I sang heartily. I was singing away, and the water became bearable, even enjoyable. I sang my own lyrics as I became oblivious to the discomfort. Making up the words as I went along, I sang, 'Que rico el agua (How beautiful the water is) ....It's so good to feel clean again', and so on, adding a positive spin to the whole experience. The girls stopped laughing and whispered amongst themselves.

That morning was utter chaos. Most of the time, I didn't know where half the girls were. I couldn't keep track of them all on the huge 2,500-square-meter property. Six of the older girls were getting ready to walk to school. They knew when they had to leave the house. Others were doing their washing in the laundry, while some were in the kitchen preparing breakfast. All without supervision.

Outside was a small group of young girls playing in the dirt; Carli was one of them. The first time I saw Carli, my heart ached. She looked totally neglected. Her hair was matted, and she had a bald patch at the back of her head, similar to that of a baby left lying on its back. Her clothes were dirty, and she reeked of urine. This 8-year-old child had a speech impediment which, combined with her husky voice, caused the other girls to mimic her. In spite of her unkempt appearance, Carli's smile stretched from ear to ear, and she was beautiful to me.

Carli had been allocated the task of rounding up the girls at mealtimes. When breakfast was ready, she stood outside the dining room and yelled at the top of her lungs, 'Desajuno, desajuno (Breakfast, breakfast)!' She repeated this in her loud husky voice over and over relentlessly.

This morning was no different. Carli ran up the stairs from her dusty play area into the dining room to check if she could alert the girls. Given the go-ahead, her voice just about reached to the end of the valley. Everyone hurried into the dining room. Some of the girls looked like they had just jumped straight out of bed, their thick mops of hair still tangled. The six older girls in school uniform were still tying up their hair as they wolfed down their breakfast. They left unaccompanied, barely saying goodbye and rushing off at 7.45 am as if they were late. I stopped Kari to question if someone normally took them to school, but she informed me that this was the norm. No other staff had arrived yet, so I let them go.

It was 9.30 am before a staff member appeared. A very pale-skinned woman in her mid-thirties arrived. She was a little too smartly dressed for the dusty surroundings, but she did wear practical shoes for the rough terrain. This poised lady spoke clearly and slowly, introducing herself as Manuela, the teacher. From that first encounter, as soon as she spoke, I knew we were going to get along. I could actually understand what she was saying, and her first statement was, 'Welcome to Peru, Hermana Bridget.'

It was Manuela's role to help the girls with their homework, and she knew how to handle them well and how to keep them focused. The girls showed great respect for her and seemed to do as she asked almost straight away. Manuela only worked every Wednesday and Friday until noon. I was sorry to see her leave so early that day and a little disappointed to learn that her routine was to go straight home after taking the younger girls to primary school. The morning with Manuela seemed to disappear quickly, but after she'd gone, a couple of hours on my own seemed to drag until Jahnique arrived.

All the girls attended the one and only school in the local area, which was a Catholic school, a ten-minute walk from the house. In Peru, there are two shifts for school children, the morning shift at 8.00 am and the afternoon at 12.30 pm. Generally, the children that attend the afternoon shift had some sort of employment during the morning. In our case, the younger girls attended the afternoon shift simply because that was when a staff member was available to take them to school.

Manuela had dropped nine children off at school, which left me with a manageable number of eleven. Those who remained were children who were not eligible for enrolment at school because they didn't have a birth certificate. The girls sat around two tables in the dining room and were very helpful in showing me their school books and explaining where they were up to. I was grateful, as I had never done home-schooling before. I soon found that not all were at the same level, and they worked directly from textbooks. Some shared a textbook, and others had their own individual book. I simply needed to set tasks out of the textbook and oversee their work, helping them with any questions.

I noticed that Carli was missing; the girls informed me that she couldn't read or write and that she never attended school. I went looking for her and found her playing alone in the dirt at the bottom of the block near the laundry. 'Carli', I said softly, 'you have to come and join the others.' She responded, slow in speech, 'I don't have any school books, and I just want to play.' I smiled and told her, 'You still need to come with me, Carli, but you don't need any books. I just want to comb your hair.'

'No, no, Hermana, it's too knotty', she whined.

I responded persuasively, 'If you allow me to comb your hair, I will try my very best not to hurt you.' She wasn't convinced, and I spent a good while coaxing her until, eventually, we walked through the dorms to pick up a comb and headed back up the rickety stairs, hand in hand.

On return to the dining room, I found the girls fighting and squabbling over the use of an eraser, and they had made very little effort to do the work set for them. I realised that they couldn't be left for long without supervision. They settled down quickly and began their work while I began combing Carli's hair. It was a slow, tedious process combing a tiny section at a time, but Carli didn't seem to mind. Instead, she enjoyed the attention. The finished hair needed a good wash, but when Carli resisted, I didn't insist, and we both agreed, 'Another day!' Instead, I plaited her greasy hair, which helped a little. When all the other girls saw Carli's braid, they too wanted a braid, but again I said, 'Another day!'

Like a whirlwind, the days swept through, bringing with them a mass of endless challenges. The first days, in particular, were the worst. The cupboards were bare, and we were running out of water. The house was in disarray; a mad house with no rules, no discipline, and no structure. Total chaos would be an understatement to describe that first week. Each day seemed to reveal more and more of the disorder, the poor nutrition, and the appalling conditions at the house.

Managing the girls was tough, especially when I was on my own, which was every night, most evenings, and every weekend. Working alone was not something I had anticipated, nor the sleep-deprived nights. The incredibly high risk of accidents was another thing that had never crossed my mind.

My list of jobs for Eddy was growing rapidly, but Eddy was never anywhere to be found, especially when it came to starting the generator, and when I did find him, he was arrogant and hard to deal with.

The girls were accustomed to chatting amongst themselves well into the night, and with a large gap above the plywood walls, I could hear every word. This kept me awake, and others too. But the girls were not used to any kind of boundaries and were very defiant at times. They would quieten down initially when I told them to go to sleep, but then they would recommence within minutes. Their whispers, quiet at first, grew louder and louder until I told them again. This pattern of behaviour repeated itself until the early hours of the morning.

The biggest source of frustration was the large bundle of keys that Pastor Luis had handed to me before he left. The girls had each been given a key to their door, and the doors had locks that, when slammed shut, were automatically locked. Consequently, the girls would accidentally lock themselves out all the time, and nearly always, at a crucial moment, they would come running to me, urgently wanting the spare key, often just before leaving for school. This would inevitably make everyone late for school as I fumbled through the vast number of identical keys, rarely finding the right one straight away.

In Peru, the most bizarre thing about the public school system is that the iron school gate closes at 8.15 am, locking any latecomers out. Many a time, I stood knocking on the school gate persistently until someone responded. Sometimes it would take up to half an hour of constant knocking, which turned into frustrated banging. By then, a crowd of other latecomers piled around us, all hoping to be allowed in. I spent countless frustrating hours pleading through the little peephole in the iron gate for the door to be opened, just so the kids could attend school. After some months, I became known for my relentless banging on the door, and the gate was opened much sooner!

The first things on my list for Eddy, *the master builder*, whom I noticed always avoided eye contact, were to remove the locks and to fix and relocate the generator. After hunting him down, I requested that he remove all the door locks from the girls' rooms. His response was simply, 'No', as he began to walk away.

'How come?' I asked, surprised at his rudeness.

'I don't have the right tools for that', he said as he continued walking off, 'and I need permission from Pastor Luis.'

The girls found their own solution to the key problem by scaling the plywood and scrambling through the gap over the top. They often bruised themselves, and it was dangerous, not to mention the shoe marks and the damage to the walls. Carli's bedroom, in particular, was dreadful as the plywood around the door began to bulge and sag. The frustration I experienced dealing with shoddy building materials and unreliable people was close to distressing.

Although the generator was deafening, being without electricity was worse. I never imagined that living in the dark would be so hard, but in reality, it's a big deal! Our candle-lit evenings were very short, reading was impossible, and TV was out altogether. The batteries in the CD player seemed to be flat most of the time, just like those in my laptop, and there was no way of recharging them.

The generator was broken more often than not, and each time I searched for Eddy, I had to corner him so he couldn't walk away mid-sentence.

'Are you able to fix the generator?' I asked respectfully.

His response was a curt, 'No!'

'Do you know anyone who can?' I said, trying to stay polite.

'No!' he said belligerently.

'I don't know why it's in the kitchen', I said enquiringly.

As if speaking to a developmentally delayed person, he replied, 'Because if it was outside, it would get stolen.'

Ignoring his ill manner, I said, 'How could anyone possibly steal such a heavy machine – and it's broken anyhow, so can you please move it outside?'

'No', he said as he edged around me, laughing and mumbling something under his breath. After that conversation, I felt sure that Eddy hated me, but I had no idea why. I was also left wondering about my safety and realised I didn't even know the police emergency number in Peru. There was no way of looking anything up, no landline or phone directory; everything was word of mouth. The kids didn't know either. Manuela was my best source of information, and I made a note to ask her.

Eventually, Eddy did find someone to fix the generator, but the supposed mechanic looked more like a homeless man, and he charged a hefty fee. He did actually get the motor started, but it functioned for approximately four hours before the same problem occurred. The second time, a real mechanic came, but he charged close to double the previous fee, and this time, it lasted a whopping twenty-four hours! My personal cash was dwindling fast, and Pastor Luis was off the radar; I could never contact him, not even in any emergency. I had tried to purchase a mobile phone but was told I needed to provide proof of identity and address by means of a utility bill, with my name and address on it, in order to purchase one. Those were the rules in Peru.

One morning I found there was no water. I couldn't even wash my hands after using the toilet! With no mobile phone and no idea when Pastor Luis might show up, I was in a bit of a predicament. I hadn't seen or heard from Pastor Luis for days. The girls told me that he ordered water once a week, but they had no idea of how he did it.

In emergencies, Eddy's mobile phone was to be our mode of communication. When I finally tracked him down, he was of little help. The usual problem: no credit, insufficient funds. I gave him some money to get credit, and off he went with his brick-phone in his hand to catch the green bus into The Porton.

Meanwhile, the sun was up early that morning, and it was turning into a very hot day. The reality of not having a single drop of water hit me like never before. I was concerned that the girls would suffer from dehydration. We couldn't even have breakfast, which was normally porridge made entirely on water; milk was a rare luxury. Thinking ahead, I realised that there would be no lunch either since we couldn't wash or cook the rice or veggies.

Knowing that the pastor wasn't even aware of our situation, I realised that I had to do something. In desperation, I grabbed some buckets and organised three girls to help. We each carried an empty bucket and walked to the nearest neighbour's house, only five minutes away. It was difficult for me to ask for anything. On top of that, I had never met the neighbours before. I felt awkward explaining our situation, but I did manage to ask if we could borrow some water. I promised that we would return it as soon as we had a delivery ourselves. Fortunately, the woman agreed, and at least for the interim, the dilemma was resolved.

Carrying those heavy buckets home, even though the distance was short, was hard work!

Everything was running late that day. No one had had a wash, and the high schoolers were unable to make breakfast. They went to school without anything in their stomachs; instead, I had given them a "gold" coin to buy something at the school tucker shop.

Although Eliza and Meridian tried to help me make breakfast, they had no idea; they were just kids. Meanwhile, the rest of the younger girls, all eighteen of them, ran riot while I was busy in the kitchen. The day was off to a bad start, and I seemed to be chasing my tail.

Hours later, Eddy returned with credit on his phone only to inform me that the battery was flat. Frustration levels were rising, and Manuela was on a day off, so I couldn't leave the house; I was beginning to feel helplessly trapped.

After breakfast, we couldn't do the washing up. The water had run out already. The girls were constantly demanding attention, not only to help with homework but to supply their needs for minor things like pencils, erasers, and the like. The house didn't have an emergency "kitty", so there was never any money for unforeseen expenses. My headspace was occupied trying to solve the problem of an empty water tank while at the same time trying to deal with the girl's needs. Their school supplies seemed almost insignificant compared to the gravity of having no water. The water problem became all-consuming and took precedence over everything else.

The routine on Manuela's days off was for Raisa (the cook) to walk the primary girls to school around midday and at the same time escort the high schoolers back to the casa (house). This short window of time with a fewer number of girls was much more manageable, at least until the high schoolers arrived. Once they arrived, the constant demands kept me distracted, and 2.00 pm came around quickly. As soon as Jahnique arrived, I informed her of the water shortage and asked her to call Pastor Luis. She explained that her mobile phone had no reception in the area and that the one-and-only service provider wasn't hers.

My only option was to go to a public phone box myself and call Pastor Luis. Jahnique, a little apprehensive about me leaving her alone, gave me some directions to the water supplier's office, just in case, and off I went. Like Eddy, I too caught the green bus to The Porton, where I found the nearest locutorio (public phone). I rang Pastor Luis, but his secretary answered the phone, informing me, 'Pastor Luis is attending a court case at present. You can try again in an hour.' I couldn't just sit on my hands for an hour, so I decided to try to sort the problem out myself.

When I found the water supplier, he told me that I could only buy water in the mornings and I would have to return the following day. I desperately tried to reason with him, explaining, 'The water is urgently needed at the refuge, where there are twenty-six girls who are suffering from dehydration already.' I literally begged him to make an exception. He responded with great sympathy, saying, 'At this late hour in the afternoon, I won't be able to sell anything less than a full tank of water.'

'But that's exactly what we need', I said.

'You don't understand', he replied, 'it will cost you seventy soles, and it won't all fit into your tank.'

'I don't care', I said, 'I will pay for the full tank, and you can fill some buckets and keep the rest.' A win/win deal resulted, as he could sell the leftover water the next day.

For the evening meal around 7.00 pm, which was always a light meal, Raisa served up the most disgusting concoction I had ever tasted; it was a type of salty, watery porridge, not unlike breakfast. It reminded me of the gruel served to Oliver Twist in the Charles Dickens story. I couldn't stomach it and was surprised to see the girls happily hoeing it down. In the dimly lit kitchen, I was able to dispose of mine in the bin before anybody noticed. My grumbling gut reminded me of the two packets of biscuits I had purchased on my outing earlier that day. I had left one packet in the kitchen and went to get it but, like the toilet paper, it had vanished, and no one knew anything about it. The second packet of biscuits was in my room, but I couldn't move without an entourage of girls following me, so I tried to forget about it.

Raisa was gone, and as usual, all the washing up was left behind. Every night the girls would argue and squabble over who was to do what in the kitchen. After a couple of incidents of infighting, I decided to step in and involve everyone in a joint effort. I gave each girl a specific task to do. The chore of washing up was more fun and got the job done, but it seemed to take forever. I clearly needed a better plan.

Whenever I left the room, even to go to the toilet, the girls noticed and followed me. Still, when I explained what I was doing, telling them that they didn't need to tag along, they weren't satisfied. Moaning and groaning, they insisted on coming along, but I insisted all the more that they remain. Still, their groans persisted. It was only when I said that I would be back with something special to share that they complied with my wishes. Blackmail was the only thing left that seemed to work.

When I returned, the chaos was no different from any other time, but with a packet of biscuits in hand, it was a little easier to grab their attention and restore some order. Slowly the tumult began to decline as I noticed Flo quietly sitting up straight in hopeful expectation. I handed her a biscuit, and the rest of the girls soon caught on. I needed to talk and put some changes into place, and finally, I was able to do so while their little mouths were occupied. That's when I re-introduced the pseudo- mike again. I talked about the bad habits I had observed and how we were going to overcome them.

Poor hygiene, combined with the fact that the girls shared each other's shoes and clothing, caused terrible fungal infections to spread rapidly. Diarrhoea was rife, and the girls suffered from all manner of ailments, including ringworm, tapeworm, and head infestations.

Hygiene hadn't seemed to improve because no matter what I said, the girls just did not want to shower. They'd convinced me that the water was too cold in the morning and had persuaded me to let them wait until later in the day when it was warmer; a reasonable request it seemed, but before long, I discovered that they never did get around to showering later in the day. At most, the girls had a quick cat-lick at the sink, and I found it hard to keep track of who did and who didn't wash at all. When they were all quietly munching away on the biscuits, I commenced speaking. 'Please don't steal the toilet rolls', I said persuasively, 'so there won't be any need to use the curtains again.' Yes, somebody decided to use the curtain when the toilet paper wasn't available. Embarrassed giggles rose, and with blushing cheeks, they all pointed the finger at each other.

Settling them down and moving on, I informed the girls of the importance of hand-washing, especially after using the toilet. I explained, 'Dirty hands is probably the reason why you all have diarrhoea.' I was careful and told them, 'It's not really your fault since you didn't have any soap or towels.' They seemed reasonably accepting, but no comments were made, and it was unusually quiet.

I continued, 'This is all going to change because you will have your very own soap and a brand-new towel each'. They cheered, 'Yeay!' and seemed happy with this. I was on a roll and continued with great animation. 'You can even have a shower because you don't have to use your dirty clothes to dry yourselves. 'Yeay!' I cheered, but alone this time. They remained silent. The subdued look on their faces didn't sit well with me, so I asked, 'Are there any questions?'

Carli blurted out, 'Do I have to have a shower too?'

'Yes, even little girls need to shower', I responded with a big smile while handing her the mike.

'Every day?' Carli exclaimed in a remarkably high-pitched voice for her.

'No, not every day, maybe every second or third day', I assured her. Some girls sighed with relief, while others grumbled under their breath.

I continued to explain that because there were only four showers, I would make a shower roster to keep track of everyone. This didn't go down well and brought sighs of dread to some. Trying to ignore the negative responses, I talked about the problem of flea-infested heads. I started scratching my head with exaggeration to illustrate how uncomfortable it was and said, 'I have fleas too. I want to get rid of my fleas, so I have to get rid of yours as well. I will buy some anti-flea shampoo for all of us.' At this, some girls started to protest and groan.

Amelia grabbed the spoon and complained, 'The mattresses are full of fleas.'

Then Kari chirped in, 'Can we all have a new mattress too?'

They all laughed. I laughed with them for a

moment, then I tried to continue, 'Oral hygiene is important...'

But Meridian, one of the quieter girls, interrupted, shouting out, 'Can you sing a song for us?'

I hesitated, suspecting this was a diversion tactic, but in that moment of hesitation, the girls began to chant over and over, 'Que se cantar! Que se cantar! (You have to sing! You have to sing!)'

Obviously, they'd had enough lecturing. I tried to hush them down by taking the spoon, saying, 'I don't know what to sing.' It was impossible; they just continued chanting all the louder. Meridian tried to raise her little voice above the din, but I couldn't hear her. I passed the spoon and motioned to the others to listen. Repeating her words, she said, 'Sing what you sang in the shower.'

'OK, OK', I conceded, and as soon as I gave in, there was complete silence. 'English or Spanish?' I asked.

They all unanimously exclaimed a definite response, 'English, English!'

'Hmm! What can I sing in English?' I couldn't even remember all the words to the song I sang in the shower. Then Eliza, with a delightful chuckle, said, 'Sing, Aflan, Flan, Flan, Eneski.'

'Que?' I responded, totally confused. After some clarification, I discovered that what she really meant was, "A flag flying high in the sky".

'OK', I said and began to sing...

'There is a flag flying high from the castle of my

heart, from the castle of my heart, from the castle of my heart…'

Looking around as I sang, I could see their angelic little faces. They were so still and wide-eyed as their countenances beamed in the dim, lamp-lit room. I was moved. It was as though they were in some sort of trance, just gazing. I invited the girls to try to join in, and they did try. It was quite funny how they made the English sounds, but the words were all wrong. I encouraged them for trying. As soon as I finished the song, the girls began to chant again, 'Otro, otro, otro (Another, another, another).' I really wanted to hear them sing, so I made a deal. I said that I would sing one more song, but only if someone would sing a Spanish song for me when I had finished. To my surprise, many hands went up as they cried out, 'Yo, yo, yo (Me, me, me).'

My first choice was Herleena, to start us off. I explained that Herleena would start but that they could each have a turn at starting a song, and then we would all join in. Herleena sang from her heart, and the others joined in one by one until a beautiful chorus of harmonizing voices could be heard. Truly, I felt like I was in the presence of angels. It was just glorious! They sang one beautiful song after another, and I didn't want it to end.

I lay awake that night, reflecting on all the goings-on over the past few days. All the frustrations with Eddy and the pastor and all the things that had been irritating: like the keys, the noisy generator, the cold showers, and the dreadful food. Then the beautiful singing harmonising audibly in my ears seemed to buoy up my resolve. Every annoyance just faded into insignificance. How I had felt at that moment in time far outweighed all the frustrations and difficulties. I knew that God was encouraging me. I was able to thank God for the broken generator and for the singing, knowing that one thing would not have occurred without the other.

I recognised that it was for such a time as this that I had come to Peru. The girls and I were experiencing that same closeness with something bigger than ourselves. Sharing our lives and our hearts in this way was truly an incredible encounter. Each time the tangible presence of God was unmistakeably right there in the midst of us, I was captivated, and so were they.

Chapter Twelve

OVERWHELMING TRIALS

Journal Entry:
San Juan de Lurigancho, Peru
20th June 2005

Peru is proving to be much harder than I had ever anticipated. Apart from the difficulty of organising and figuring out the discipline for so many young girls, with very little help, I have the added pressure of dealing with a pastor who is constantly letting me down. He lies compulsively, or he is suffering from short-term memory loss, I'm not sure.

Another disturbing factor is that this man seems to be detached from the reality of the conditions in the house and from the daily needs of the girls.

Although we couldn't listen to music, the discovery of our voices turned out to be something very precious. Every evening after dinner, in the dim candlelit room, we all joyfully participated in the singing. We found great comfort and camaraderie in those nights of singing together; sometimes, we just didn't want it to stop. The difficult days did at least end in this beautiful way, and we went to bed content.

The mornings, however, were different; they nearly always began with a rude awakening of some sort or another. If it wasn't the water trucks blasting their horns at 6.00 am, it was often a loudspeaker blaring through an amplifier. Sometimes traditional Peruvian music played, and sometimes it was someone yelling out about their goods for sale, 'Bananas, bananas baratos, bananas', or, 'Chancho, chancho barato y fresco, chancho (Bananas, pork, cheap and fresh).'

Minor accidents were common around the house. One afternoon a tremendously loud smashing sound of breaking glass boomed through the whole house! I ran to the scene to find a very bloody child, pale as a sheet, and blood spurting out of her slashed wrist. Instantly I grabbed her wrist with my bare hands to apply pressure and sat her on the floor before she fainted. The bleeding stopped while I held on, but I couldn't let go, not for a second. The girls around were in shock and looked petrified. I asked them calmly to get a blanket and a tea towel, but they were unresponsive. The second time I asked, I raised my voice, and they hurried off.

The cut was dangerously deep. After binding the girl's wrist with the tea towel, I enquired of the others as to what had happened. Apparently, the window was stuck, and Blanca had tried to force it open when it suddenly became free and slid up with a thud. The force caused the pane of glass to shatter, and shards of glass fell down, slicing her wrist on the way. Both wrists were exposed; it could have been much worse.

Jahnique had just left half an hour earlier, so I was on my own. Once the wound was secured and a blanket wrapped around Blanca, the rest of the girls seemed to settle down. They were a captive audience and listened carefully to my every word. 'Blanca will need stitches', I said. 'I will have to take her to hospital, and Herleena will be in charge while I'm gone.' I could see by the look on her face that Herleena was a little reticent, but at fifteen years of age, she was the eldest girl in the house, and I had no choice. I gave clear instructions that they *all* had to do whatever Herleena said. They nodded in unanimous agreement. Then Herleena seemed to relax a little.

We prayed together before Blanca, and I stepped outside into the pitch-black night. No pavements, no lamp posts, not even the moonlight was visible; it was a nightmare stumbling over the rocky ground. Even the bus stop was hard to find, and I had no idea where the hospital was.

To my relief, I found Jahnique still standing there at the bus stop. She'd missed her bus. She could hardly believe what had happened when I told her, and she had no qualms about showing me the way to the hospital.

After waiting with us for an hour in triage, I encouraged Jahnique to go home and asked her to inform the pastor what had happened. Almost another hour passed before we saw a doctor. Without even looking at the wound, he gave me a script and sent me to the pharmacy window. There a long queue moved at a snail's pace with just one person serving. Finally, on reaching the window, I was given all the items written on the script: the sutures, alcohol swabs, antiseptic spray, syringe and local anaesthetic; even the dressing and bandage.

Told to wait outside the doctor's room again, we sat patiently. Blanca was called to have her wound stitched, but I was told to wait outside. I tried to insist on going in with Blanca, but they flatly refused. While waiting, I rang Pastor Luis on a public phone in the hospital. I had no success as the phone just rang continually. Blanca ended up with five stitches and a pressure bandage, but before the doctor gave final clearance, he sent us to wait in yet another long queue, this time, at the cashier's window. I was required not only to pay for the consultation but also for the dressings, the syringes, and even the local anaesthetic. On two other occasions, I tried to ring the pastor, but his daughter or Pilar answered the phone. It seemed that Pastor Luis was a busy man. When I explained that I urgently needed to talk to him, I was told by Pilar that apart from being an associate pastor at the Cathedral de Fe in Lima, Pastor

Luis was also a psychologist in a busy practice. The best she could do was to pass on my message. That sinking feeling returned with the realisation that I was truly on my own.

It was almost midnight before we made it back to the casa in the pitch-black night, and most of the kids were anxiously waiting up for us. Alarm bells began to ring loud and clear about the situation that I was in.

Another couple of days passed, each one with its own troubles. Jahnique, an indecisive person, was apprehensive about many things. She was a great help to me, but she was reluctant to make any decisions independently, her reasoning being that she only worked part-time and didn't know what was going on. Jahnique would consult me about every little detail; even when one of the girls got out of hand, she would come to me instead of dealing with it herself.

Eddy was a worry. He caused me no end of strife. He was difficult to find at the best of times, especially when a job needed doing or when we needed to get the generator started. Everything was problematic for him; his heart just wasn't in his job. On the few occasions when the generator was functional, if I didn't pull that chord, he certainly didn't.

The difficulty was that the motor never started on the first attempt. On one particular evening, each time I tried to pull that chord, it sounded so close to starting but not close enough. Determined not to give up, I would pull the cord even harder. Eventually, the motor would either start, or the cord would jam; and when it jammed, it jarred my back terribly. After a few repeated jarrings, the pain in my back was so severe that I had to stop. When I was done in, the three older girls, ever helpful and ever desperate to watch TV, attempted to pull the chord too. Each time the promising sound of the motor reviving tempted them to pull again, and again, until they were in a lather of sweat. But that promising sound eventually fizzled out into nothing. After a short break, I tried again, giving it my best shot, but it refused. I had to give in to the excruciating pain in my back. The stubborn motor triumphed, and I succumbed to taking strong analgesics to relieve my pain.

I tossed and turned most of the night, trying to get comfortable. Then in the early hours, alerted to the sound of distraught children crying, I stepped out of bed cautiously, still with niggling pain in my back. Thinking another accident had happened, I tried to hurry up the stairs, but the sound grew distant, and I realised it was coming from outside. I opened the front window and saw Eddy's two young boys standing below. They were crying convulsively and incoherently blabbering something over and over again.

I told them to calm down because I couldn't under-stand what they were saying. Between their sobs, it sounded like, 'Estan muerto, estan muerto (They're dead, they're dead)!' I thought they must be talking about their guineapigs, so I yelled out insensitively, 'Go tell your mother.' The poor little tykes only grew more distressed and cried out even louder,

'They're dead; they're dead!'

'Who's dead?' I asked.

'Pappi, Mammy', they sniffed through copious snot and tears, 'they're dead.' The two distraught little figures standing in the dark seemed so fearful. I put my dressing gown on immediately and went outside, taking my torch with me.

I held the boy's hands and said, 'Show me.' They led the way towards their flimsy little hut at the back of the property. Their crying calmed down a little as they hurriedly pulled me along.

The door was ajar, and I knocked hard several times. I had never been inside their place before and was hesitant. It was so quiet. I felt unnerved, but the insistent tugs on either side ushered me forward. I took courage and yelled out, 'Soy la Hermana Briggitt!' No answer; it was still deadly quiet. I let go of the boy's hands and pushed on the door. The door slowly creaked open, and I ushered the boys in, following them close behind.

I heard a deep, eerie growling sound, which made the hair on the back of my neck stand up. Shining my torch in the direction of the growl, my beam of light landed on Raisa's face. Her eyes remained closed and unresponsive to the light. Next to her, face-down on the bed, lay Eddy. For a brief moment, I thought that they really were dead. Trying to process what I saw, I approached very slowly. The closer I got, the louder the growl, and then a strong whiff of alcohol invaded my nostrils. The empty rum bottle next to the bed confirmed my suspicions.

Eddy snored into the mattress with his breathing obstructed; he sounded like he might suffocate. I couldn't leave him like that. I tapped him on the shoulder, but no response! I shook him firmly, calling his name repeatedly, and still no response! Turning to Raisa, I tried to arouse her instead. In a comatose state, her pupils did at least respond to light. She was stoned drunk!

I knew, unlike their needy children, that they were both alive and well. To reassure the boys that their parents were *just sleeping*, I rolled Eddy onto his back. Using my nursing skills, I firmly rubbed my knuckles hard on his sternum. This invoked a short-lived but violent thrashing of the arms, a favoured response to pain. 'See, he's not dead', I assured them.

The boys were still scared. I couldn't leave them there. I brought them into the main building that night and settled them down with a blanket on the couch. I left the two inebriated ones to sleep it off, and I went back to bed. I was unable to sleep; far too many things kept me awake. It seemed like I was on duty 24/7, and I knew I would soon burn out if this continued. I had to get away from the demands of everything, including the constant needs and wants of the girls.

The next day when Manuela arrived in the morning, I organised some time off. Manuela was very capable; she often used her own initiative, and I knew she would manage without me. With no communication from the pastor, not even in response to Blanca's accident, I felt annoyed and decided to chase him up. During the limited window of freedom afforded by Manuela's presence, I went to The Porton.

Arriving at the locutorio, I called the pastor, but once again, I was informed that he was busy on another call. Determined, I said, 'I can't call back in an hour; I will wait!'

'He may be a while', the secretary said.

But I was firm and said, 'I'll wait until he is free.'

When I did finally get to talk to him, it took me all my effort to stay calm. The first thing I asked was, 'Did you receive any of my messages?'

'Yes', he said casually. 'Is Blanca all right?'

'Yes, she is now', I said, 'but I am concerned about leaving the girls without any supervision at night. I didn't expect to be working alone.'

'Herleena can be left in charge. She is quite capable', he responded.

'She is a minor, and I really feel I need more help', I said.

'You have Jahnique and Manuela', he said, 'and Eddy and Raisa.'

I felt myself getting furious and responded, 'Eddy is unhelpful. He refuses to do anything. I found him drunk one evening, and neither Manuela nor Jahnique are there during the night', I responded.

'What about Amelia and Herleena? They can help too', he claimed.

'Pastor Luis', I said firmly, 'they are minors.' I paused, but there was nothing but silence. I couldn't contain myself, and all my frustrations came spilling out, 'The tank ran dry, and we didn't have a drop of water. There is not enough food in the house, and the kids need school supplies, and no money has been allocated to cover anything.' More silence followed, and I added, 'We haven't even been to church for two Sundays in a row.' Again, the silence continued, but I had said enough and quietened myself.

After a long pause, he finally responded, 'The water shouldn't have run out; it normally lasts seven to ten days.' He complained, 'You must be using too much.'

Shocked at his response, I felt myself getting upset and tried to explain, 'The girls have skin infections and diarrhoea as well as flea-infested heads, and I am trying to improve the poor hygiene.' He didn't respond.

After a short silence, I told him I had purchased a tank of water, paid the hospital bills, and covered the cost of the repairs to the generator as well as a few other food items out of my own pocket, and that I felt we needed to have an emergency kitty in the house. He responded, 'I will reimburse you on my next visit to the house.'

'When are you planning to visit?' I asked.

'Perhaps one day next week', he responded.

'And in the meantime?' I questioned.

'Try to make do with what you have', he said.

'What about the food situation and the school needs?' I asked.

'Raisa has money for food', he said, 'and I will bring some school supplies with me. I must go now. Is there anything else?'

'Yes', I said, my mind flooded with a million things, 'the door locks are a problem, and I'd like to have them removed, but Eddy said he needs your permission, and he hasn't got the tools.'

After a short description of the problem, he agreed, saying, 'Purchase a screwdriver for Eddy, and tell him he has my permission.'

'OK, thank you', I said, somehow feeling relieved.

'I really must go now, goodbye', he said hurriedly.

'Also, before you go', I responded just as quickly, 'I need to organise a day off.'

There was silence again at the end of the phone. It lasted so long that I thought he had hung up, then he said, 'When do you need a day off?'

'Every week', I said, 'starting now!'

'We can talk about this on my next visit', he said unfazed. 'I must go now.' And that was it. He hung up.

I had no one to talk to about how I was feeling, and I really wanted to call Greg. In desperation, I had a look around the market to see if there were any second-hand mobile phones, but there were none. The time difference made it a bad time to call right then, so the best I could do was to send him an email. I found an internet café, but when I tried to express myself in writing, it sounded so unreal. I needed to talk, so I just organized a date and time for a call the following week. I was determined to get the time off somehow.

I purchased some food, but I could only buy what I was able to carry on the green bus. I decided to keep a record of all my spending, but the sellers looked at me as if I was mad when I asked for receipts. I had to keep track of the purchases in my head. The bumpy ride home was standing room only, and it was quite a struggle with the bags. It seemed like nothing was easy.

With the cooperation of Manuela, Jahnique, and Herleena, I organised every Wednesday off. Jahnique changed her Tuesday to Wednesday, and Herleena covered for the two hours in between Manuela and Jahnique's shift. This wasn't the ideal option, and I wasn't sure if I could survive being on my own all day with the girls on Tuesdays, but there wasn't any other choice. With the uncertainty of Pastor Luis ever showing up at all, I didn't hold my breath waiting for his approval.

A crazy teenage boy in the adjoining cubicle yelled a warning out loudly across the room. 'Sniper on the roof!' he cried, and to avoid the bullets, his body made a thud against the thin partition separating us. I jumped with fright and looked into his cubicle, half expecting to find his body on the floor.

The disturbing commotion turned out to be the boy playing computer games with his friends scattered around the room. I found it hard to think with all the distractions, but I had no choice. I was waiting to call Greg, and in the meantime, I wanted to check my emails and charge my laptop. I dared not leave the laptop out of my sight for fear of it disappearing. I noticed that it attracted far too much attention from onlooking envious eyes.

The computers lined three of the four walls so that everyone faced a wall. It was a very hot day; the small, dingy room with no windows and no ventilation was sweltering hot, even with the door open. The old computers with sticky and missing keys, combined with the poorly lit room, caused no end of frustration when it came to writing emails. Some of the letters on the keys weren't always the letters that appeared on the screen either. The @ was number 7 and vice versa, but eventually, I got used to the keyboard, and I managed to tolerate the yelling and bouncing around. The first thing I worked on was making a list of the girls' names and creating a shower roster. I still had some time left to respond to emails until suddenly, mid-writing, the lights went out. It was a total blackout! The email I had begun was lost! I just sat in the dark and felt like crying.

Someone was scuffling around the room, and I feared for my laptop, but it was so black I just sat waiting for the lights to come back on. They never did. Instead, the owner appeared with a candle and my laptop in hand, explaining that he had forgotten to pay his electric bill. The relief of seeing my laptop diffused the exasperation I was feeling, and I thanked him profusely and left.

WORKING BY CANDLE-LIGHT ON MY LAPTOP

Compelled to find a way to call Greg, I asked around and discovered the nearest place was thirty minutes away by bus. With plenty of time for the call, I caught a bus and set off. It didn't take long to find an internet café. This one was much quieter, which allowed me to have the headspace I needed to think. The computers were better, and the environment was less oppressive. There were even printers available, and I was able to print the rosters I managed to complete. I still had time to spare. Close by, I found a bite to eat at a place which I had noticed near the bus stop where I alighted. It was called Norky's, the Peruvian version of MacDonald's. There I enjoyed a wholesome lunch. Wholesome, that is, compared to Raisa's cooking.

The highlight of my first day off was not the lunch or the internet café, it was what followed when I went back to the internet café a few doors down. Hearing Greg's charming Aussie accent on the end of the line made life inexplicably better. Just hearing my native language and being able to speak it was so refreshing. I shared my woes with Greg, and he listened patiently and empathetically, but he seemed worried, especially after I told him the drama of finding Eddy in a drunken state. Greg told me to be careful with Eddy and to keep my guard up at all times. He even suggested that I keep something I could use as a weapon if needed. 'A baseball bat or a chunk of wood', he said. I laughed at his suggestions and thought he was joking, but Greg was very serious. I told him there was nothing I could think of to use as a weapon. He made me promise I would find something. It was only when I promised that I would put the broken wooden leg off a chair under my bed that he would tell me his news from Australia.

Greg's update from Sydney made me feel like I was in another cosmos. Our conversation was like a healing balm to me. It brought back balance into my chaotic world and helped me to realise that he really did care for me. I didn't want him to worry, so I didn't tell him everything. Instead, I spoke at length of the beautiful experiences I'd had with the girls and all the positives I could think of. It was hard to end the call. But when we did, I felt strengthened and ready to face another week.

The changes and the rosters weren't very popular, but I had to establish order in the house. When I re-organised the bedrooms and told the girls that they would be buddied up with a younger girl and share the same room with their buddy, that didn't go down well either: the teenagers quickly realised that this meant they couldn't chat into the early hours of the morning.

Fair warning of the new rules was given well before they were put in place. Other measures were taken if and when the older girls ignored my request to blow out their candles by 9.00 pm. The candles were confiscated. Because the kitchen had always been dangerously overcrowded, I put up a sign over the door to remind the younger girls to stay out of the kitchen. It said, 'Only 12-year-olds and over allowed in the kitchen.'

To make sure that the washing up after each meal was efficient and to get the house in ship-shape condition, I introduced a cleaning roster that ensured that all the work was equally shared; even the younger children had light duties. The biggest problem was that the girls realised that I could actually keep track of them, and they didn't like that at all. Also, the buddy system disturbed them because it meant responsibility for the older girls and accountability for the younger ones. None of them were happy.

Soon there was rebellion in the camp. The girls, all but a handful, decided that they didn't like routine, and they didn't want the responsibility. Some girls even ran away, but the rebellious ones who stayed only stayed to make my life hell.

During the next few days, the rebellious girls seemed to infect the ones who had been agreeable. It was mass mutiny, and it all became so very wearing. Chores were left half done, bickering and answering back increased, and morale was low. When I went upstairs looking for the girls, they went downstairs; when I went downstairs, they ran upstairs. If it weren't for the evening meal, I would never have managed to get the girls all together in one place. What really upset me the most was that the girls showed little desire to pray, and gradually even the singing was affected. Their heart just wasn't in it anymore. Instead of singing together, the ringleaders asked for permission to go to bed early, and they only asked because it was so dark they needed a candle. We had lost the power of unity. With fewer voices and the decline in morale, it just wasn't the same.

By the end of a disastrous week, I was devastated. I prayed for wisdom and wondered if my expectations were too great? I wondered if the girls may just need some incentive, and I lost sleep trying to think of one.

I had to do something before it was too late. I decided to make a "Rewards Chart". That was something I had done with my own children, and it seemed to work. In our gathering of the evening meal, I showed them the chart and explained how it worked: at the end of every day, next to each girl's name, if she completed the allocated task, a happy face was drawn, and if she didn't, a sad face was drawn. At the end of every month, the girls who had a minimum of sixteen happy faces could look forward to an evening out at Norky's. (I assumed the cost of all rewards.)

Some girls were excited about the chart, and they really tried to make an effort. Others didn't care and defiantly ignored the rules. The house did start to look a little cleaner, and slowly I could see an improvement in personal hygiene, though the fleas were always a challenge.

At the end of the month, less than a handful of girls managed to achieve sixteen happy faces. I took the small group out to dinner while Jahnique stayed back with the girls, who didn't try hard at all. When they were left behind, they couldn't believe it. They had obviously had little or no experience of having to face the consequences of their actions.

Jahnique gave the girls extra jobs to do while we were out enjoying ourselves. Unaware of this, when we returned, the small group of girls raved about how great the chicken was and how they even had ice-cream for dessert and how much fun they'd had—this only rubbed salt in the wounds, and the rebellious ones were furious.

From then on, whenever given a sad face, these girls would try to cheat. Sometimes they crossed out the sad face; other times, they bitterly contested and argued with Jahnique. They were relentless, so much so that poor Jahnique was coerced into revoking her decision, and she would cross out the sad face and replace it with a happy one. When I saw this and realised what was happening, I said nothing right away; at the end of the week, I again explained the rewards system and revealed that there would be a new, smaller weekly reward. I informed the girls that it wasn't that hard; all they had to do was to follow through with the rosters. I also made sure they understood that if a face had been crossed out or changed in any way, I would assume it was a sad face without question. I heard girls sniggering at that point.

To encourage the others, I enquired about what kind of things they would like as a small reward, provided they met their quota of happy faces. Most of the girls liked this and were keen to shout out what they wanted. The most popular requests were chocolate bars or biscuits. One girl wanted an egg, a fried egg for breakfast. Another wanted some milk. I was amused when one girl asked for some clothes pegs. I made a careful note of the things they craved for and promised that I would follow through if they did.

This short-term incentive seemed to have a more

positive effect on some girls but not on others. I was sure they all longed for something, but I couldn't reach all of them. A small handful of girls claimed that they didn't want anything. Still, at least the back-chatting and arguing with Jahnique would cease.

Dealing with the daily challenges of the girls, as well as the many upsetting incidents with Pastor Luis was tough, but the situation worsened further when I discovered some unsavoury truths that left me speechless.

I felt an incredible lack of support and needed to communicate with someone from the church. The Cathedral de Fe in Lima was supposed to be the supporting church for CEDES, and when many Sundays in a row had passed without any mention of us attending, I called the pastor. I requested that we plan a visit on Sunday. Pastor Luis was against the idea. He explained, 'Cathedral de Fe is a long way to travel with so many girls; it's two long bus rides into Lima, and I don't have enough money for the bus fares at the moment.'

After a pause, I inquired, 'How come you don't have enough money?'

He explained, 'The funding normally comes from the U.S., but it's been delayed, and I can't reimburse you for the water, let alone the bus fares. I assure you that we are expecting the funding to arrive any day now.' I was so desperate to communicate with anyone in authority at the church that I offered to cover the cost of the bus fares. I half expected that he would find another excuse, but to my surprise, he agreed. We arranged to meet at the church the following Sunday.

Time moved slowly that week; each day seemed long and drawn out. Finally, the day arrived and we were about to set off to attend Cathedral de Fe in Lima. After a short pep talk about behaviour and rewards, twenty-six girls and I set out of the house for the first time in what seemed to be an eternity. The girls were super excited and difficult to manage. I decided to pair them each with their buddy and remind them of their responsibility to one another. Herleena and Karina, who knew the way and became my guides; I could never have done it without them.

Each bus arrived jam-packed, and with so many of us, we couldn't fit on. We let the bus go to wait for another, hopefully with a little more room. After letting the next bus go, I realised it was not going to happen. Time was ticking over. If we were ever going to get there, we had to split into two groups.

Herleena accompanied the older, responsible girls while Karina and I took the younger ones. Hot and humid, with standing room only, our warm bodies were squashed against each other during the jerky bus rides. Then, after an hour and a half of this horrendous trip, the worst happened. Eliza heaved up violently over the other passengers, and the smell of vomit in the stinking heat was almost unbearable. The windows were all closed, as Peruvians are fearful of draughts. I was glad that I was standing at the other end of the bus because I didn't even have a tissue handy. Those in the line of fire were very understanding and tried to help by shuffling the vomiting child past other passengers nearer to the open door to get some air. That's just where I was standing. I had stood there purposely to make sure that none of the girls fell out of the doorway on the crowded bus. I never imagined this scenario.

The church was huge, with over a thousand in the congregation all praising and worshipping as we arrived. We were late. I couldn't see Pastor Luis, so we took the back two pews, trying not to disturb the singing. Later I noticed him sitting at the front, side row with a number of other associate pastors.

During the service, there was no acknowledgement of the refuge CEDES and not a mention of our presence there. I felt it was odd that no one approached us after the service either. I asked the girls if they knew anyone, but they didn't seem to. Apparently, only a small number of them had attended and only a few times.

We remained seated and waited until the church was almost empty before Pastor Luis finally approached. After the stony, cold greeting, I asked, 'Is your church aware that a volunteer has arrived from Australia to look after the girls at CEDES?'

With a flash of anger in his eyes, he snapped back at me, 'There are much more important people than you attending this church, and they don't seek recognition.'

In disbelief, I glared at him, but he was unfazed, and with his piercing defiant stare gazing back at me, I felt extremely uncomfortable. I looked away, upset; I said nothing. His cruel remark cut deep, and I was on the brink of tears. But I needed to make sense of it, and I convinced myself that this must be one of those strange cultural differences. I calmed myself and tried to let it go. Scanning the empty auditorium, with no other pastor in sight, I turned my attention to the girls. They were getting restless and teasing each other. It was all too hard to seek out any other person in leadership. I just gave up and began to organise the girls for our trip home.

We made our way outside, and Pastor Luis followed. I talked about the terrible trip and how Eliza had vomited on the bus, but Pastor Luis, with great scepticism, responded, 'It's normally an easy trip for me; I only catch two buses, and I never have trouble getting the girls on the bus.'

I asked him to accompany us to the bus stop, suggesting that perhaps we had taken the wrong bus and that he could show us the correct one. We stood at a different bus stop; the girls noisily, but the pastor and I were coldly silent. Shortly after, the bus arrived. Pastor Luis hurriedly piled all the girls onto an already full bus, but it was impossible, they didn't fit, and they all had to pile off again. I said nothing. I just waited. When a repeat of the same thing happened with the next bus, I just watched in amazement, and I knew then that I was not dealing with a rational person. A good while passed, letting one bus go after another, and the girls started to complain that they were hungry. That's when Pastor Luis agreed that we should split the group. By that stage, he was desperate to get rid of us. In the end, we caught three buses and finally arrived at the casa hungry and exhausted.

The following week, Jahnique relayed a message from Pastor Luis informing me that he was looking for a local church for us to attend. I knew something was terribly wrong, but I didn't know how to handle it. I was just relieved that we would never have to make that trip again.

For a while, we had our own church service in the living room at the casa led by me, but the girls were less than keen. Some weeks later, early on a Sunday morning, the pastor dropped in unexpectedly with a pick-up truck to take us all to a local church. We weren't prepared, but the girls scurried around, trying to get ready in a hurry. I hesitated and asked if it was legal to transport kids in this way. He assured me it was only fifteen minutes away, and it was fine on the back streets. He was determined: 'I thought you were desperate to go to church', he said.

'I am', I replied and went to get ready.

In spite of the humiliation of being herded onto the back of a pick-up truck like cattle, it was nowhere near as bad as our last ordeal getting to church. I didn't think we would all fit, but we stood squashed in tight, and even Pastor Luis somehow fitted in. No one complained. The girls even thought that it was exciting!

TRANSPORT TO CHURCH WITH LUIS GUIZADA

Manuela and Jahnique did their best to occupy the girls with colouring competitions and spelling games during the school holidays, but the girls rarely left the house, and it seemed that there was nothing for them to look forward to.

We had enjoyed singing and praying during the evenings, but even that was dwindling away. On the long, boring Sunday afternoons, when I was "all" they had, the girls were getting stir-crazy, and it wasn't much fun for me either.

One particular Sunday, I seemed to be spending most of my time separating the girls from murdering each other. Since there were insufficient funds to take the girls out anywhere, I decided to take them on a hike up into the local foothills of the Andes. I made sure to take my compass with me so we didn't get lost. It was an extremely hot afternoon, as always, and we only had three empty two-litre containers to fill with drinking water. The girls grumbled about carrying the bottles, so they passed them around like hot potatoes sipping at them continually. Within a short space of time, the water was gone. The girls figured if they drank it, they wouldn't have to carry it. The further up we climbed, the more the girls complained bitterly about the heat and the dust. I told them they shouldn't have drunk all the water so quickly and ignored their protests.

Very soon into the hike, when we reached the second ridge, the landscape began to change. Before us, we could see layer upon layer of grey, rocky slopes separated only by a white mist. It was spectacular. The air was less contaminated, and we could see blue sky above the mist. When we looked behind us, all we could see was the mist covering the valley below. There was no sight of the casa, nor any visible sign of life. We had ascended through the mist and now stood on the peaks above it.

The girls were tired and thirsty, but they were also fascinated by the terrain. They were a little disorientated and concerned we might be lost. I assured them that if they didn't stray off, all would be well. We continued at a snails-pace; before long, they were moaning and groaning, desperate to get back to the casa. I insisted that we continue and progress upward. In fear of getting separated, they followed close behind.

Within a short distance, the whining started again. This time, I explained that we would only turn back if they all stopped complaining and if they promised to stop bickering and fighting at the casa. They would have agreed to just about anything at this stage; all were happy to make a solemn promise on a hand-shake. So, we turned back.

DUSTY FOOTHILLS OF THE ANDES: SAN JUAN DE LURIGANCHO

It was a slow but extremely quiet descent. The girls were exhausted by the time we reached the casa. They immediately quenched their thirst and, full of dust and perspiration, crashed on their beds. The house was in perfect peace for the entire evening.

During the peace and quiet, I reflected on how the girls had responded; I felt sorry for them. Perhaps, I'd been too hard on them? Remembering my own girls during the summer school holidays in Australia and how they had a swimming pool and easy access to the beach and many other places, I felt compassion towards the Peruvian girls in San Juan de Lurigancho. They had nothing! That night I thought of the TV and decided to try once again to get the generator started. I pulled the chord as hard as I could, and miraculously it started the first time, but it only lasted for a moment before it died again. It sounded so promising that I pulled one more time, again with all my strength, but it jammed. My back wrenched, and I was in excruciating pain. All my efforts were in vain!

Chapter Thirteen

BREAKTHROUGH

Journal Entry:
San Juan de Lurigancho, Peru
27th June 2005

I'm shipwrecked and treading water. Every now and then, some ruthless words or some malicious act pulls me under. I'm drowning but I'm not destroyed. Because I know that God is faithful, somehow my head is above water. I know that there is a reason for all of this and I stay afloat.

Pastor Luis, "the man of God", is prone to telling lies; he's also dangerous. I must warn Greg about this unbelievable situation.

The funding from the U.S. never appeared, and I had no support from anyone in Peru. I only had access to my own personal money through the international ATM. Fortunately, I was able to keep in contact with my home church in the Central Coast, keeping them informed of the situation by email. They, in turn, sent regular funds, but because I didn't have an ID card, which meant that I was unable to open a bank account, the funds had to be paid directly into Pastor Luis's account.

The funding provided to me didn't improve. On top of not reimbursing me for the things I was asked to pay for, Pastor Luis continued to make more requests for me to pay for the daily living costs of running the house. He claimed that the funds from the U.S. were in the bank but were held back for some reason unknown. He never discussed the quantity of funds received from Australia except to say that it wasn't enough to cover the costs.

Alarm bells reverberated like never before. The problem was that the children's basic needs for food, water, and medical treatment were not being met; school fees were overdue, and the girls were prevented from taking their end-of-year exams as a result. The pastor was never around; I was the only Johnny-on-the-spot, and I paid for what I could.

The weeks passed, and still, no money had arrived. Pastor Luis dropped in randomly to ask me to cover another cost, and although he was in a mad rush to leave (as always), I confronted him. I asked more questions about the financial situation and noticed that he became uncomfortable, only responding loosely and never really divulging any information. Finally, I said, 'Pastor Luis, I don't have any more money!' Looking at him square in the face, I asked, 'What would you normally do in this predicament if I had not been here?'

Sharp as a razor, he responded, 'I would have to get a loan from the bank and then pay it with interest from the U.S. funds when they arrive.' His facial expression never changed as he added, 'The interest is very high, and the money should be cleared any day now.' I found it hard to believe he could lie in such a convincing way. Perhaps I wanted to believe him, I don't know, but I covered the costs with my own personal money again.

The time dragged by until finally, my day off arrived, and I was so looking forward to talking with Greg. A call came through Eddy's phone; it was Pastor Luis. He informed me that two new girls were on their way in a taxi and that they would be arriving in approximately ten minutes. I protested and told him it was my day off and I was not prepared. I insisted that we really needed to plan the arrival of new girls.

He totally ignored me as if I had not said a word and continued, 'The new girls are sisters. The youngest, Angelica, is three years old, but her sister, Yakira, is sixteen.'

'But, Pastor', I affirmed in disbelief, 'you know that

there is a shortage of staff and there are no extra beds, or sheets, or towels!'

Unaffected by my urgent tone, Pastor Luis calmly interrupted, saying, 'It's just a matter of shuffling the girls around. They can share a bed.'

I was beside myself, and I blurted out, 'I have a bad back, the house is full, some girls are already sleeping two to a bed, and who is going to take care of a 3-year-old?'

He assured me that he had spoken to Jahnique and to Manuela and that they had agreed to pick up some of the responsibilities. He seemed to have an answer for everything. When I reminded him that it was my day off, he said, 'These girls need your help. Their needs are greater than yours. You must consider them.'

I backed down, feeling selfish, and in a less urgent tone said, 'It would have been better if you had coordinated this with me. As it *is* my day off, I *do* have plans.'

He became coldly arrogant and retorted, 'I am in charge, and I don't need to consult you about anything.' His voice was stern as he continued to assert himself, 'You are just a volunteer, and I will have the final say.' He then hung up. I stood there, powerless and deeply troubled. His heart seemed cold as ice, colder than anyone I had ever known.

Jahnique remained with the rest of the girls while I went to sort out the room and improvise on sheets for the new girls. I barely had time to collect my thoughts and take some medication for my backache when suddenly there they were. Angelica stood clinging to her big sister, looking extremely frightened. Some months later, after reading their case-history, I reflected on that day and felt really sad. Their first impression of the solemn-faced foreigner could have been so different if I had known. I was never given any paperwork on the girls. It was only later, after hounding Pastor Luis for it, that I read their case history. Angelica's mother was incarcerated during her pregnancy, and Angelica, born in prison, spent her first years with her mother and the inmates. At age three, however, alternative arrangements had to be found. Angelica's half-sister, Yakira, had been estranged from her teenage mother since birth and had met her sister for the first time only recently and only as a result of her mother's need to find a babysitter for Angelica. The woman who had taken in Yakira could not manage a second child and brought both girls to Pastor Luis.

Pastor Luis never even showed up that day of their arrival. When Manuela arrived, I learned that she had had no prior knowledge of the new girls. It was the same with Jahnique. The next time I saw Pastor Luis, I confronted him about this in the presence of Manuela. He dismissed it by blaming my language skills, saying, 'You obviously misunderstood me.' Without batting an eyelid, he grinned and moved on. He explained that the reason he had come in the first place was to inform us of the fundraising idea he had. Apparently, there were huge sacks of old donated clothes in a storage space above the showers, and he requested that we have a jumble sale on Saturday, the very next day.

The thought of balancing on a chair and handling heavy bags was unbearable to me. Immediately I politely declined, explaining, 'My back is still sore, and there are no other workers to help on the weekends.'

He looked at me, the grin still affixed, 'You won't be needed', he said, 'Jahnique has volunteered to help the girls, and Eddy and Raisa will help too.' Then he produced a stack of flyers out of his briefcase and sent the girls out, unaccompanied, into the local community to hand them out. I felt demoralised and that the girls were being exploited. His actions were beyond reason, and I couldn't wait for him to leave.

Early next morning, while still making breakfast for what had become *the lawless crew of girls*, I could see through the window that a queue of people was already forming outside. The queue was growing at an alarming rate. I spoke to Eddy and Raisa, but they had no knowledge of the jumble sale and were about to leave. Immediately, I phoned Jahnique using Yakira's phone, this time. Jahnique knew nothing about the jumble sale, and she had other important plans organised for that day. I then tried to call the pastor, but, conveniently, he didn't answer his phone.

I looked out the window again, and the queue had grown to stretch out the whole length of the property. Nervously, I called the pastor again, but to no avail. I asked Herleena to tell the people it was cancelled. To my surprise, without complaint, she complied and went to the gate. 'Problem solved', I thought. Breakfast was finally ready, and we sat down to eat. Through the dining room windows, I could see that the queue had not gone away; in fact, it was still growing. To this day, I don't know what Herleena actually said to those people! When asked, she told me that she had delivered my message.

What to do? I had no idea, nothing was ready, and the queue was not going away. To my amazement, Ruby and Amelia offered to help. I soon realised that they had an agenda of their own. Their offer of help was conditional; they wanted a cut of the profits. I thought about this for a moment and realised I was in no position to argue. I agreed, but only if they sold enough clothing to cover what they were asking. They agreed and immediately made a start on sorting out the clothes.

When the other girls heard what was going on, they all wanted to help. I made the same deal with all of them. There was an unusual air of excitement, and the mutiny had all but faded away, at least for the moment. The girls worked hard, struggling with heavy sacks of clothing, dragging them up the awkward stone stairs. I couldn't do much with my back, but I tried to help where I could. We spread the old clothes all over the dining room tables and on every available surface. Clothes were stacked high and even spilled onto the floor. The dining room was a shamble, but it was worth it; the jumble sale was a huge success.

JUMBLE SALE

By the end of the day, I was feeling very sore and tired. The girls and I gathered in the glow of the lamplight after dinner. I began to quiet them and express gratitude for all their help. With animation, I told them that we had made over four hundred soles, and I dished out their cut, as agreed. I was hoping that the day's event might clear the atmosphere in some way. I spoke enthusiastically, saying that we could all go to Norky's for dinner with part of the money, and they seemed happy. Then I said that I would like to give thanks for the great success of the jumble sale, and I bowed my head and began to pray.

After a short prayer, I waited expectantly. It was deadly quiet. No one was willing to break the silence. I waited in the mystery of this silence, but with each second that ticked over, I felt that nothing had changed. The girls were not willing to pray, and I felt extremely sad.

The stillness lingered; I really didn't know what to do, so I quietly began to pray again. I closed my eyes and earnestly prayed, 'Help us, Lord. We need You, Father.' I prayed for the girls by name, one by one. The tears welled up in my eyes and streamed freely down my face as I tried to continue. But, deeply affected by all that was happening, I was overcome by emotion; I couldn't speak. No matter how hard I tried, I just couldn't regain composure, and I sobbed my heart out uncontrollably.

This weak reaction was unimaginable to me: Bridget, the strong, crying pathetically in the presence of a bunch of girls. I couldn't face them. I kept my eyes sealed as if somehow this would hide my shame. In my darkness, I wanted the ground to swallow me up. Then something extraordinary happened. I was touched gently on my shoulder by a small hand. On the other shoulder, another hand rested, then another, and, in the stillness, I heard quiet sobs. My eyes were sealed, but I felt their presence surrounding me, and I knew that they, too, were crying. Kari softly began to pray. Between sobs, her words were almost incoherent. But I managed to understand that she was saying she was sorry. Herleena, Vera, and Noelia followed suit, along with most of the girls.

They asked God to forgive them, and then they asked me the same. I was overwhelmed by this change in attitude, just when I thought I was done for. That moment turned into a pivotal point of change in my life and in theirs. I asked them to forgive me, and reconciliation was sweet. We had an understanding. That night was the beginning of redemption for many. I thanked God. I knew then that God had a plan for each and every one of those girls. I knew that 'His grace was sufficient for me; his strength was made perfect in my weakness.'[1]

I knew that everything was going to be all right.

My backache became severe. I really needed to see a doctor or at least get some physiotherapy, anything that would help relieve the pain. The medication I had was no longer helping, and I could hardly manage the steps. Although I had medical cover, there was a six-month waiting period before I was eligible, and the thought of those jerky, uncomfortable bus rides into Lima was more than I could bear.

The little exposure I'd had with the doctors in the local clinics was enough to put me off going there. I prayed and hoped to wake up feeling pain-free every morning, but it only seemed to get worse. Then Kari handed me a flyer, which she had received at school. It said an American medical missionary team was in San Juan de Lurigancho, and they were giving free treatment to anyone who needed it.

The next day I knew that I had to brave two buses

to get to the clinic where the American team was, but at least it wasn't as far away as Lima. The first person I saw was a registered nurse named Jan Daigle. She spoke softly, and she was listening carefully. Jan gave me some strong analgesics to take on the spot and told me to relax.

She was inquisitive and curious to know why I didn't get someone else to pull the cord on the generator. I told her about Eddy, and she asked more questions. The more she asked, the more the story unravelled and the more shocked she became. Then Jan called some other members of the team into the room, saying, 'You have to listen to this.' I had thought that she meant my symptoms, but she really meant the situation at CEDES. I found myself repeating a lot of what I had already spoken of until a sharp pain stabbed my back.

'What about my back?' I said, 'That's really why I'm here!' Jan gave me a good supply of strong medication; she then asked if the medical team could pay a visit to the refuge. I was delighted! I explained that the girls were on school holidays, so that would be amazing. When Jan mentioned that they had a drama team who could entertain the girls, I was speechless. The thought of a visit and getting help with the girls lifted my spirits immensely; my eyes welled up, but this time with tears of joy. We settled on a day that very week. I walked out of that clinic feeling so very encouraged, and for the first time in weeks, pain-free.

As soon as I returned to the house, I couldn't wait

to tell the girls. They had been so cooperative and helpful since that night of tears, and I was happy to have some good news. In anticipation of the American visitors and with great enthusiasm, the girls cleared away the plates and happily cleaned up the kitchen. Later I heard one saying to the other, 'Hello, how are you?' then, 'Good, thank you, and you?' They were cheerfully practising some English phrases. English was a struggle for most of the girls, with the exception of Kari; she was very smart and took a shine to the English language.

We were all elated to have something to look forward to; the girls never stopped talking about the upcoming visit. When the day finally arrived, their squeals of excitement echoed across the yard as Raisa and Yvett hollered out, 'Ya vienen, ya vienen (They're coming, they're coming).'

I went down to greet the team, and the girls helped to open the gate with all the younger ones trailing behind. The air was buzzing; lively clowns dressed in vibrant colours waved madly out the windows as the bus slowly drove into the grounds. We welcomed the visitors enthusiastically and helped them with helium balloons and large colourful puppets, and all sorts of equipment.

The girls led the team to the living room, where they set up their sound equipment, while I organised Karina and Ruby to help in the kitchen with preparing the popcorn and soft drinks the team had brought.

The show began. The girls were fully entertained by interesting mimes and slap-happy clowns, and we were having so much fun. We laughed and laughed – it was all so wonderful! I had to capture the moment and thought of my camera. I rushed to my room to get it, and instantly everything changed. To my shock, the camera was gone! The case was there, but it was empty. Immediately, I checked my laptop and found the same thing; just an empty case!

I sat on my bed puzzled at first, but then it hit me; someone had been in my room and been through my personal things. Suddenly, my whole world caved in. I thought about the few possessions I valued now gone, and a sharp, stabbing sensation returned to my back. The laughter and the happiness in the background faded, and my joy turned into misery. All I could do was weep.

I couldn't figure it out. No one apart from Pastor Luis had a key to my room, and he hadn't been to the house for some time. I tried to control myself and told myself, 'They're just material things; they can be replaced.' But the tears kept coming. Just then, in my peripheral vision, I caught sight of a figure standing at my doorway.

A clown with a painted smile stood there and softly asked, 'Are you OK?'

I was silent and cried into my hands, trying to cover my anguish; I couldn't speak. The clown approached. 'What's wrong?' he asked, trying to console me with an arm around my shoulder. I gazed up to observe the juxtaposed grin. Somehow, the bizarre absurdity of the serious expression behind the painted smile made me stop crying, and I was able to speak.

Just talking made me feel better. Especially in my own language. The girls had no inkling; they were in another reality where their spirits were high, and I didn't want to spoil it. I quickly composed myself and tried to put the incident behind me, at least for a time. The clown did his job well, and I returned to the laughter but with a heavy heart.

The "New Covenant Creation Ministry" team left behind an image of the God they served, and we were all so very much encouraged. We were sorry to see them go. But in fact, this visit initiated the beginning of a long and meaningful relationship between us over the ensuing years.

The next day I contacted Pastor Luis to inform him about the theft, and to my amazement, he came to the house straight away. He felt sure that the perpetrator was Eddy since he had given Eddy notice of termination just the previous week. It seemed that Eddy was the likely suspect to me too, but I really wasn't sure. Pastor Luis accompanied me to the police station to report the incident, and he encouraged me to name Eddy as the prime suspect. It was at that point that I became suspicious. I never saw my computer or my camera again, and Eddy left on a bitter note. I was very cautious with Pastor Luis from that day.

I felt very unsettled in the weeks that followed and

slept with the wooden chair leg close to my pillow. Pastor Luis must have sensed my uneasiness; he began to show concern about my back injury, something he had never done before, and he turned up at the house more frequently. On one occasion, he even brought some tools to repair a broken bed. Not fully convinced of his goodwill, I was suspicious of his motives. I suspected that he was trying to build some rapport before Greg's imminent arrival.

Good communication was almost impossible at the locutorio in The Porton, partly due to the boys on their computer games and partly because of the unreliable connection. The line often cut mid-conversation, leaving me high and dry on so many occasions. I decided to brave the two bus trips for the better locutorio.

I lived for that weekly call to hear Greg's voice at the end of the line with his encouraging words. Our conversations kept me afloat in the rapids of that raging river. Greg had often referred to himself as my logistical support person, but even in those early days, I knew he would become much more.

Initially, I only wanted to talk about the good things, about the breakthrough with the girls and the return of angelic singing, but then I began to share the scary bits: how upset I was when my personal space was invaded and my belongings went missing. I tried to hold back some of the unpleasant things because I didn't want to put Greg off, but I didn't want to be deceptive either. In the end, I found myself telling him everything. I blurted it all out in one big, ugly heap. I told him about the bathrooms with no doors and explained that he would probably lose all dignity in Peru. I described the reality of living in the "house that Jack built" and the overwhelming feeling of being very isolated. I also revealed the truth about the unreliable pastor who was a compulsive liar. The hardest thing to tell was how foolish I had been to loan money to the pastor. Greg responded with a long-drawn-out, 'Wow!'

After a few seconds of thoughtful silence, I affirmed, 'I wouldn't blame you if you didn't want to come. I seriously want you to think about all this, and over the next week to process it and reconsider your decision.'

Greg responded quickly, saying, 'I don't need to think about...'

I stopped him from speaking and urged him again, 'Just take the time to digest everything and reconsider with your eyes open so that you can make an informed decision.'

'OK', Greg said, 'but I am coming, and I will be telling you the same thing next week!'

Greg was both concerned and understanding; we ended our call by praying together, and I felt strengthened once again. Those calls were a lifeline to me.

Meanwhile, the situation between the pastor and me deteriorated. Our main mode of contact was by phone. There were so many problems, and Pastor Luis often shifted the blame for something he failed to do by insisting that he had instructed Manuela or Jahnique to do it. As a result, the girls and I were without the very basic needs such as water, electricity, and even food at times.

Because the pastor's visits were so random, and he never answered his phone, it was difficult to sort out the problem of school fees. At the end of term, the school, again, threatened to exclude the girls from exams until fees were paid. I approached the principal to explain and tried to negotiate, but he insisted that I pay not only the current debt but also the outstanding debt for the previous term too.

I asked Manuela to approach the pastor in his consulting rooms about the problem. He emphatically claimed that I had agreed to pay this bill, and again he claimed that my level of Spanish had caused some misunderstanding. The problem remained unresolved; another week passed without any contact from the pastor, and I refused to pay the fees. Consequently, the girls missed taking their exams again. They were upset, and I began to feel uncertain myself whether or not I had done the right thing. I felt guilty! Wednesday couldn't come around quick enough; I needed to talk to Greg. Finally, even before a 'Hello', Greg said, 'Nothing has changed; my answer is the same as last week; I'm still definitely coming.'

'Really, you're really coming!' I said in admiration. I was so glad and so relieved; I had had thoughts of catching the next plane home if he decided not to come. It was just wonderful news. I began to realise how determined Greg really was in his resolve both to follow Jesus and to come to Peru. His steadfastness is one of the many traits I love about him.

We talked about many things, including the school fees. Greg confirmed it was the right thing to do and suggested that if funds weren't covering basic needs, then perhaps the girls should be in a public school. Greg was logical in his approach to problem-solving and always came up with a solution.

In spite of being upset about lagging behind at school, the girls didn't complain. They were so different in their attitude towards me and couldn't do enough. They continually tried hard to get happy faces on the chart and to help out where ever they could. To make the goal of an evening out at Norky's more achievable, I lowered the benchmark.

Knowing that Greg's mind was made up to come to Peru, I began to prepare the girls for his arrival. In the evenings, I took the time to talk about him and gave the opportunity for the girls to ask any questions they might have. I showed photos of Greg and told them about his quiet character and thoughtful ways, and I explained that he didn't speak any Spanish. The girls were curious and asked lots of questions; they wanted to know how we met, when we were going to get married, if we were going to have babies, and lots more. They also wanted to know how to address him. Eventually, they decided on calling him "Broder Greg" (their English version of brother).

Some of the girls felt that they already knew Greg and were excited about him coming, but others were fearful and dreaded the thought of having a man in the house. Because of this, I felt that it would be better if Greg didn't stay at the house. I investigated the accommodations outside, but there was nothing close by. The makeshift shed where Eddy had lived had no plumbing and was almost collapsing, and was not an option. After some thought, I concluded that Greg could definitely not share the toilets and showers with the girls and me. There was no privacy whatsoever. Looking for a solution, I wondered about the storage shed outside. It was full of junk, but the small room stood independent of the main house and not too far away. The good thing was that apparently underneath all that garbage in the corner was a shower and a toilet. The storage shed was the only practical option where Greg could stay.

The girls helped me clear out all the broken furniture. I discovered that the plumbing wasn't connected, and there was no base to the shower. A crude pipe jutted out of the brick wall where the showerhead should have been, and the cracked toilet bowl with no toilet seat wasn't connected to anything.

I had a handyman fix the plumbing as well as insert

a curtain rail to provide an enclosure for the shower. The handyman also put a lock on the door and helped me to move a bed from the main house. When he re-assembled the bed inside the room, he found that the length of the bed was just a couple of inches less than the width of the room, whichever way he placed it. It was such a tight fit that it was very awkward to put the screws back in. The only way he could do it was to insert them from underneath, back to front. The final touches were the new Peruvian bedspread, the new shower curtain, and the curtain I made to hang over the window. The little shed looked so much better when the crack in the glass was covered. By the time we were done, it had started to shape up and look reasonably cosy.

By the end of the month, most of the girls managed to earn the prize of dining out. Many of the girls had never been taken out before and were extremely excited. As they got ready, they talked about what they were going to wear; some were anxious about how they looked and how to fix their hair, others worried about their shoes being old and daggy, while others were more concerned about whom they would sit next to and what they would eat.

Noelia lingered around the open doorway of my room as I was putting some make-up on. She seemed nervous, like she had something on her mind. Then sniffing deeply, she said, 'Hmmm, what's that beautiful smell?'

I still had the bottle in my hand. 'It's Chanel No.

5', I said as I motioned her over; I squirted some onto her neck. Slowly she breathed in the fragrance with great delight and then disappeared down the hallway. The next thing I knew, a bunch of very excited girls were crowding around my doorway asking if they could have some of that lovely smelly stuff too. With amusement, I sprayed one girl after the other, joking around about how they would have to fight off the boys; they all bubbled over with laughter, some with embarrassment but loving every minute.

This set the stage for a great night out and put everyone in good spirits. Channel No.5 is no ordinary perfume; it seems to have some magical effect on the psyche and always lifts the mood. Whenever we went out to dinner after that night, we always had the ceremonial squirt of my favourite perfume; the girls lined up so patiently, I think they loved it as much as I did.

That first night out with so many girls, I felt the need for a prep-talk. Clearly defining my expectations of conduct, I warned them that if they weren't on best behaviour, this would be their last night out. Partnering the girls with their buddies, I insisted that they show respect and courtesy to one another. I explained how dangerous the roads were at night and asked that they hold hands and not let go of the younger girls at any time.

We had a wonderful night out; the girls were no trouble at all. I was utterly amazed at their impeccable behaviour, especially getting on and off the busses; they stayed with their buddy the whole time, there was no pushing or shoving, and when they had a seat, they surrendered it for an adult. I noticed onlookers watching them get on the bus two by two in an orderly fashion; they seemed quite impressed. I was so proud of them.

Chapter Fourteen

SIN'S TRAGIC LEGACY

Journal Entry:
San Juan de Lurigancho, Peru
5th July 2005

> *The anticipation had been rising over the past week,*
> *and the day of Greg's arrival was an exciting one. The*
> *girls talked to him all at once. They just didn't get it*
> *that he couldn't speak Spanish. Greg was overwhelmed*
> *with all the unsolicited attention. He couldn't slip*
> *away, even to use the bathroom, without being*
> *followed. Out of sheer embarrassment, Greg found*
> *ways of communicating pretty fast. He was generally*
> *well accepted, but a small group of girls were shy and*
> *standoffish. They kept their distance.*

On the third of July, Greg finally arrived. The girls were overexcited and nervous at the same time. Each one introduced herself with a handshake and greeted Greg in English with the few phrases I had taught them. After their initial address, they kept talking to Greg in Spanish at a very rapid pace.

Greg was a little shell-shocked into silence at first because the girls bombarded him with questions all speaking at the same time. They would repeat their questions over and over until Greg made some attempt to give an answer. Although I helped to translate, Greg was quick to learn and he became very good with sign language to make himself understood.

The daylight seemed to fade early that evening. We hadn't used the generator for some time, but we had grown accustomed to the lamp light and even found it to be quite cosy. For Greg it was different. Not used to this realm of darkness, the sudden blindness was a nuisance and he stumbled around in the shadows; the stone steps being particularly difficult. It was all so unfamiliar to him.

In the dim candlelight, the girls cooked the evening meal as they had done since Eddy and Raisa had left. Greg asked me what kind of soup it was, but the dull light made it hard to distinguish so I shone my torch on his spoon as he was about to put it into his mouth.

We could hardly believe our eyes when we saw a wriggling cockroach squirming on it's back on his spoon. My stomach turned, and I groaned in revulsion, but he just quietly flicked it onto the floor and carried on eating.

'It's just protein', he said. That was Greg, no fuss!

Me, I just couldn't eat anymore and pushed my plate away.

The girls and I had grown to really enjoy our evenings together, talking, praying, and of course singing to our hearts' content. They were quality times of bonding and good feelings towards each other, and that night was no different. The girls had prepared a presentation for Greg with some special songs that they wanted to sing for him.

Greg had some notion that he could remain a little detached from the girls and just be logistical support around the house. That first night, however, he was somehow unwillingly drawn in, much more than he had expected or even wanted to be.

Perhaps it was the enthusiasm of the girls, their angelic voices, their sorrow, or the light that shone from their faces. I don't know. All I know is that he was deeply moved. I could see it in his eyes. Something much bigger was drawing all of us together during those times of singing; we had a deep mutual respect for each other. It was like we had one heart and one mind, and it was wholesome.

The following morning, I discovered that Greg had had a terrible night. In San Juan de Lurigancho the average rainfall is around one inch per year; it hardly ever rains. Ironically, it had rained during the night. The roof leaked and thoughtfully dripped on his pillow.

Greg told me that after a long struggle with the bed he gave up trying to move it. Instead he decided to top-and-tail. Then, just as he was about to drift off to sleep, he was startled by something landing heavily onto the flimsy tin roof. 'It sounded like a leopard noisily prowling around', he said.

'So I sat up in bed and lit a candle.' He continued, 'I saw the shadow of an enormous cat moving across the roof above me'.

I interjected before he could resume: 'Oh, that's *Puffy*, it's a huge feral cat that often comes looking for food; we feed it because it's good for keeping the rats at bay. Its long hair makes it appear bigger than it really is, that's why we named it *Puffy*'.

Greg laughed and went on to tell me of a vision he'd had. 'I imagined that my bed was a tiny raft floating in the dark abyss with uncertainty all around, but the warm glow of the candle was comforting and gave me hope'. He said, 'I was exhausted, I must have then dropped off to sleep'.

There were many irritations and frustrations for Greg; language was just one of them. With no percolated coffee to start the mornings, he was having withdrawals.

Fed porridge for breakfast and beans for dinner with no shops close by was his worst nightmare. Cold showers were a shock, but the biggest blow would have to be the bad news about Pastor Luis. There was something I had learned just before Greg's arrival, and I didn't know how to break it.

Journal Entry:
San Juan de Lurigancho, Peru
1st July 2005

Something horrible!

He lives a lie and commits sexual child abuse. I have seen their eyes weep bitterly and heard the secrets of their hearts laid bare. Their sense of worth battered to pieces; they cover their faces with shame. Their wounds seem incurable.

Just a couple of days before Greg's arrival, Manuela's phone rang. It was a call from the senior pastor, Arturo Ramos, from the Cathedral de Fe church asking for me. This was the first time I had ever heard from anyone from the church. He wanted me to attend an important meeting. At that meeting, I was given a copy of a letter from the church, addressed to Pastor Luis, and I was asked to read it. The letter said that Pastor Luis was under investigation because he had been accused of sexual abuse by one of the girls at CEDES.

I was shocked. I didn't know how to respond. Pastor Ramos explained that Pastor Luis had already received a copy of the letter. He advised me to take no action but to wait because it may be a false accusation. Initially, I didn't believe it! Pastor Luis had three daughters of his own. He was rarely at the house. How could I not be aware of it? How could it be true? I took Pastor

Arturo's advice and waited, knowing that Greg was soon to arrive.

I couldn't put it out of my mind, and while we were talking about the uncertainty, I told Greg the devastating news. He was speechless. We barely had time to discuss the matter when we heard the girls yelling, 'Pastor Luis, Pastor Luis.' A taxi was driving towards the main gate, the horn tooting; sure enough, it was Pastor Luis. Greg and I looked at each other wide-eyed. It was such an abnormal situation.

While walking towards the gate, Greg quickly muttered, 'Don't say anything. Just wait to see what he has to say.' I nodded, opened the bolt, and we dragged the door open. Introducing Pastor Luis to Greg, I could barely look him in the eye. He said nothing about the letter, his mood was cheerful, and his pseudo smile had a good workout. Either he didn't know that we knew anything about the letter, or he was indifferent.

I found interpreting very stressful from the start. The welcoming words, the over-confidence, and the pleasantries all seemed so false. Pastor Luis came across as ever-so-charming. He addressed nothing of importance. Instead, he made superficial conversation with Greg, asking the usual questions about his trip and his first impressions of Peru. It was as if everything was running smoothly. I had so many questions but asked none; I just observed very closely. After a short time, Pastor Luis looked at me and asked, 'Are you unwell? You look a little pale.'

'No, I'm just tired', I said. He then stood up and

excused himself, explaining assertively that he had business to attend to. Then he went. Once again, we were speechless as we watched his taxi drive off. As we hauled the gate closed, Greg and I looked at each other long and hard; it was the most bizarre feeling. All I could say was, 'Welcome to Peru!' We both apprehensively smiled. Really, we felt very much out of our depth.

Later that night, Greg and I discussed the situation more fully when the girls were all in bed. We didn't know which girl was involved nor how serious were the allegations, so we decided to wait until the end of the week, as Pastor Arturo had suggested. During that week, Manuela approached us and said that she needed to talk to us in private. She told us that Kari had confided in her about an incident where Pastor Luis had attempted to kiss her on the lips.

That evening we talked to Kari in private. When I explained that we needed to ask her a few questions about Pastor Luis, she was immediately afraid and unwilling to speak. Kari just stood silently, looking downward. She was uncomfortable, and her embarrassment was obvious. I spoke softly and explained, 'We don't want to judge you, Kari, or the pastor, but it's important to know the truth.'

Kari clammed up, reluctant to look us in the eye. She became inward-focused and said nothing. After waiting a few moments in reticence, Kari began to weep, and silent tears fell. I tried to comfort her by putting my arm around her shoulders and reassuringly said, 'Oh Kari, don't get upset. Go and think about it, and if you want to talk, we are here to listen.' She nodded and hurried out of the room.

Kari approached me after dinner the next evening and asked if she could speak with me, but without Greg. This time she opened up and confided in me. She explained that the pastor had tried to kiss her. I responded casually, 'Isn't that normal in Peru? We always kiss when greeting.'

Kari quickly exclaimed, 'It was not a normal kiss Hermana, it was on the lips, and he touched my breasts.' Covering her face with both hands, she began to cry. I tried not to be emotionally drawn in and waited for her to calm down. When she did, I asked, 'Where did this happen?'

'The first time it was at his office', she said, continuing to explain, 'the pastor had offered me a job doing office work and answering his phone.'

I clarified, 'So it happened more than once.'

'Yes', she said, looking down again.

'Where did it happen the next time?' I asked

'At CEDES', Kari answered with her eyes fixed on the floor.

'When was this?' I questioned.

She hesitated, and by the anxious look on her face I knew she had detected the doubt in my voice. With an air of hopelessness and a deep furrow between her eyes, she said, 'It happened before your arrival, Hermana, and when you came, it never happened again.'

I asked, 'Did Pastor Luis ever try to kiss any of the other girls?'

'I... (pause) Ask them; they know everything!' she exclaimed with a scowl. Kari obviously felt that I didn't believe her.

'Kari, I believe you. I'm just trying to find out more information', I responded.

'The other girls saw, ask them', she said insistently.

'Saw what, Kari?'

'I don't know', she responded nervously.

'You must know, Kari. It's OK, you can tell me.'

But it was as though her lips were sealed, and Kari remained silent. I ended the conversation there. Except I had one last question, 'Which other girls should I ask?'

Their story unfolds…

Half asleep, Meridian drags herself out of bed to go to the toilet. Her eyes adapt very quickly in the dark as she makes her way there. Excited whispers and giggles alert Meridian to the fact that something is going on. She hears Kari trying to hush the girls, 'Shhhh, shhhh!' But it's too late, Meridian's curiosity is aroused, and she strains her ears all the more. It's deadly quiet for a moment; then the stifled whispers begin again. Moving effortlessly, as though she could see in the dark, Meridian follows the sound.

She sees three older girls stooping down, leaning against the brick wall, and she realises that they are peering through a hole. 'What are they looking at?' she wonders. Herleena pushes Kari out of the way to look through the tiny gap between the bricks, but Kari pushes back, refusing to give way. Meridian is intrigued and approaches quietly and says, 'Let me see, let me see.'

Startled, Kari jumps to a standstill and instantly leans her back against the hole in the wall saying in a loud whisper, 'Go to bed, Meridian, you should be asleep.'

'Why are you whispering?' Meridian asks loudly.

Kari, almost in a panic, covers Meridian's mouth with her hand. 'Shhhhh! Be quiet!' she whispers frantically.

'Why?' Meridian muffles through Kari's fingers. Meridian is only half the size of Kari, but she's a feisty little girl.

'He might hear us', Kari responds as she grabs Meridian by the shoulders and guides her in the direction of the dorm. 'Back to bed, Meridian, you're too young for this', Kari says quietly but assertively.

Meanwhile, as they go, Herleena crouches down to look, and Amelia leans over her, hoping for a turn. Transfixed, Herleena's eyes widen. Open-mouthed, she begins to blush. Amelia successfully pushes her away to see what's going on. Amelia remains silent for a few seconds, and then she can't look anymore. The two girls stare at each other in complete silence, as if unable to process, then Amelia walks off whispering, 'I'm going to bed.' Herleena follows without saying a word.

Not sharing the same room, they go separate ways.

Each climb without a sound into their respective beds, but neither can sleep. Amelia stares at the ceiling pensively. Herleena tosses and turns, but neither of them wants to talk about it. It's too embarrassing!

We hadn't seen Pastor Luis since he first met Greg on arrival, and because we knew the girls were safe, we waited a few more days. But there was no phone call. We tried to contact Pastor Arturo on several occasions, but with no success, and felt sure that he was avoiding us.

In the meantime, some of the other girls had confided in us, and although they were very much entangled in this web of deception, Kari was the only one who was willing to testify against the pastor. Perhaps because Kari had escaped his attempts to seduce her, she felt strong enough to speak about his advances and was willing to make an official denuncio (police report).

Karina and Ruby were less fortunate. Pastor Luis had convinced them that he loved them and that his actions were an expression of his love. In their thinking, he was the only person who really loved them and cared for them. He was the one they depended on, and they just couldn't betray him. They were totally mixed up about his affection towards them.

After speaking with the girls, we knew with certainty that Pastor Luis was guilty. It was an impossible situation, but we suspected that he might be planning to exit the country and knew we had to take action. Manuela counselled Karina and Ruby, but they fully believed the lies fed to them by Pastor Luis. I tried to support them while at the same time agreeing with all that Manuela had said in regard to the wrong that the pastor had done by them. They just didn't want to hear anything bad that was said about the pastor. They couldn't bear to think that he didn't really love them. He had filled their heads with lies and false hopes, and now they were left confused and thinking that we were lying. They remained loyal to the pastor even to the point of ganging up on Kari to persuade her not to take action against him.

On 10 August 2005, Greg and I assisted Kari to write a statement, and with Manuela we accompanied her to the closest comissaria (police station). A young man, Detective Hanalocca Moreno (whose nickname was Mono Loco), was very keen to hear Kari's story, the reason being that he had already received a statement from another girl, Dolores, a 15-year-old. This girl, who had once been a resident at CEDES, was claiming that Pastor Luis had sexually abused her while she was there. The detective informed us that an investigation had been underway for some time. We asked if the Cathedral de Fe had instigated this investigation, but he knew nothing about Cathedral de Fe.

Talking with the detective about the events was bad enough for Kari, but even though she insisted that the pastor had only kissed and touched her, it was necessary to undergo an internal medical examination. Kari, not prepared for this psychologically, needed time and flatly refused. Manuela tried to persuade her, insisting that without her cooperation, the case was weak. Eventually, Kari agreed that she would at least think about it.

After a sleepless night, Kari agreed to have the examination and, not wanting to risk her changing her mind, that same morning, instead of sending her to school, we took her to the medico legista (legal doctor). The other girls in the house were unsettled when Kari didn't go to school that day, especially Karina and Ruby. They started to spread malicious gossip about Kari.

The unease between the girls at the house worsened, and the younger girls, who knew very little, heard whispers and rumours. The tension soared when Kari found out that Karina and Ruby had phoned Pastor Luis on their way home from school. She found that they had warned him and reported everything they knew to him. Kari became anxious when she knew that they had told Pastor Luis about her going to the police.

We gathered the girls together to have a meeting. We reassured them that Kari had not done anything wrong, while at the same time, we were very careful not to say anything negative about the pastor. We made the point that if he was innocent, he had nothing to worry about.

After a week or so, Greg and I contacted Mono Loco because nothing seemed to be happening. He explained that he was waiting for the pastor to go to CEDES, because under Peruvian law, it was essential that he was arrested on the premises where the abuse took place. The detective tried to persuade us to help him by making a call to the pastor and luring him to visit CEDES. He would then make his arrest as soon as we informed him of the details. Greg and I were reluctant to do this in case there might be some kind of serious retribution, so we refused.

The days passed long and slow until early on Tuesday morning when we received a phone call from Jahnique on her day off. Pastor Luis had just called her to tell her that he was on his way to CEDES to have a meeting with all the staff, and he wanted her to be there. We thanked Jahnique and explained we would contact the police and that it was not necessary for her to come. Jahnique breathed a sigh of relief, 'Gracias Hermana - Vaya con Dios', (Thank you – God Bless), she said; she seemed glad not to be a part of the plot. Instantly, we rang Mono Loco, who told us to wait for the pastor. 'Stay calm, and act normal', he said.

Most of the girls were at school, but there were a handful of girls still at the house, one of them being Kari. When I informed them that the pastor was on his way, Kari took a sharp intake of breath and began to groan in absolute dread. The others noticed her anxiety, which transmitted to them, causing them to be fearful too. Kari was by then pacing around in circles of panic. I told her that everything would be all right and that she could stay in her room if she wanted to. I then gave instructions to all of the remaining girls to go to their rooms once the pastor arrived and to stay there until he left. They were so jittery that they instantly scattered and hid away in their rooms. The girls remained there the whole time, peering out of their windows. The anticipation was extremely stressful for all of us.

A taxi approached, tooting its horn as usual. Greg went to open the gate, but I was too nervous and stayed in the dining room. I was surprised to see that Pilar was with Pastor Luis. She had never come with him before. Her expression was serious, with a deep frown on her forehead and a vague unfriendly look in her eyes. Pastor Luis wore his frozen smile with confidence and greeted me as normal with a kiss. I stiffened when he touched me; it was impossible to "act normal". The pallor in my face gave me away once again.

'Are you ill?' the pastor asked.

'No, no, I'm just not one-hundred per cent', I replied.

'We really cannot continue fighting with each other, Bridget', he said almost sympathetically. Then he began talking about our working relationship; he went on and on about how difficult I had been, and he began to scold me and tell me that I lacked accountability. I just sat there listening in absolute bewilderment. Both Greg and I sat in a daze, hardly knowing what to say as we quietly listened to his bizarre reprimand.

Within minutes, two intimidating, dark figures with balaclavas (full-face masks) aggressively burst into the dining room. I jumped with fright; for an instant, I thought that they were the pastor's "hit-men" who had come to rough us up. Then, looming over the pastor, stood a man at each side of him. One of them spoke assertively and asked, 'Senor Luis Alberto Guizada Diaz?'

'I am he', the pastor responded indignantly.

Immediately, each man grasped an arm and pulled him up to his feet. 'Come with us, sir', the masked men demanded.

Pastor Luis, as if detached from the enormity of what was happening, calmly said, 'There must be some mistake', and he didn't move. The men then roughly began to drag him towards the door, and he stumbled. Without stopping, one of the men grabbed the back of his pants and yanked him to his feet, forcefully continuing to haul him out the door.

Pilar was flustered, her eyes wide with shock as she rushed after them. I will never forget the stunned look on her face as she glanced over her shoulder in expectation of us following. It was distressing. She was absolutely horrified; she desperately said, 'Come on, we must help him.' Greg and I remained glued to our seats, still trying to process what had just happened.

We just gazed at each other for a moment, lost for words. Somewhat relieved to see the back of Pastor Luis, we went over to look out the window. We saw him, suspended by his arms, feet dragging along the dusty ground, being sprinted across the yard, past the taxi driver and outside the gate, then bungled into an undercover police vehicle. The car sped off, leaving a huge dust cloud. Pilar, trailing behind them, entered the taxi and disappeared into the haze of dust in hot pursuit.

The following day when both Manuela and Jahnique arrived, we didn't need to inform them of what had happened: they informed us. Apparently, the front page of the newspapers had a photo of Pastor Luis with the headline, "The Face of a Child Molester". The story, given regular updates every hour, was the spotlight on national television too. The ears of those who heard it tingled. This predominately Catholic country revelled in the sensationalism of an evangelical pastor turned bad.

I felt sorry for Pilar and her three children. They would have heard and read all kinds of merciless accusations made about their husband and father; accusations that he was involved in extortion and fraud, that he was a liar and a psychopath, and that there were as many as six children abused by him.

In one sense, not having electricity at the house was a good thing. We didn't have any exposure to the news on television, and this meant that the girls were sheltered from all the bad publicity.

Over the next few days, Jahnique, Manuela, or I gathered the girls to debrief them before they went to school. Manuela had explained about the pastor's arrest and that an investigation was underway. We tried to clarify any confusion and answer the many questions they had, and we tried to prepare them with answers for their peers as well as the teachers.

Most of the girls were anxious about the arrest; some were relieved, and Kari expressed that she was glad. Karina and Ruby cried. They couldn't believe what was happening to their beloved pastor. We tried to reassure them that everything would be all right; if the pastor were innocent, he would go free. We asked all the girls not to talk too much about it at school, and we reassured them that the house would continue *as normal*. In reality, nothing was *normal*. The future was very uncertain, but we couldn't tell them that.

Around lunchtime one afternoon, after Manuela had left, a van arrived with the logo "TV Peru" on the side. No horns tooting, the van very quietly parked just outside the makeshift fencing. Two people walked around to the small side gate with the bell.

Greg, Jahnique, and I quickly discussed our strategy, Greg affirming that we must be careful and preferably not speak to the press before getting legal advice. We agreed. The last thing we wanted was to face litigation from the accused.

Jahnique and I went to the gate, and Greg followed. A young woman with no sign of a camera asked for me by name. She then asked permission to come inside and film the children to confirm that they were safe. I politely refused, saying, 'No, that's not possible as we have to consider the privacy of the children.'

She asked if she could film the premises, but no

sooner than I said, 'No', she quickly responded, 'Do you have something to hide?'

'Of course not', I said, 'but I would prefer to seek legal advice before being filmed.'

'Can I ask you a few questions *off the record*?' she asked. I saw no harm and agreed. Her first question was, 'How do you know the pastor.' I told her briefly about my first visit to Peru, how my pastor in Ecuador had given my phone number to Pastor Luis, and how he contacted me asking for help.

'Why did you come here?' she asked.

'I came as a volunteer missionary worker to look after the girls', I responded. The young woman went on and on with so many questions. Eventually, I decided that standing at the gate wasn't the appropriate place. I explained exactly that, but she was very persistent. After answering a few more questions, I ended the conversation. She conceded and left.

Although we couldn't watch the news ourselves, Jahnique kept us updated with each new broadcast. A few days later, I was shocked when she told us that she saw Greg and me on national television. We were on Channel 13's television show "Link with Hilderbrant". The popular journalist, César Hilderbrant, talked about the arrest and showed footage of Greg and me arriving in a police vehicle at the station just after the arrest. Jahnique said Luiz Guizada was sitting in handcuffs in the background, looking very forlorn with Pilar next to him. Jahnique had also seen herself on TV in the filming of our conversation at the gate when the van from *TV Peru* came. Apparently, the young woman had had a hidden lapel camera, and it was rolling from the moment the gate was opened.

During the frenzy of the media, we had a visit from the Fiscalia de la Nacion (National Prosecutor), whose role it is to defend the law and human rights. Firstly, their investigation of CEDES had already begun with the public registry, where they had found that the refuge had not been registered or accredited. Secondly, they interrogated Greg and me separately, and then they interviewed each of the girls individually, and both Jahnique and Manuela.

The fiscalia informed us that the refuge would be closed and that all the girls would be "farmed out" to other NGOs. The thought of the girls being separated was heart-breaking, and we asked if there was any possibility that we could start the process of accreditation. The fiscalia was very helpful. He told us that we would need to create an association of our own and that the process was complicated. He explained that the first steps would be to get a good lawyer, to contact MIMDES (Ministry of Women's Health), and to obtain approval from INABIF (Department of Children's Services). He also said we would have to demonstrate that we could cover the cost of running the refuge.

Just a day after the fiscalia's visit, Manuela, emotionally drained by the whole saga, didn't want to be associated with the casa anymore. She gave short notice and left by the end of the week.

A daunting task lay before us, and all we really understood was that we needed a good lawyer. How to find one was another thing. Amazingly, after watching the Hilderbrant report, a doctor named Ruth Albarado contacted us. Ruth was the lawyer (doctor of law) who represented the other girl, Dolores, who had testified against Luiz Guizada. Ruth was also the founder of a refuge named *Hogar Agape,* and she was well familiar with the process of accreditation with both INABIF and MIMDES.

We will always be indebted to Ruth; she was kind and patient, and without her help, we would never have known what to do. Although she had a busy schedule, Ruth organised and even accompanied us on our first interview with the officials. There is no doubt in my mind that it was her good reputation with MIMDES and her influence when she spoke on our behalf that compelled the officials to give us a chance.

The decision to close the refuge was revoked, and we were given six months to present our case and obtain accreditation. Ruth introduced us to Rocio Acosta Leon, another lawyer whom she highly recommended. Rocio was of immense help to us with the ongoing legal issues and the plague of red tape.

The following surreal weeks revealed an amazing contrast in the different reactions of the people around us. La Comunidad (the Leaders of the Community) paid us a visit. They came to offer us possession of the property and the land on which the refuge stood. Apparently, land purchased by anyone in the community could be repossessed in the case of improper behaviour and either resold or freely given for the good of the community. No one in the community actually owned their property, but rather they had "possession" of it. We accepted the offer, and the Comunidad transferred the land into our possession completely free of charge; they even covered the transfer fee to have the legal papers drawn up.

On the other hand, the locals met together, and it was suggested that they should tear down the refuge brick by brick! Total strangers approached us in The Porton to inquire if we were the people they saw on TV. Their attitude, more accusatory than inquisitive, made us nervous, but with no other Gringos in the vicinity, we could hardly deny it was us. They asked lots of questions and seemed suspicious when we weren't forthcoming, but it wasn't something we wanted to talk about in the street with unfamiliar people. Later, we learned that when the locals had gathered to talk about the "ugly" incident at the refuge, some suspected that Greg and I were involved and wanted to take the matter into their own hands. When we heard about this, Greg and I half expected to be "stoned", and we wondered if we should buy a one-way ticket home before it was too late.

In a wave of roller-coaster emotions, our faith was tested, and our flesh seemed weak, but we knew in our hearts that we couldn't abandon the girls. The bonds between us were strong. We prayed and reflected on God's promises that He would be with us; he would never leave us nor forsake us. We reflected on how God establishes a spiritual bond between Himself and all of His children, the kind of bond that can't be broken. And then God gave us an encouraging scripture, Revelation 3:8: 'I know your deeds. See, I have placed before you an open door that no one can shut. I know that you have little strength, yet you have kept my word and have not denied my name.' Greg and I were no longer afraid but instead found strength and experienced new courage to stay and fight the battle. We knew it wasn't just a battle against people and bureaucracy.

The locals continued to keep a close eye on us, but contrary to our expectations, the idea of two Australians coming halfway around the world to help some needy kids and then to find themselves caught in a maelstrom of difficulties had somehow caught the imagination of many people. Lawyers, social workers, and other organisations rallied around us to give their assistance. Even the military contacted us to donate desks and chairs for the children.

We struggled to write about the bad news to our home church; it was not pleasant reading, but we had no choice. We wrote as best we could about the situation and about how the scripture given to us had inspired us to pick up the pieces and persevere. As a result, our pastors and the church were right behind us, encouraging us that we would have their full support.

At the casa, our focus was to provide the girls with a

safe environment where they could grow and learn to trust once again. Settling the girls down emotionally was our top priority, but there were so many needs. Providing stability was just the beginning.

In order to cut all connections with CEDES and the negative media that went with it, we changed the name of the refuge to Hope House. Our new association was to be called by the same name. However, the bad media about the infamous Luis Guizada left its mark; all donations from the United States were cancelled immediately. (Not that they ever managed to get past Luis Guizada's personal bank account in the first place). Apart from the Central Coast in Australia, we had no other support. The monthly check from the House of Praise Christian Church, combined with individual supporters, became our lifeline and, for a while, kept us afloat.

Greg and I tried to regain the support once received from the United Methodist Church in the U.S., but having been deceived by the ex-pastor who pocketed their cheques, they could not stand to be associated with CEDES any longer. We kept trying to raise funds with new donors, including Rotary International Peru, but we had little success, and our freedom was limited due to inadequate staffing.

We had to make some difficult decisions. Pulling the girls out of the private school was the first, but we knew it was necessary. We talked to the girls about public school, and they understood the situation; they cooperated happily. The toughest thing for them was the ridicule they faced when they had to wear their old school uniform to the new school. Still, they never complained; they were just thankful to be going to any school at all.

For months, we strived only to make ends meet, but even the basic needs were hard to manage when donations were low. We approached the Cathedral de Fe church for help, but they virtually slammed the door in our faces, totally ignoring our plea and the needs of the girls. Instead, they chose to protect themselves by staying in the shadows and pretending we didn't exist.

With insufficient funds, we were no longer able to pay wages to Jahnique. She worked hard on a voluntary basis for a while, but eventually, she had to leave for paid employment.

With just Greg and I left, the workload became stressful, and the situation seemed bleak. There was nothing in our former professional training or life experiences that could have prepared us for this situation.

The monthly cheque from Australia barely covered the cost of food and water, let alone the legal cost of accreditation. Often, we ran out of money well before the end of the month, and then we used our own personal funds, but even that didn't cover all the costs. Sometimes we had nothing!

In desperate times, we never knew if we could put food on the table for the next meal. It was one thing to go without food for ourselves, but to see the children go without was extremely difficult. But the girls never complained. They were an inspiration to us. Accustomed to having nothing, they improvised and somehow managed to make much out of little. Milk was diluted with water and salt used instead of sugar on the porridge. The girls were resilient, and with creativity, they kept the hunger at bay.

During those times, we discovered that having nothing was a prerequisite for the miraculous. When we had used up the last of the rice, and there was absolutely nothing left to cook for the evening meal, at the eleventh hour, with all our options exhausted and the cupboards completely bare, a miracle happened.

It was late in the day, well after dinnertime, on the cusp of growing dark. Greg and I were lighting the kerosene lamps, knowing that the girls would go to bed hungry; we looked at each other and felt dismal. Suddenly, we heard a tooting horn outside. It was a van on the other side of our gate. It had 'PRONA' written on the side of the van. We had no idea who or what PRONA was, but the girls became excited and shouted repeatedly, 'It's PRONA, it's PRONA', as the tooting continued.

We went to the gate and approached the driver, who explained that PRONA was the Proyecto Nacionál de Alimentación (National Food Program) and that they had a delivery for Hope House. They were a government program designed to eradicate hunger in Peru. Three men unloaded two 50 kg sacks of frijoles (black-eyed beans), one sack of rice, six litres of oil, and a sack of sugar. We signed the paperwork, and they told us that they would bring the same delivery every second month. It was dark and late by the time we had a meal on the table, but we didn't go to bed hungry that night, and we all gave thanks to our God. We were so, so very grateful.

Every day for months, the girls boiled the frijoles with rice for lunch, they made tacu tacu (frijoles burgers) for dinner, and they fried the leftover frijoles for breakfast. We had frijoles coming out of our ears. And no one complained. We did, however, look forward to when the funds from Australia arrived once a month when we splurged on chicken and were able to purchase some eggs. Before the money ran out, we made sure we purchased condiments and red-hot chillies to enhance the flavour of the very bland frijoles. Determined not to be disheartened, we prayed together, and we trusted, even when it seemed like there was nothing on the horizon.

Although the financial struggle continued, we had a good rapport with the girls, and they really did pull together during those difficult times. They just wanted someone to listen to them, to play volleyball with them, and help with their homework. Greg and I did what we could, and the girls knew that we cared, and that was enough for them. Actually, Greg and I didn't do much – just being there was sufficient. The girls felt accepted, they felt loved, and they were happy!

Laughter came to reside in the house, and the invisible wounds in their hearts began to heal. The girls began to share their deepest thoughts, dreams, and feelings with us with no fear of rejection. They grew in self-esteem and became emotionally stable. Everything broken in CEDES was slowly being restored in the safe haven of Hope House.

On Sundays, we didn't have the bus fares to go to church, so we created our own service in the living room. We had tambourines, a triangle, and some shakers (donated) as well as our harmonious voices, and we openly worshipped our God with all that was within us. We each participated in uninhibited prayer, and God showed up every time. It was glorious! We were very, very content.

After our Sunday service, since we couldn't afford to go anywhere, we developed a habit of taking the girls hiking in the nearby foothills of the Andes. Most of the girls grew to love our trekking adventures because Greg made them so dynamic. In anticipation of this, each Saturday, we would plan for the big day out by cooking a double portion of the usual frijoles and rice as well as boiling the drinking water. Each girl carried her own portion of food and water. Having water with us meant that we were able to set off earlier and stay longer.

These memorable treks became something we all would look forward to. With Greg leading the way, there was a sense of excitement and freedom. Greg took us much farther up the mountains than I had ever dared to go. The parched, dusty terrain showed little signs of life apart from the tiny lizards and the odd scorpion; they somehow were able to survive up there. Once past the mist, we came across unusual, breath-taking landforms. We also found tall vertical rocks placed in circles, ancient hieroglyphics etched into large boulders, and even some ruins with broken pottery and other relics strewn around.

TREKKING ADVENTURES IN THE LOCAL HILLS

Having crossed various dry river beds littered with scorched white snail shells, we made the most curious find—a human skeleton with a small backpack lying next to it. All the way home, we engaged in deep conversations, debating the endless possibilities of what may have happened to the poor soul.

On one occasion, just a couple of hours into the trek, Veronica, the leader of the pack that day, discovered some concrete steps. It was most unusual to see anything but dirt, rocks, and ancient ruins in those hills. We all followed a very excited girl all the way up to the top of the steps on a steep section of the mountain. There, perched at the very top, was a construction site. The unfinished building had an inscription, which read Santo Domingo de Guzman University. The girls were excitedly running around investigating the site, then Veronica, still very excited, headed down the rough, concrete steps. As she ran, her little legs couldn't keep up with the momentum she gained on the steep slope. Inevitably, she fell, tumbling head over heels down the hard steps, and her body just kept on rolling. We all looked on in horror! When her body reached a final halt, she screamed and screamed so loudly. I was a distance away from her and was so relieved to hear her screams; I knew she was alive. When I finally got to her, the deep gash in her shin was down to the bone. On examination, I could tell that the bone wasn't broken; she was fortunate; she could have had multiple fractures.

I had my first aid kit (as always). I was able to patch

her up by applying antiseptic powder to the gaping wound and binding it together with a bandage, which at least kept the dust out. Although Veronica was in a lot of pain, with a little encouragement and an arm around the shoulder of a girl on each side, she managed to hop all the way down that mountain. The girls were very helpful, they all rotated in turn to bear the load, and they didn't complain. We made the slowest descent ever and then split up at the bottom. Herleena took most of the girls to the casa while Greg and I took Veronica to the hospital. We spent numerous hours yet again waiting in various lines in the emergency department; while waiting, I purchased my very own stitch remover to avoid the same wait all over again in ten days! Veronica ended up having fifteen stitches.

Chapter Fifteen

BEHOLD A NEW THING

Journal Entry:
San Juan de Lurigancho, Peru
10th December 2005

The struggle to keep food on the table remains. We are experiencing shortfalls in many areas, and for now, we are carrying the load. Life in Peru is one big battle. Even getting married is a complex procedure fraught with red tape. The legal component is excessive, but the actual reception and catering is only a tenth of what an Australian wedding might cost.

Even so, our finances are hard-pressed and we don't know how we're going to get some dresses for the girls. It's looking bleak, maybe they won't be coming; that's if we ever get to the end of the paper chase.

L ife went on, but it seemed like we were adrift in a leaky boat, never having time to repair the hole, only to bail out the water before we sank.

Financially, nothing changed; we continued to live by faith, and we saw God's hand move in amazing ways.

I was kept busy managing the daily challenges of the girls, supervising in the kitchen, attending parent-teacher interviews, sewing and giving English lessons, making trips to the markets, and a ton of other things.

Greg's time was equally filled, constructing an incinerator pit, a chicken coop, a new vegetable garden, a watering system (using grey water), and more.

He became Mr. Fix-it, repairer of beds and tables and leaking toilets.

He moved the generator out of the kitchen, and when he discovered Dengue in the water tank, he cleaned it out. He even custom-made a lid for the tank that kept the mosquitos out.

Truly, there was no end to the hard work he did to make the refuge safe.

Together, Greg and I often took the older girls to the markets while the others were at school.

One time we bought half a dozen chicks only a few days old, and in no time, they seemed to be laying eggs for us.

GREG WORKING ON THE WATER TANK

Even so, the rude awakenings continued to happen. One morning, a loud thud followed by some serious screaming and crying woke me up. Eliza had fallen backwards from the top bunk and split her head open. She needed stitches and remained in hospital overnight with a concussion. The suture remover I had purchased was invaluable; I sterilized it by boiling it and using it over and over again.

Meanwhile, Rocio ploughed through the legal nightmare of setting up a new asociación and of acreditación with MIMDES and INABIF.

The changes at Hope House and in the lives of the girls were evident to all. Even the social workers from INABIF, when they brought new girls to the house, spoke highly of our home.

One day without announcement, a supervisor from INABIF came to us to tell me about the 14-year-old girl she had brought with her. She explained that the girl, called Zoila, was the estranged half-sister of Kari. They hardly knew each other, as they had only lived together in the very early years of their lives. Zoila had attempted suicide on several occasions. The supervisor felt that the connection with Kari and the positive environment at Hope House might give Zoila the will to live.

Zoila was not on any medications, and she was able to look me in the eye, so I knew I could work with her. I discovered very quickly that Zoila had no boundaries. She was unruly, and she was used to getting her own way.

I took great pains to help her settle down and show her that I cared about her, but Zoila just wasn't a happy young lady; she made life difficult for herself and everyone around her. She didn't like getting up early, she didn't like doing her chores, and she didn't like cold showers. Neither did any of us, but we complied, and I knew she was capable of doing the same.

The smiley faces on the chart meant nothing to Zoila until the day I handed out bars of chocolate for rewards. When she didn't get one, she became angry and threatening. Zoila, a master in manipulation, threatened to kill herself and then somehow climbed up on the three-storey roof to jump off. I knew she didn't want to jump. She just wanted a chocolate bar. I was relentless in following through on natural consequences, which she well knew, and told her, 'Broken bones can be quite painful, glad they're yours and not mine', then I walked away and ignored her.

Another time in the kitchen, when Zoila grabbed a butter knife and threatened to slash her wrist, I told her she would need a sharper knife and motioned to hand her one. She knew her threat was powerless and declined. In time, she observed how the rest of the girls, even Kari, seemed to be happy. After some painful confrontation and missing out on all sorts of privileges, Zoila eventually decided to give in. The first time she picked up a mop, we all cheered and gave her much appraisal, and she found that she liked it. She discovered that she felt much better about herself. In the end, Zoila learned to own her actions and to be responsible. She became a great help in mentoring the new girls.

Olivia, another girl who lacked confidence and self-esteem, was so terribly shy that she could barely open her mouth to speak. Her sad face never smiled, and she wore a constant frown. She was a silent presence around the house who didn't join in any of the activities but instead stood silently watching everything. Day after day, Olivia stood on the sideline watching us play volleyball, until one day Zoila stopped playing and stood on the side with her. After a few days of repeating this, Zoila had the ball on the court and simply motioned to throw it to Olivia on the side. After a pause, she threw the ball, and Olivia actually caught it. With minimal persuasion, Olivia then joined us. This was a first for her, but Olivia soon discovered that she was good at volleyball. As a result, she grew in popularity. Gradually she began to blurt out a word or two on the court, and eventually, not only her voice but also her laughter filled the house. Her whole countenance changed, and she began to bloom. Her transformation resembled that of a tiny bud slowly revealing its petals and growing into a beautiful flower, one that had the most amazing colours.

Given time, nearly all the girls responded well, and love was always the main ingredient. The lack of material resources truly had no bearing on what really mattered to these girls. Greg and I were learning from the girls that a "sense of belonging" was the most important thing to them. We learned that to be loved, to have mutual respect, sharing life, and just being there for each other were the most valued of all things, the things that money cannot buy.

The end of the year was fast approaching, and to accomplish the legalization of the refuge in the period given was going to be difficult, as there were still lots of matters to deal with. There were policies to be read, public registration compliances to be met, civil defence regulations to comply with, as well as MIMDES and fire safety requirements. We were sinking in a mound of paperwork. On top of this, and justifiably so, our home church decided that it would not be a good idea to become the association in control of Hope House. They did not want to take on the responsibility of a refuge from so far away, so they advised us to find a Peruvian group that might already have an established association of their own.

After an extensive search, the Christian and Missionary Alliance Peru (CMAP) church came to our rescue. They offered to support us not only with the umbrella of their association but also with their help to form a multidisciplinary team of Peruvian professionals to help us at Hope House. They had many good ideas regarding fundraising, and they were willing to assist us in meeting the necessary ongoing needs of the girls. We felt the weight of responsibility lifted from our shoulders and became confident that with their help, we could meet the new challenges that lay ahead.

When the CMAP church discovered that their association would need to go through accreditation with MIMDES, they requested that we hand the property and all the buildings over to their association. We were happy to do this, and our home church gladly agreed, so we began the process of legal transfer. Our subsequent weekly meetings confirmed that they would cover the legal fees involved and half the cost of the transfer fee. However, at the actual time of the transfer, the association of the CMAP church was temporarily unable to meet the costs, and they asked us to loan them the money. Greg and I drew up a contract to loan the money, and we paid their portion out of our own pockets.

The weeks passed, but our financial struggle continued. None of the fundraising ideas were followed through on by the CMAP church's association, and, in reality, nothing much changed. We were still struggling to keep afloat financially. Although we tried to remain hopeful, the demands from the CMAP church only seemed to increase. We were required to bring the children to attend church services every Sunday morning in Lima. That meant the gruelling trip on three buses each way. Apart from bus fares to church, the association had not yet provided assistance with anything else. We were expected to create individual care plans, document all our activities and interactions with the girls, and provide receipts for all our purchases, including small items. The promise of help with a team of staff never eventuated, and with no other staff, the workload only became greater. Greg and I could never have a day off, and we felt that their demands were unrealistic.

We had interludes of sanity whenever the short-term mission groups came with New Covenant Creation Ministries from the United States. I began to recognise familiar faces like Jan and Richard Dagle, Laura Reynolds, Don and Joy Norris, and Cath Davies, as they were the ones who came most often; they grew to love the girls as much as we grew to love them. The drama team entertained the girls, and we had a wonderful break. Their visits were medicine to the soul every time! They lifted our spirits and enabled us to escape the reality of our struggles, even just for a short time. They also brought with them a medical team, and in the space of three hours, eyes were checked, teeth pulled, and general health examinations were given by a very efficient team of professionals.

The arrest of Luis Guizada was known even in the United States, and the teams were very empathetic towards us. Pastor Bruce Carter brought with him a significant donation collected from his congregation, especially for Hope House after they had heard the news of the arrest. He also hired a bus and invited all of us out to dinner at Norky's. The girls, Greg, and I were so happy to be invited to share a meal with the team. The excitement on the bus was high as the girls joyfully sang non-stop, all the way there and all the way back. They talked about those visits for a long time afterwards.

The one-off donation helped to fill the kitchen cupboards with food as well as treats, and it provided for many of the immediate needs. It was truly a reprieve, but in truth, we knew that we would soon begin to struggle with the ongoing day-to-day costs. Greg and I shared this difficulty with Pastor Bruce, and we spoke about the demands of the CMAP church. Before he left, we prayed together about the situation. We felt hopeful and encouraged by his prayers and his promise to help us in any way he could.

In the meantime, we did finally get some help from the CMAP church. Fiorella, a voluntary worker, Fiory for short, was sent to us to fill the role of tutor. Fiory played the guitar and enjoyed singing with the girls; she also seemed to handle them firmly, so she fitted in well. Her arrival came as such a relief for me because until then, our rule to never leave girls alone in male-only company meant that I could never go anywhere without taking all the girls with me. With Fiory on board, I could go out, and Greg and I could actually take some time off together. It was heaven!

With some breathing space, Greg and I began to think about our wedding. The date we had in mind was Valentine's Day 2006. On our first day off, we went to book with our minister at the CMAP church. He explained that we must have a civil wedding before we could have a church wedding. On further enquiries, the marathon of forms and other requirements made it look impossible to complete in time for that date.

Providing the correct documentation for the civil marriage was horrendous. Our passports weren't sufficient identification; we were required to have birth certificates too, and copies wouldn't do; only originals were accepted. In my case, I had to write to Ireland for my original birth certificate, and because my passport was Australian, I had to provide a certificate of citizenship. Not something I had thought to bring.

Once gathered, all the original documents had to be translated into Spanish by a specific government translator, and then they had to be photocopied, stamped, and signed by the Australian Consul himself.

After that, the documents had to be legalised by a notario (justice of the peace), and the Australian consulate had to provide a certificado de soltero (certificate of being single) for each of us. Even though we had already provided our certificate of decree nisi (divorce), we still needed to prove that there was no impediment to our marrying. That meant placing an announcement of our wedding in the daily newspaper as a seven-day-old clipping from the paper needed to be attached to all the forms.

After that, we both had to attend a medical examination at a specific government hospital and pass it. Finally, we were required to attend two sessions of prenuptial workshops, which were compulsory. They were also very amusing. Then, bingo, we were ready!

Once the date was booked with our minister and locked in with the civil authorities, we asked Fiory if she could look after the house while we took a week off for our honeymoon. Fiory agreed, and then we booked a trip to Aruba. When we announced to the girls that our wedding date was set for 14 February 2006, they were very excited, but when they realised it would be a formal wedding, they were mortified. The thought of attending in their jeans and flip-flops was a huge disappointment. I tried to assure them that it didn't matter what they wore, so long as it was clean, but they were not convinced. We really wanted the girls at our wedding no matter what they wore, but they didn't feel the same; they didn't feel good about wearing old jeans and faded T-shirts to a wedding. The problem was, there were insufficient funds to purchase dresses for all the girls. It wasn't looking good.

The next day, in our early morning devotional, the girls prayed fervently that they would be able to attend the wedding and that God would provide some decent clothes to wear. Greg and I felt awful, but the costly paper trail of documents left us with insufficient funds, and we were unable to cover the cost.

The wedding day was fast approaching, and the girls were down in the mouth about attending in their old clothes. It was just before Christmas, and we had an extra donation from Australia. We had to prioritise, and it was difficult, but we decided to cover the cost of replacing the generator. We needed the power back on for many reasons, especially with the Christmas school holidays coming up, so we felt it was more important.

Hope House was ever-changing. Some girls were reunited with family, two new girls ran away, and Reyna and her sister Elena waited for the court to issue their discharge papers. They would soon go to live with their uncle. We were down to only nineteen girls. I wasn't sorry because school holidays were around the corner, and it was the long break; they didn't go back until early March. I was praying that we would get some more help by then.

We never really knew who would come knocking on the gate of Hope House; there were many unexpected surprises. Flo and her younger brother Matias had been found at home alone and were now being led through our gate by a social worker. They had been locked inside a tiny 3x3mt shack with no electricity, food, or running water. They were in a fearful state: bruised, hungry, and dirty. A neighbour had alerted the police about a theft, and this was followed up by a social worker being sent to the house. When it was discovered that the children were not enrolled at any school, they were taken into care and sent to us.

Initially, we weren't sure about taking Matias, but he was only five years old and such a gentle, shy child. The dreaded thought of him being separated from Flo and being bullied in a boy's home was too much. He became the first boy at Hope House; he was so adorable that the girls smothered him with love and affection.

It was months before their mother turned up to visit, but when she did, she became emotional and showed genuine concern and affection for her children. Flo and Matias reciprocated that love in their delight to see their mother. When I discovered that this woman had walked seven kilometres to visit her children, I invited her to stay for lunch. Flo's mum, Naida, hesitated when I asked, 'Why didn't you catch the bus here.' After a moment, Naida blushed with embarrassment and said in a soft voice, 'I don't have enough money for bus fares, Hermana.' She was a simple woman who could not read or write, but she was obviously quite proud. Nevertheless, Naida managed to find work as a cleaner, working long hours for a very small wage. As we talked over a meal, she shared her story. It was apparent that she barely managed to put food on the table, let alone pay for school registration and uniforms. When Naida's husband left, Matias was just a baby, and since then, she had struggled to feed the family. Naida admitted that she often had to leave Flo and Matias while she went to work, but she insisted that she always left them enough food to last the day.

'One day', Naida began, 'I found my kids in a neighbour's house. The neighbour complained that they had stolen money from her and she threatened to call the police if it happened again. I was afraid and felt that I had to teach them a lesson to stop them repeating the offense'. Naida swore that this was the first time she had ever beat her kids with a belt. She had to go to work the next day, so she locked them in the house to prevent the same thing from happening. The food she left was eaten in one hit, and by the time evening came, the kids were hungry again. That's when the social worker arrived at the house.

MATIAS INSIDE THE OLD SHACK

One afternoon, a middle-aged Peruvian woman knocked on the gate. Some of the girls recognised her and ran to the gate to greet her. The woman responded in such a warm and friendly way, hugging and kissing the girls. She stood, a girl under each arm, with misty eyes and was obviously very upset. Introducing herself as Doctor Sophie Salamanca, she told me that she had seen the arrest of Luis Guizada on the news. She was unable to hide her shock as she spoke.

She exclaimed, 'How could he do such a thing!' She held the girls tighter as she broke down and cried. It was awkward with the girls present, so I invited Sophie in. She composed herself and followed me.

The only private place was my office, which was also my bedroom. I took her there and she closely examined the girls' artwork covering the walls. 'I just need reassurance that the girls are all right', she said, 'and I had to see for myself.' We talked at length and I set her mind at rest. Her tears revealed her deep compassion towards the girls, and I felt a genuine affinity with her.

Sophie explained that she was the director of a German group, the Fundacion Wilhelm Oberle, who had supported CEDES. She went on to say, 'I know these girls and I want to help; what do you need?' I was taken aback, lost for words, yet my mind was racing trying to think. Many thoughts flashed through my mind: the wedding, Christmas presents, food, school supplies, and a myriad of other things. After a long silence, I replied, 'There are so many needs; I don't know what to ask for.'

'What do you need the most?' she asked.

Without much thought, 'It's almost Christmas', I said. I hesitated. She nodded as if to encourage me, and I continued, 'Christmas was one of the best times for my own girls at home. I spoilt them with new clothes and shoes and presents. If I could, I would do the same with these girls. I would have a special Christmas dinner and treats, and presents and new clothes.'

'You can', she said softly as she pulled out her check book. She wrote a cheque for $2,000.US and handed it over to me with a huge smile. I couldn't believe it. Overwhelmed, my eyes filled up; I could hardly find the words. Sophie didn't need words, she just put her arms around me, and I felt that she fully understood. This was the beginning of a valuable relationship between us. That very week, I took the girls out shopping. I made several different trips over four days, taking a small group of five or six at a time while Fiory took care of the remaining girls while I was gone.

The girls were a pleasure to shop with. None of them were fussy, they seemed to like everything they saw, but trying to buy dresses with Christmas and a wedding in mind was hard. The girls were bubbling over with excitement to be buying something brand new. They wanted to keep the first dress they tried on; in fact, they didn't want to take it off. Instead, they pranced around the fitting rooms unable to take their eyes of their reflection in the full-length mirror. We had a lot of fun shopping! Searching for shoes and accessories was met with the same excitement – and it was easy.

All the girls were finally fully decked out and I was over the shopping blitz, happy to be finished. That's when the girls persuaded me to purchase a Christmas tree. How could I not!

My daughter Carmen arrived early for the wedding; I was so happy to see her and talk to her and hug her. I truly did miss her. I was so proud of the way she was… a lovely young lady with a lovely warm personality. I felt sad that Anna didn't come to my wedding, and I couldn't stop thinking about it. I tried to fight the negative self-talk by making up excuses for her, but my mind went into overdrive and I didn't want to think about it anymore. I pushed the sadness away, somewhere deep into the unconscious.

A few days later, Greg's three sons, Luke from Dubai, Patrick from South Korea, and Nick from Sydney, arrived. This time it was Greg's turn to wrestle with his feelings as one of his offspring was missing too. I knew he was disappointed even though he didn't like to admit it.

Greg's boys planned to take their dad out on the night before the wedding, but they promised to get him to the church on time. Once they left, I took the opportunity to show Carmen my wedding gown. It was kept out of sight in my room so that Greg didn't get a glimpse of it. Carmen and I got to talking about all sorts of things; I was so grateful for her and the effort she made to be there.

Fini and Leslie from my home church in Australia, had also arrived, to my delight. Leslie was out with a group of girls when Fini knocked on my door. Carmen and I were still chatting when she joined us. She too hummed-and-hawed over the dress. Then our conversation came to a sudden halt, after Fini asked me a simple question, 'How are you feeling Bridget?' She said as she made eye contact. In that moment of silence, out of the blue a surge of emotions dampened all the good feelings, and I felt overwhelmingly sad. Thoughts of Damian invaded my head and I became very sensitive.

The more I thought about him, the worse I felt. I knew that getting married meant "the end" of my devotion to Damian, and I struggled to let go. I knew that I loved Greg, but I also loved Damian. How could I deal with this conflict of feelings?

I just could not reconcile the conflict. At that moment I became aware of the music playing in the background; it was the theme song from the movie *Titanic*. I recalled the end of the movie when Jack died. I couldn't go through with the wedding. Not without first burying Damian. As the song continued playing, in my mind's eye, I could see Damian sinking down to the bottom of the ocean until he disappeared. As he sank, the sadness I felt created an overwhelming pain in my chest, but the lyrics of the song continued, 'The heart must go on'. A kind of strength surged into my heart and, for the first time, I told myself, 'Yes, you can live without Damian.' I thought about Greg and felt at peace again. My whole mood changed. Greg was my man.

The morning of the wedding was nothing less than a disaster. My worst fears had come upon me. The water tank had run dry. In all the business of the past days, I lost my mobile phone and allocated the job of ordering the water to Fiory. She must have forgotten. I feared that this might happen.

On this scorching day, the girls were running around frantically trying to find bottles of drinking water to wash in. I was feeling dreadfully hot and sticky, but there was nothing I could do. I tried to console myself, knowing that I could have a shower later in the hotel, but I felt like crying.

'It's no good crying; you have to improvise', I told myself. At least I had washed my hair the previous day. Carmen came to the rescue and fixed my hair up some-how; she did a great job.

The girls, without even a drop of water, were all upset and complaining. Their emotions were high, and they didn't know whether to laugh or cry. When Fiory arrived, she insisted that she had ordered the water, so I asked her to ring the water supplier and, 'Demand, beg, do whatever you have to do for a delivery.' She did exactly that, but the tank of water didn't arrive until after 11.00 am, only an hour before the bus was due to pick us up. When the water arrived, there was a stampede. The girls fought tooth and nail to get into the shower first. (What a turn-around!) For me, it was too late as Carmen had already done my hair and was in the process of doing my make-up.

The chartered bus arrived, tooting its horn from a long way off. Some neighbours had gathered around the open gate to peep inside. Nineteen little princesses excitedly piled onto the bus. Carmen and Veronica helped me with the long train on my wedding gown as we also made our way across the dusty ground to the bus. It suddenly hit me that I was getting married, I was really getting married!

I couldn't believe my eyes when I boarded the bus and saw the girls sitting there, poised, calm, with beaming smiles. They looked so radiant, so colourful, and so very happy. How did this angelic sight emerge from the chaos of a few moments ago? I will never know!

We set off to the Hacienda Tres Cañas in Ate Vitate, which was just over an hour's drive away on the bus with no air conditioning. Tres Cañas, an authentic replica of a typical Andean hacienda, was set on acres of stud farm with Peruvian Paso Horses, 100% purebred.

The large colonial gates opened automatically, and we drove through. It was like driving through a time warp; magically, we were surrounded by lovely green gardens with an abundance of bougainvillea and rustic buildings… such a contrast to the dry, dusty atmosphere of San Juan de Lurigancho.

We piled off the bus, arriving a little late, a little nervous, and very excited. The girls' long silky dresses of various pastel colours complimented my cream-coloured gown. Adorned with a mixture of sequins and diamante accessories, we sparkled in the sunshine. Then music began to play.

I could see Greg on the other side of the beautifully manicured courtyard waiting with his boys. They looked like "Men in Black" with their dark glasses and black suits, but extremely handsome.

The bridal party in all its glory walked slowly down the winding path to the soundtrack "My Heart Will Go On" by Celine Dion. We continued past the fountain, through the lush greenery, until we reached the men. I looked at Greg and felt so happy.

'Wow!' I thought. Just then, Greg said, 'Wow!' It was like he read my mind. I'll never forget it.

During the ceremony, we were asked to verbalise a promise to each other. Greg promised that he would always love me and take care of me. I promised that I would love him just as much on his bad days as on his good days.

We exchanged rings, and rolling my veil back, Greg kissed me. The knot was tied, and we were man and wife.

OUR WEDDING

The mood was relaxed with this intimate group of fifty guests, including family, close friends, and all the girls. Sophie came with her husband and enjoyed watching the girls perform some of their favourite dance routines and sing their songs.

After the ceremony, we were led to an open field where many chairs set the stage for the Paso Horse Show. The magnificent horses captivated our attention with their dancing steps and disciplined bows. Then it was time to feast on the best Creole and Peruvian cuisine I have ever tasted and sip on fine wine while the girls had their fill of ice-cream and chocolate.

After dancing the night away to the sound of salsa music, the wedding came to a close. Fiory and the girls were ready to board the chartered bus to be dropped off at the casa. Finally, after lengthy goodbyes and many long hugs, we felt a mixture of relief and apprehension; parting with the girls was unexpectedly difficult. We had never left them with anyone before, not overnight! It was foolishness. The girls were happy for us, and we knew they would be safe with Fiory. Noisy shouts of well wishes carried out the windows, petering into silence as the bus pulled away. Then we were alone; all the challenges and disappointments of Peru were on hold for now, and we spent the next ten days on the beautiful Caribbean Island of Aruba, just being alone!

Chapter Sixteen

AMBUSH

Journal Entry:
APEC Conference: Arequipa, Peru
10th May 2008

Greg and I attended the APEC (Asia-Pacific Economic Cooperation) conference hoping to learn more about how to empower our girls to reach their full potential. The "Women Leaders Network" was the specific subject of interest that was aimed at unleashing the potential of women entrepreneurs by providing support and networking with organisations such as ours.

After a full-on day listening to several panel discussions, some other delegates invited us to a meal. We met some of the speakers and discussed all sorts of things from advocacy to innovative strategies for strengthening women, and we made some good contacts.

*An excellent meal served with freely flowing pisco sours
made us feel thoroughly spoilt. It had been a great day
in all, but we were feeling just a little exhausted and
decided to leave early. Heading off, we waited outside
for a taxi. Within a moment it came and then
everything changed.*

W e had no idea of the route back to the hotel,
but we did know that Arequipa was made up
of many alleys and back streets, so we were not
concerned when the cab drove through the small unfamiliar roads.

We both relaxed in the back seat of the small cab,
happily chatting away until suddenly it stopped in a
blind alley. Before we knew it, two men jumped in, one
on each side of the car, virtually landing in our laps.
Another man jumped in the front passenger seat. They
covered our eyes with their hands and yelled frantically,
'We only want your money! We're not going to hurt
you.' They kept repeating this over and over.

With no room to move, I felt absolutely helpless.
The man's fingers exerted so much pressure on my eyes
that I was in pain. I cried out, then a hand covered my
mouth, but the pressure on one eye caused excruciating
pain. I felt smothered and confused; it was like a bad
dream.

The situation had changed so fast that I couldn't
process what was happening, but I knew it was real.
Grasping at the hand over my mouth, I tried pulling it
away to speak. I mumbled through his hand, 'My eye,

my eye! You're hurting me!' Immediately, to my relief, the pressure eased and then a blindfold was placed over my eyes. I quietened down and became aware that there was no sound from Greg.

I couldn't see anything through the black cloth, so I reached out for him and felt his arm, grasping it tightly. I heard his voice whisper, 'Are you OK?' as he touched my hand. 'I am now', I responded, 'What about you?'

'Yes, just keep calm', he said. I clung to him desperately; feeling for his face, I realised that he too had a blindfold on. While driving, the men searched us and emptied out all our pockets: our wallets and watches, my wedding and engagement rings, and my gold chain – all taken.

After a good twenty minutes, the car stopped, and we were told to get out. They gave instructions for Greg to get out one side and me the other, but I refused; I thought they were going to murder us, or worse. I got upset and raised my voice whilst grasping tightly onto Greg's arm. 'I'm not separating from my husband', I yelled. Someone pulled on my arm, insisting, but I retaliated in a shaky voice, 'You have taken everything, is that not enough? Do you want blood too?' The pulling stopped, and I continued more boldly, 'Have you no conscience?'

The man's aggressive voice furiously said, 'Shut up, shut up; I will bash you if you don't shut up.' Overcome with emotion, I just cried like a baby on Greg's shoulder. I felt so helpless and fearful. Greg was calm. He said, 'We can't do anything in the confined taxi space, but we might have a chance of fighting them if we get out.' I was afraid and wouldn't let go of Greg's arm.

A kinder voice persuasively said, 'We just need your pin numbers to the credit cards, and then we will let you go.' I translated for Greg and then responded, 'We can give you the pin numbers here in the car.' But he didn't want that; he just wanted us to get out and go into a building.

I appealed to the kind voice, saying, 'We are missionaries, and we are here to help your people.' Then I asked him, 'Can we just have a minute to pray?' Surprisingly, he agreed.

Never in our lives had we prayed with such fervour and, in my case, tears. Greg was composed and strong, which really encouraged me. He prayed for strength to overcome and for protection; I prayed for wisdom and guidance. After our prayer, I told Greg that I didn't want to fight. I said, 'We might end up in a hospital or worse.'

Without telling me what he was going to do, Greg began to negotiate in his broken Spanish, promising them that he would do whatever they wanted if they let me go. I shuddered at the idea. Fortunately, they refused, but they did agree on something. They allowed us to get out of the car at the same time, on the same side. Clinging tightly to Greg's arm, led like two blind people, we got out of the car. Stumbling on rubbish and empty bottles, we shuffled along through a gate and up some narrow stairs until we reached a brick wall. Ordered to sit down on the ground, I felt for a clearing near the wall, but it felt dirty and disgusting. Still, we sat without question.

As soon as we sat down, they asked for the pin numbers to the three visa cards they had found. We gave them willingly. Maybe too willingly. They said they would 'waste' us if we were lying. Then the angry voice asked if we had read the papers last week about the Israeli tourist that was robbed and left in a pool of blood. 'That was me', he claimed, 'and I can do the same to you if you're lying.' We were given a second chance to be honest, but we weren't lying.

I listened to their conversation while they rummaged through Greg's briefcase. They spoke coarsely, cursing with every second word, and were harsh even with each other. One of them had slurred speech like he was on something, or perhaps he was developmentally delayed. Their low-life dialogue sent a shiver up my spine; I knew they were desperate men.

I heard them talking about the camera and the cell phone. They were removing the memory card and microchip when a quarrel broke out. The men didn't know how to use the ATM machine. They thought that a signature was needed to withdraw cash and were arguing about which one of us would go with them to the bank or whether they should take both of us. Their plan was to wait until the morning for the bank to open. One argued it was too dangerous to take both of us.

I spoke up and interjected, 'You don't need a signature with the pin number.' Complete silence fell for just a moment; I imagined them looking at each other with glazed eyes. Then much exchange of words between them broke the silence, and they turned the conversation to me. They asked questions about how to use the card. I explained, and they asked the same questions, and I explained again – then finally they got it.

Two of the men left, and the other two stayed to watch us. We sat there huddled together, not knowing if we would ever survive this ordeal. It was so quiet except for the sound of their movements and our whispers. We decided to pray again. We reaffirmed our faith in God and claimed His promises, and then we were encouraged by some scripture verses we recalled. A calmness came over us, and we even sang a song quietly, but one of the men hurried towards us and kicked our feet. In no uncertain terms, the angry voice threatened to harm us if we didn't shut up. We did, immediately.

After a time, one of the men broke the spell of silence; he approached us and asked in a considerate voice, 'Where are you from?'

Simultaneously, we spoke. Greg said Sydney, and I said, 'Australia.'

'What language do they speak in Australia?' he asked.

I answered all his questions about Australia before he moved on to ask about the photos he had seen in our briefcase. I told him that they were photos of Hope House and the girls we lived with. After a short silence, he asked about the work we did and how long we had been in Peru. Before I could finish answering, the two other men burst into the room, and that was the end of our conversation.

I heard the men mumbling something under their breath; they purposely didn't want us to hear. They seemed reticent, then one man said, 'We couldn't get any money out of the machine.'

I knew there was money in the accounts and told them, 'That happens to me sometimes; the ATMs run out of cash, and I just try a different machine.'

With less intensity, the man asked me to explain again how to use the machine. I realised that they were embarrassed and almost child-like in their understanding, so I spoke to them with simpler words at a slower pace. After painstakingly repetitive instructions, they went off a second time.

The same man who had talked to us approached again, and this time he sat on the ground near our feet; I felt his elbow leaning against my shin. He began by saying, 'I believe in God.' He continued, 'I'm sorry for doing this to you; I wouldn't have done it if I knew you were missionaries.' This lawless man seemed sincerely remorseful. He went on to explain, 'I am an uneducated man with no work and no opportunity to get work, and I have a family to feed.'

Dumbfounded at his candour, I found myself sharing a little about my childhood. I told him of the hunger I had experienced and how my mother would beg, borrow, or steal to feed us. I said, 'I understand.' He was very quiet. I told him softly, 'Necessity must!

We do things out of necessity.' Complete silence followed, but I felt that something was happening inside his heart. In the positive air of silence, I felt it was appropriate to say nothing and pray for him.

I silently prayed and waited. After a few moments, I gently said, 'You know, we really do understand, and we forgive you.' Another silent interlude passed, and then he spoke with certainty in his voice, as if unmoved, and his response was bizarre. He began to advise us how to avoid this situation in the future, and he explained the difference between "official taxis" and "unofficial taxis". His words gave me hope that there was, in fact, a "future", and we would eventually be released.

The men returned, but again they had failed to withdraw any cash. After many conversations and explaining everything again, they went off to try for the third time. This time they finally succeeded to get the cash. I was strangely happy for them. They were such incredibly simple people and were boasting about how they had emptied all the accounts. It was a huge amount of cash to them. I kept quiet and allowed them to revel in their bragging. They had no idea about daily limits, and I wasn't about to fill them in.

Moments later, I heard them arguing; three of the men wanted to get rid of us; they were afraid that we would go to the police. The fourth man whose voice I knew became our ally. He stood up for us and began to persuade the men otherwise. 'They haven't seen our faces', he said. Footsteps approached, and I felt a presence close to my face, and then nothing. It was silent.

The familiar voice in the background said, 'See, they can't see nothing.' Then the angry voice in my face said, 'I will personally kill you if you go to the police.'

I remained calm and told him a convincing story of how useless the police were. It was convincing because it was true. I told him how we went to the police the last time we were robbed, and how they detained us for hours to fill out countless forms, and how in the end, they did absolutely nothing. By the time I was finished, he was satisfied that we would not even consider going to the police.

They argued again but purposefully in a more constrained, muffled way so that I couldn't hear. I wasn't sure what they were going to do. Without explaining anything, just a 'Vamonos (Let's go)', the men led us outside to the car and bundled us in – and drove off.

The familiar, reassuring voice told us that they were going to let us go and instructed us on what to do. When the car stopped, we were told to get out, leaving the blindfolds on, and we were to hug and kiss each other with our eyes closed. Greg shuffled out of the car, with me grasping onto his arm as he went. One of the men led us a few steps from the car and thrust the briefcase into my abdomen, which I grabbed with both hands. I felt a push on my back pushing me towards Greg. I clung to him tightly. I was terrified and did exactly as they said. As I kissed Greg, the blindfold was suddenly snatched off my eyes, but I kept them shut tight. I heard the sound of the car screeching off and then nothing. It was deadly silent; they were gone.

Hesitantly we opened our eyes and found ourselves in a dark, desolate alley with no idea where we were. Greg revealed a ten-sole note in his hand. One of the men had thrust it there; it was enough money to pay for a taxi to safety.

We walked to a main road, and within ten minutes, we were back in our hotel room. The most amazing thing was that when we looked into the briefcase, we found all our credit cards, the memory card, and the sim card, along with all our photos and documents. We looked at each other in that look of speechless amazement – hugged each other – and knew it was good to be alive!

Impossible to sleep, we reflected on the whole incident the remainder of that night. We gained a new appreciation of each other and felt valued by God. Our faith strengthened so much that all the current struggles we faced seemed paltry. Greg felt like he would never complain again, and I felt almost invincible as if I could do anything, go anywhere, and ultimately be protected and safe.

Each new day seemed like a day we could have been denied. The experience showed us that we were ready to meet our Maker and that even if the situation had turned bad, the final outcome would still be good.

We came away from Arequipa with a different understanding of the behaviours and attitudes of desperate men. To be mugged by uneducated, impulsive men trying to scratch a living in a harsh country with little or no social welfare, compared to being attacked by someone who doesn't like the colour of your eyes or has had a bad day, is so vastly different.

In the strangest of ways, the incident turned out to be a good experience!

Chapter Seventeen

GOD'S SUCCESSION PLAN

Journal Entry:
San Juan de Lurigancho, Peru
5th January 2009

> *Greg and I value the growing relationship we are*
> *experiencing with Pastor Rodney Spears and his wife,*
> *Rebecca. This missionary couple from Ohio, U.S.A.,*
> *have demonstrated their love-in-action and have*
> *become a powerful influence in our lives as well as the*
> *lives of the girls. They have graciously allowed us to*
> *share our load with them and we have come to cherish*
> *our times of prayer together.*

After the Arequipa experience, we continued our work at Hope House with a new passion for God and a zest for life. Due to lack of staff, however, and with every waking moment occupied by the girls, we were limited in what we could do outside the home. Mostly confined to the casa, we were spurred on to rise up early in the morning and pray. Every day, long before the girls stirred, we circled the perimeter of the property, claiming back the territory that the enemy had stolen and declaring the Lordship of Jesus Christ over it. Some days we were able to walk around the perimeter several times. Because there was no fencing or walls on the boundary line, we could see when the girls were up and mulling around the grounds. That's when our prayer walks ended.

For some months, we continued praying in this way, claiming the blood of Jesus over each girl by name and earnestly asking that *every* girl would come to know the love of God in a personal way. We began to see God's grace at work, and the more we saw, the more we prayed. The more we prayed, the more we saw God's hand moving. Our prayer life soared as we witnessed the power of God changing the lives of each girl; and changing the situation at Hope House.

The girls brought home flyers one day, informing of outreach meetings by a new Baptist church planting in the local area. The church, to our surprise, was only a short bus ride away. Seizing the opportunity, we attended every meeting, taking all the girls with us. Nika and Carina gave their hearts to Christ during different meetings, and from that time on, they wanted to attend church every Sunday. All the girls looked forward to Sunday mornings at the Baptist church, and a great number of the girls grew strong in their faith as a result.

Different organisations began to hear about Hope House and stepped in to help us. Before long, we had some volunteers as well as a housemother working the night shift. This made a huge difference to us as we could look forward to spending an entire weekend all to ourselves. Our weekends were amazingly calm and peaceful; we actually had time for each other—time to relax and do absolutely nothing if we chose, and we even had time to sleep in. We often stayed in Lima on Friday and Saturday nights returning on Sunday afternoon.

One Saturday, we were invited to a BBQ hosted by the Australian Consulate. There, we met Rod Ward, who worked for Rio Tinto at the time. He, in turn, invited us to visit his church, which we eagerly did the very next day. We were delighted to receive a warm welcome from the "Union Church of Lima", and more importantly that it was an English-speaking church. Our time there certainly brought spiritual refreshment to our souls; it was incredible to hear a sermon in our own language and to have fellowship with other missionaries.

We started attending a Bible study on Friday evenings with a German couple, Ada and her husband

and made several English friends. I joined the choir, and within a short time, the mission team of the Union Church began to make regular visits to Hope House. This led to many helpful contacts and ongoing financial support.

One such contact was a Peruvian organisation (already established in Lima) which ministered directly to kids living on the streets. Greg and I joined this group, and every second weekend we became involved with the ministry, going out on the streets from night-time to the early hours. Strange things happened on the streets of Lima late at night; marketplaces converted into places for drug addicts, homosexuality, transvestites, and all manner of sexual perversion. We knew the dangers as we walked the streets at ungodly hours, but we felt safe under God's covering. Many of the street kids were nicknamed Terokaleros, as they were heavily involved in glue-sniffing (Terokal). Some were out of control, while others were so far gone that they were hardly able to make coherent conversation. These kids had been subject to all kinds of violence and sexual abuse, even from older kids in the street gangs. Terokal was their way of escape. Breakthrough was extremely difficult. For me, it was heartbreaking.

It wasn't long until we left the despair of the almost hopelessness of the streets to those who were better able to cope with it, but we made sure that they knew where to bring the girls. Our focus returned to Hope House, where hope really did thrive.

Another contact was with Markham College, one of the most prestigious international schools in Lima. It seemed to me that Lima was full of extremes and contradictions. We moved from the hellish existence of the destitute street kids to the outrageous indulgence of the diplomat's kids. The deputy principal, David Massiah, who attended the Union Church, invited Greg and me out to dinner with some other people from church. Over dinner, he asked us to share about Hope House with his year-ten students, or as they were commonly referred to, Markhamians. We were surprised when this secular school offered their Markhamians an opportunity to visit the casa as part of their community service. Even more surprising was that many of the kids took on the challenge. These very privileged kids were really stepping out of their comfort zone because San Juan de Lurigancho was considered a dangerous, high-risk area, so much so that their parents insisted on sending their personal bodyguards along with them. Ironically, our girls were feeling fearful and a little inferior at the idea of meeting such superior kids, as they mistakenly thought.

The first group of Markhamians arrived, bringing presents of school supplies, and our girls surprised them with their gifts of humour, wit, and intelligence. Our girls, who felt that Hope House was their comfort zone, were bemused that these kids were out of theirs. They laughed at each other's fears initially, but by the end of the evening, they were laughing with each other.

We desperately needed to build a wall around the property to keep the rabid dogs out and to stop theft. When voluntary mission teams from Colorado and Georgia arrived, we talked about this need and together we planned the project "Adopt a Wall". Individuals from churches back in the U.S. provided for the cost of building a small section of the wall, eventually raising enough funds to purchase the entire building materials necessary.

On their next visit, a large group of mainly young people came with New Covenant Ministries; they worked hard and accomplished much. A huge brick wall, three metres high, surrounding the 2,500-square-metre perimeter of the property was in place by the time they had finished. The entire property was finally secured. The same group beautified the dorms and the living room with a facelift of fresh paint, and best of all, they demolished the eyesore of a swimming pool. When Greg and I witnessed that pool being smashed to pieces and crumbling down to nothing, it was such a good feeling. At the end of the day, we all stood by the rubble and prayed to acknowledge God. I was left with a symbolic image of the plans of the enemy being torn down and stamped out. I shared the imagery with Greg and the team. It was a triumphant moment! We were all elated. The teams came to do their utmost, expecting nothing in return, and I don't know if they will ever realise how much they meant to us.

MISSION TEAMS PRAYING BY THE RUBBLE

By the end of 2009, we were able to develop a multidisciplinary team and, with many extra hands-on-deck, the quality of care improved immensely. Greg and I had more time to focus on the house rather than in the house. We decided that since the CMAP Church had still not paid their debt and had let us down so badly that we would ask them to hand the property back to us. Surprisingly, they agreed. From there, we worked hard on establishing our own association. We called our officially accredited and newly registered association Asociacion Hogar Nueva Esperanza (Association: New-Hope House).

On the home front, Greg's mother, Sue, almost ninety years of age, had been battling cancer for some years, but she had been in remission when Greg left for Peru. The news that the cancer had returned was devastating. This time, Sue needed to have surgery. We didn't know whether she would survive the operation, and we immediately began to organise a trip for Greg to be there with her before, during, and after the operation.

Sue not only pulled through, but she made an amazing recovery as well. Soon the time came for Greg to return, but he felt guilty leaving his mother and yet guilty for being absent from us in Peru as well. Sue knew this when Greg asked, 'Do you want me to stay?' She responded, 'No, Greg, not now, but when I do need you, I will let you know.' Leaving his frail mother was one of the hardest things he'd ever had to do. Greg, being an only child, was torn, but his mother graciously made it possible for him to go.

Over time, the situation with Greg's mother became more pressing, and Greg travelled back and forth various times to support her. Both Greg and I knew that we would have to return to Australia before long. Greg knew it was good management practice to plan for one's own replacement, and I knew it was sensible, so we began working towards it. New blood, as they say, but actually finding another generation proved far more difficult than we had anticipated. All the hopeful candidates seemed to fall by the wayside for one reason or another. The model of a married couple managing Hope House on a voluntary basis was unworkable in the Peruvian context. The Peruvians just didn't have the same support or the resources that overseas missionaries have. They basically needed a full-time wage just to survive. We had to look further afield. Nevertheless, when we did this, there were no North American missionary couples to be found, or any couple for that matter, that was remotely interested or available.

Consequently, in March 2011, we changed the model. The new model of a director, preferably a single person, would work a forty-eight-hour week and would be paid a fair wage in return for professional management. With this model in mind, we began to search, and it seemed to offer more potential for success as a number of applicants did apply. Even so, our search took some time. We felt that perhaps we were being too picky and became more liberal by dropping our preference for candidates to have an evangelical background. Soon we employed a young Catholic lawyer, but just for a probationary period. She was keen to assist from a humanitarian perspective, but her values and beliefs caused some confusion and even division among the girls. It really didn't work at all.

Finally, an applicant with all the necessary tertiary qualifications came highly recommended by our good friend and pastor of the local Baptist church, Rodney. He couldn't speak more highly of Geraldine Valenzuela Azaña as he had known Geraldine since she was a child, and he also knew her parents.

Geraldine, a softly spoken but confident young lady in her late twenties, began in-house training in all aspects of the administration of Hope House. She had a caring disposition, and she worked well with both the staff and the girls. Geraldine proved herself to be both diligent and competent within a short period of time.

Just a couple of weeks into the commencement of Geraldine's training, I received an urgent phone call from my sister Carmel in Australia. She told me that my daughter Carmen had been involved in a very serious car accident and was in the hospital.

Distraught, I booked the next possible flight back to Sydney, leaving Greg to cope with Geraldine's training. I knew that Greg would find this to be quite a challenge because of his level of fluency in the language, but I also knew that he was more than capable of dealing with challenges.

Carmen went through a difficult time, but she had an excellent prognosis, and I was glad to be there with her. We spent a lot of time together during that recovery period. I had come to realise just how much of Carmen's life I had missed out on. So much happened, and I wasn't there for any of it. Initially, I wanted to turn back the clock, but then I reflected on all that had happened in Peru. I thought about God and His sovereignty, and I knew that I could trust Him with everything. I believed that He would turn this situation around and bring some good out of it, just as

He had done with the situation in Peru. I knew that nothing was going to get in the way of God's plans for Carmen's life, and I began praying for her more earnestly.

While in Australia, I could see an alarming deterioration in Greg's mother and urged him to return as soon as possible. Geraldine's probation period had to be cut short, and her training brought to a sudden halt, but this didn't deter her from accepting the position. She commenced as directora on a permanent basis just a few weeks before Greg's departure.

On 30 June 2011, Greg arrived back in Australia, and his mother passed away three weeks later. Their time together was short, but it was a precious time of reconnection, and he was truly grateful for it.

During our seven years in Peru, over one hundred girls and just four boys walked through the doors of Hope House. Not every girl was a success story; sadly, some even ended up back on the streets just as angry and fearful as when they came. They were not affected at all, as far as we could see. My heart grieves for those ones. Others were somewhat heartened but preferred to go their own way, perpetuating their mothers' lifestyle and succumbing to the trap of having several babies to different fathers. They somehow stumble through life, never really knowing what stability looks like, but then, it is their choice. God has graciously given free will to all of us.

The rest were moved in such a deep way that their lives were fundamentally and permanently changed. These girls learnt about self-worth as well as responsibility, and more importantly, they didn't just learn about Christ, they learnt to *relate* to Christ himself. It was that personal relationship that made an unmistakable transformation of their lives. We saw them flourish and begin to grow in their identity in Christ. The healing in their lives was more than evident, and we even witnessed a ripple effect overflow into the lives of some of their estranged families. All of this could only be attributed to the amazing grace of God.

We ensured that Yakira and Angelica paid regular visits to their mother in gaol. As a result, they shared all that was happening at Hope House, bringing photos of special occasions such as Angelica's first day at school and birthday celebrations, and they talked about their own experiences during the singing. After years of witnessing to their mother, eventually, she accepted Jesus. This led to a notable change in her behaviour at the prison, and she had a positive influence on the inmates. Yakira's mother started a Bible study group among the inmates, and she was highly commended by the wardens for good behaviour. So much so that her sentence was reduced significantly, and she was released on parole. The first thing she did was to visit the refuge; this young woman was so appreciative and wanted to tell us all about her life-changing experience. We knew only God could bring about such change, a change so profound that it would carry into eternity. As soon as her parole had finished and after much red tape, she eventually gained custody of her two beautiful girls. This was just one of the very happy endings that we were fortunate enough to see.

ANGELICA: FIRST DAY AT SCHOOL

Currently, Yakira is happily married to a devoted

husband and loving father. They have one child and one on the way, and they maintain close contact with Angelica and her mother. Angelica continues to live with her mother; she is sixteen at the time of writing, attending high school, and hopes to do further studies.

Many girls missed out on years of education through exploitation in the form of forced labour. At Hope House, these girls were being encouraged and were given the opportunity to study; some even began to excel at school.

Fannie was one such girl who, sometime after arriving at Hope House, made the huge decision to trust God. She had missed three years of schooling, but once she started attending school consistently, she committed herself to studying, and there was no stopping her. Fannie was so keen and worked very hard.

After a couple of years, and with a little help from our tutor, her dedication paid off. Fannie miraculously beat all the odds stacked against her. She not only caught up, but she excelled and eventually made entry into university.

With less than fifty percent of girls in Peru actually finishing high school, this was extremely rare. Fannie was the first girl from Hope House to ignite the hope of other girls ever achieving University entry.

BRIDGET WITH FANNIE: THE NEW PREFECT

Unfortunately, in 2014, just three years after we left Peru, I received a very sad email from Fannie. She wrote that her life was falling apart.

She was struggling with no support from anyone, and far from coping, Fannie was drowning in a sea of bitterness and offense; but the email didn't make sense. I didn't understand how things could have gone so wrong. I had to wait until the next day to call due to the time difference.

Clearly, something was desperately out of balance. Fannie was not the same confident girl that I had left behind. I found myself awake and praying for her most of the night. It was a long night; 5.00 am couldn't come quick enough.

When I called Fannie, she had some devastating news. She was so ashamed of it that she found it hard to tell. But she did finally tell. She told me, through tears and anguish, what she should have told me two years previously.

While travelling home in a taxi, she had been drugged and raped. Our conversation revealed the secret struggles she had been trying to cope with ever since.

Fannie told me that she had tried to block the incident out of her head. When she found that she was pregnant, she refused to believe it. Then when she began to show, she concealed it by wearing baggy clothes and not telling anyone. She wanted no part in it, but it was too late. She felt her life was destroyed. Her intention was to have the baby secretly and then have it adopted so that she could carry on with life and study as "normal".

But that's not what happened! When Fannie's son, Martin, was born, she couldn't go through with the adoption. After a short time, she struggled to manage and became resentful towards the baby. She began to blame him for everything. Fannie became depressed and suicidal.

I encouraged her in her decision to keep Martin and commended her for sharing her story with me. I asked about her family, but it seemed that they had enough troubles of their own. From such a distance, there was little I could do; I offered prayer, and Fannie was happy to receive it.

Later, after praying with Greg, we decided to invite Fannie to stay with us in Australia. Within a short time, we had the pleasure (and the pain) of hosting Fannie with her eighteen-month-old son in our home for one year. Fannie undertook studies in language at the Sydney School of English, and, as always, she excelled, applying herself one hundred percent.

With the help of professional counselling, that year for Fannie was a season of healing and restoration. For Martin, it was the mending of broken maternal bonds, and he flourished.

At the time of writing, Fannie lives in Lima and is married to Lucio. Lucio loves Martin as his own child, and they have had a second baby boy. Fannie continues with part-time university studies, and her level of fluency in the English language is excellent.

Flo and Matias were happy at Hope House, but they also needed their mother. I realised that Naida loved her children, and she needed help to get them back. We offered her a permanent position at the casa as the cleaner, for a small wage. Naida was so happy to spend more time with Flo and Matias while at the house, and she accepted with gratitude.

During that period, Naida diligently did a great job

and proved herself very reliable, and we were able to provide the authorities with the necessary reference that she required. Her faith grew, and she began to pray with her children.

Even with help from our solicitor and getting through various psychological tests, it took two years before Naida was told that her children could finally go home.

Two conditions, however, were imposed. She had to provide a home for the children as well as submit a statutory declaration stating that she would be committed to taking her children to school each day.

Although Naida complied as far as she could, her small shack was all she had, and sadly, it did not pass the inspection; consequently, the department of child protection refused to reunite the family.

As a result of "a mother's love", the Triple B project (Building Broken Bonds) was birthed. Greg and I simply made the need known, and Naida prayed.

Within a short period of time, donations came flooding in, and a new home was built, "Invading the Darkness" being the main benefactor.

The provision of a water tank, and furnishings such as beds, sheets, a sink, and a cooker, were all purchased for the house, and at long last, the day finally arrived when Flo and Matias could be reunited with their mother.

After they left the house, all three continued to attend the local church.

MATIAS (white cap) INSIDE HIS NEW HOUSE WITH
BRIDGET AND THREE GIRLS FROM HOPE HOUSE

OUTSIDE NEW HOUSE WITH MARK, MATIAS,
SANDRA & JULIE

Currently, Flo remains single; she works in the local markets and continues living in the same house, taking care of her mother. Matias is cohabiting with his girl-friend and has a baby boy.

EPILOGUE

During our season in Hope House, we developed close relationships with the girls, gained a profound understanding of the culture, and experienced every aspect of Peruvian life. However, at the same time, we missed out on relationships with our respective families, and especially our children. We missed out on the vital years of transition from older teenagers into mature adults of most of our children... that was our biggest sacrifice. And, it was no doubt their sacrifice too!

We emerged better people, perhaps more compassionate, more accepting, and more ready to respond to His promptings in blessing those in need.

Now, in my comfortable house with my nice car and the certainty of a rich life, my thoughts dart back and forth from that country to this. I think about the girls at Hope House, the traumas they suffered, the extreme poverty, the exploitation of the most vulnerable. I think of how Matias's mum, who, in an attempt to feed her children by working long hours, actually ended up neglecting them. I think of the people exhausted and packed like sardines onto those green buses, returning home from work in the dark, night after night, with little hope of any change. Then I reflect on the wealth all around me; the waste, the excess, and the complacency towards the needs of others. I am perplexed; I struggle to find peace within. My thoughts collide in a heap of overwhelming tension, the tension of living in such abundance.

- How can I have so much when they have so little?
- How can I justify the lifestyle I live here in Australia?
- Why has God blessed me so much?

I see a need, and I want to fix it, but there are so many needs. I want to fix them all. The greatest challenge is discerning what God doesn't want me to do.

I acknowledge that everything I have is His. I thank God for the privilege of knowing Him and for the way He has so lavishly made Himself known to me. Then I ask Him: What do You want me to do with all of these blessings?

The answer comes swiftly… 'Sow generously. You have been made rich so that you can be generous.' God tells me every good and perfect gift is from above. I have been given wealth and possessions, and He will enable me to enjoy them, to accept my lot, and be happy in my work – this is a gift from God (Ecclesiastes 7:19; 2 Corinthians 9:6 and 11).

The penny drops, and I know the reason God has blessed me is so that I may be a channel of blessing to others. Now, I simply want to be that channel. So, the question is not, 'How can I have so much?' but, 'How willing am I to help others?' I no longer grieve over poverty. The poor can't eat sentiments. Instead, I do something about it. No matter how small or how big, I do according to my ability but DO I must. I will never be the same; I can never reconcile the way I live with what I have seen in South America, but I am learning to accept my lot and to replace those feelings of guilt with feelings of gratitude. The tension moves me to action. Without the tension, there is no action. So, now I can live with the tension, but only because I act on it; this action brings back the peace.

We can all be channels of positive, lasting change to make a difference in our world. Place yourself in someone else's world, even just for a few weeks, and see what happens!

Reflecting back on those years in Peru, they were the most rewarding years of my life, yet the most challenging and painful ones. Although I believe we served a specific purpose, it certainly wasn't what I expected. In spite of the bittersweet experience, I can truly say that I am grateful for it. The splendour of His grace amidst the heartache and tears was more than 'worth it!'

Did we accomplish anything? In and of ourselves, no. I believe our purpose, more than anything, was to show the girls that there is a God who loves them. God brought justice to those girls, and He alone offered a second chance.

The journey allowed us to gain a deeper understanding of ourselves and to experience peace in the eye of the storm, but it really wasn't about us. The most profound insight we gained was that God uses imperfect people; He used me, and He used Greg.

Tears...

A string of tiny human pearls,
Like raindrops from the heart;
Welling up inside us,
Deep feelings to impart...

Tears of unspeakable joy
Of happiness and bliss;
The birth of a child,
A lover's first kiss....

But then, a tear-stained letter,
From a mother in deep despair;
Weeping for her prodigal son,
Pleading with God in prayer.

Yet - most precious in the eyes of God,
Are the tears of true repentance;
Flooding our Soul with Godly sorrow,
Transforming our Will and Conscience.

Oh - cry your cries, and weep your tears,
But remember - that they are lovingly kept;
In the Crystal – clear Cisterns of Heaven,
Preserved with the tears, that Jesus wept....

Fini Kuipers — November '03
Revised — September '11

ABOUT THE AUTHOR

In 1956, Bridget was born into an Irish Catholic family, but from age five she was raised in Manchester, England.

It was when Bridget was gifted a journal on her eighteenth birthday by her eldest sister Mary that she developed a love and a passion for writing. To this day, Bridget keeps a journal of the things that matter most to her.

Off to a bad start in life, Bridget became pregnant in her early teens. Only months after a shotgun-wedding she lost the baby, and in less than one year, the marriage dissolved.

Later, at age twenty-two, Bridget married Damian and in their first year of marriage they migrated to Sydney, Australia. Together, they had two daughters: Anna, born in 1984, and Carmen in 1986.

The birth of Anna brought about a radical change in Bridget's life, which led her to a born-again experience. Damian, a professing Catholic, was unable to accept her conversion and left the marriage.

Upon becoming an empty-nester, Bridget immersed herself in mission work, and while in Peru she married Greg Bonner. Together, they ministered to the needy street-kids of Lima and established a refuge in San Juan de Lurigancho just outside of Lima.

**ASSIST THE DESTITUTE CHILDREN OF PERU
THROUGH THE PURCHASE OF THIS BOOK
THROUGH PRAYER
OR THROUGH VOLUNTEERING
AT HOPE HOUSE IN PERU
(Covid 19-Permitting)**

www.facebook.com/OneForOthers (8,120 Followers)
www.facebook.com/hopehouseperu (4,433 Likes)
www.instagram.com/hopehouseperu (3,406 Followers)

ONE FOR OTHERS FOUNDATION
are the administrators for
HOPE HOUSE
at the time of publishing.

'Hope House is a faithful and loving haven for girls that have been abused and neglected. I have been blessed beyond measure by supporting this Christian organization.'

-Laura Reynolds,
Atlanta, GA, USA

'El tiempo aquí, me ha ensenado a conocer y seguir al Jesús Cristo, a cambiar mi vida pasada, y proponerme metas con la voluntad de Dios. [In the time here, I have learned to know and to follow Jesus Christ, to change my old life, and to make new goals for myself within the will of God.]'

-Farah Garcia Contreras,
HopeHouse, Jicamarca, Perú

'Over the years, children have come to Hope House from a variety of different locations throughout the country, most from dysfunctional families, or from being left to fend for themselves on the city streets. We have seen these young children come to Hope House with sullen faces, looks of concern, doubt, mistrust, but longing for love and acceptance.

'They keep a safe distance from people to begin with. It is not long after they settle into life at Hope House that their countenance changes little by little. The very things they are worried about seem to diminish as they are cared for by loving adults for the first time in quite a long time. During our monthly visits with the Hope House family, we have seen, first hand, the changes that come along with feeling secure and accepted. The girls begin to work as a team, hold each other accountable, manage their assigned chores, and deal with the consequences when they don't complete their share of the work. The comradeship increases. Smiles, laughter, and fun far outweigh the distraught side of life in a short time. What a fantastic place to be – living in hope!

'Let me share one exciting personal story. A teenager living at Hope House shied away from the camera every time we would take photos. She is now a leader in the Hope House family and does well in school. It is such a joy to see a young lady enjoy life and become responsible. She is one of many "success" stories of the House of Hope!'

-Joy and Don Norris,
Team Missions, San Juan de Lurigancho, Lima

ENDNOTES

3. PERU'S ABANDONED

1. South America on a Shoestring, Lonely Planet; Publications Pty Ltd: 8th Edition January 2002

4. AMAZING GRACE

1. 1 Timothy 2:5 – 'For there is one God and one mediator between God and mankind, the man Christ Jesus.'
2. Matthew 23:9 – 'And call no man your father upon the earth: for one is your Father, which is in heaven.'
3. Ephesians 6:2 – 'Honour your father and mother—which is the first commandment with a promise—'

9. A LOVE STORY

1. Philippians 4:12 – 'I know what it is to be in need, and I know what it is to have plenty. I have learned the secret of being content in any and every situation, whether well fed or hungry, whether living in plenty or in want.'
2. When David insults Goliath, he calls him an 'uncircumcised Philistine' – meaning that he had not dedicated his life to Yahweh and that he was serving other gods like Dagon, Baal, and Ashtoreh. http://www.kencastor.com/2009/04/letting-the-bible-speak-its own-words.html

13. BREAKTHROUGH

1. 2 Corinthians 12:9 – 'But he said to me, "My grace is sufficient for you, for my power is made perfect in weakness." Therefore, I will boast all the more gladly about my weaknesses, so that Christ's power may rest on me.'

Made in the USA
Coppell, TX
18 March 2022

74884389R10233